From Resource Scarcity to Ecological Security

Global Environmental Accord: Strategies for Sustainability and Institutional Innovation
Nazli Choucri, editor

From Resource Scarcity to Ecological Security
Exploring New Limits to Growth

edited by Dennis Pirages and Ken Cousins

The MIT Press
Cambridge, Massachusetts
London, England

©2005 Massachusetts Institute of Technology

All rights reserved. No part of this book may be reproduced in any form by any electronic or mechanical means (including photocopying, recording, or information storage and retrieval) without permission in writing from the publisher.

MIT Press books may be purchased at special quantity discounts for business or sales promotional use. For information, please e-mail special_sales@mitpress.mit.edu or write to Special Sales Department, The MIT Press, 55 Hayward Street, Cambridge, MA 02142.

This book was set in Sabon by Achorn Graphic Services. Printed and bound in the United States of America.
Printed on recycled paper.

Library of Congress Cataloging-in-Publication Data

From resource scarcity to ecological security : exploring new limits to growth / edited by Dennis Pirages and Ken Cousins.
    p.   cm. — (Global environmental accord)
    Includes bibliographical references and index.
    ISBN 0-262-16231-8 (alk. paper) — ISBN 0-262-66189-6 (pbk. : alk. paper)
    1. Environmental policy. 2. Twenty-first century—Forecasts. 3. Global 2000 Study (U.S.). I. Pirages, Dennis. II. Cousins, Ken, 1964– III. Global environmental accords.

HC79.E5F76   2005
333.7—dc22

                                                          2004064959

10 9 8 7 6 5 4 3 2 1

Contents

Series Foreword

A new recognition of profound interconnections between social and natural systems is challenging conventional constructs and the policy predispositions informed by them. Our current intellectual challenge is to develop the analytical and theoretical underpinnings of an understanding of the relationship between the social and the natural systems. Our policy challenge is to identify and implement effective decision-making approaches to managing the global environment.

The series on Global Environmental Accord adopts an integrated perspective on national, international, cross-border, and cross-jurisdictional problems, priorities, and purposes. It examines the sources and the consequences of social transactions as these relate to environmental conditions and concerns. Our goal is to make a contribution to both intellectual and policy endeavors.

Nazli Choucri

Preface

More than three decades have passed since a research group based at MIT startled policymakers, academics, and the public with publication of a study indicating that limits to growth on this planet likely would be reached within the next century. Fueled by numerous books published in the 1960s that focused on environmental and resource consequences of continued rapid growth in population and consumption, the MIT study, and the subsequent *Global 2000 Report to the President*, forcefully called attention to a developing human predicament. These publications ignited a vigorous and persistent debate over future prospects for the human race in a world of tightening limits. On one side, a group often characterized as neo-Malthusians has argued that unrestrained growth in population and consumption will lead to widespread famine, resource shortages, and environmental crises. On the other side, a group of technological and economic optimists has countered that there are no limits to growth in ingenuity, and therefore future generations will experience a better quality of life.

We make an effort in this book to contribute to this ongoing dialogue by offering an assessment of what has so far been learned about crucial aspects of this human predicament and by using this information to explore aspects of its future. Better foresight now is critical in supporting a growing world population in excess of 6.4 billion that is pressing close to nature's carrying capacity. Anticipatory thinking and policymaking can spare humanity from potential harsh consequences of the growth trajectory that is being followed. It is much easier to manage growing problems and issues in an anticipatory fashion, dealing with them before significant damage is done, than it is to engage in remedial action later on. Just as scientific consensus on the danger of depletion of stratospheric ozone led to resolute action in the form of the Montreal Protocol, anticipatory thinking and action could help avert future dislocations, or even tragedies, stemming from global warming, petroleum depletion, or food and water shortages.

The forecasting process is unfortunately filled with risks and difficulties. There is the knotty problem of self-defeating prophecies. To the extent that pessimistic forecasts actually do galvanize people to take action, the responsible "Cassandras" can quickly become "Chicken Littles." Thus, biologist Paul Ehrlich's clarion call for action in his 1968 book *The Population Bomb* helped to sensitize leaders around the world to the need for meaningful population policies, but the subsequent success in reducing the worldwide rate of population growth allowed his critics to claim that he got it all wrong. Then there is the issue that even minimal uncertainty in forecasts is often used by vested interests as an excuse for inaction. Witness the extended delays in the United States in dealing with greenhouse warming. And there is the difficult question of complexity in the ecosociotechnical systems that are being analyzed. Things do not always work out exactly the way that they are forecast. For example, while there is a broad consensus that world petroleum production is relatively close to its peak, until very recently petroleum prices were so low as to lead some companies to shut in unprofitable wells. And the petroleum industry is still hesitant to invest large sums in exploration and development for fear that the current high prices will crash again if worldwide economic growth slows down.

In spite of these caveats, the early years of a new millennium offer an ideal opportunity to reflect on the recent past and to anticipate some of the prospects and perils of the next few decades. It is sad that the turn of the millennium, which offered a great opportunity to explore these issues further, for the most part passed with little significant research or reflection. Instead of collectively taking stock of the changing global predicament and launching bold new initiatives to deal with it, the event was mostly marked with fireworks displays and rock concerts. This book is our modest attempt to better respond to the challenges of the new millennium by assessing how well past efforts to assess global limits have done, and, more important, to look forward and anticipate how the combined forces of demographic change and technological innovation will interact with resource limitations to shape the conditions under which future generations will live on this planet.

We wish to thank our collaborators in this effort for the time and energy that they have put into this project. We owe a special thanks to The Harrison Program on the Future Global Agenda at the University of Maryland for continuing support. Also we wish to acknowledge the support of the Environmental Change and Security Project at the Woodrow Wilson Center in Washington, Citicorp, and the Office of International Programs at the University of Maryland for supporting an initial conference that first brought together the authors of these chapters.

From Resource Scarcity to Ecological Security

1
From Limits to Growth to Ecological Security

Dennis Pirages

On a March evening in 1972, a group of scientists and policymakers assembled at the Smithsonian Institution in Washington for a presentation by researchers from MIT on what they called the predicament of mankind. The presenters alarmed the audience with the central message of their new book—that "if the present growth trends in world population, industrialization, pollution, food production, and resource depletion continue unchanged, the limits to growth on this planet will be reached sometime within the next one-hundred years" (Meadows et al. 1972, 23). They then somewhat softened their message by pointing out that "it is possible to alter these growth trends and to establish a condition of ecological and economic stability that is sustainable far into the future" (Meadows et al. 1972, 24). Perhaps more important, they also pointed out with some urgency that "if the world's people decide to strive for this second outcome rather than the first, the sooner they begin working to attain it, the greater will be their chances of success" (Meadows et al. 1972, 24). Publication of this book, *The Limits to Growth,* ignited a contentious and continuing debate over the capacity of the earth's resource base and environmental services to meet growing human demands.

Increasing concern over the long-term demographic, environmental, and resource issues raised by the book, and the fallout from the first energy crisis in the mid-1970s, led then-president Jimmy Carter to issue a directive to the Council on Environmental Quality and the Department of State in May 1977, to work with other federal agencies to study probable changes in the world's population, natural resources, and environment through the end of the century. This effort produced a lengthy document, *The Global 2000 Report to the President,* which concluded that "if present trends continue, the world in 2000 will be more crowded, more polluted, less stable ecologically, and more vulnerable to disruption than the world we live in now" (Barney 1980, 1). The report identified continuing population growth, urbanization, deforestation, water shortages, energy problems, pollution, loss of species diversity, and climate change to be growing concerns as the twenty-first century approached. The report coordinators summarized their extensive findings in a letter to the president, warning that

environmental, resource, and population stresses are intensifying and will increasingly determine the quality of human life on our planet. These stresses are already severe enough to deny many millions of people basic needs for food, shelter, health, and jobs, or any hope for betterment. At the same time, the Earth's carrying capacity—the ability of biological systems to provide resources for human needs—is eroding. (Barney 1980, iii)

The MIT project and the *Global 2000 Report* provoked a strong reaction from many optimists who envisioned a much different future world. They argued that technological innovation would keep resources abundant in relation to demand for them, that environmental conditions would improve, and that looming problems could be solved by applying human ingenuity. As Julian Simon and Herman Kahn (1984, 1–2) bluntly put it in a response to the *Global 2000 Report,* "If present trends continue, the world in 2000 will be *less crowded* (though more populated), *less polluted, more stable ecologically,* and *less vulnerable to resource-supply disruptions* than the world we live in now. Stresses involving population, resources, and environment *will be less in the future than now."* This debate over growth limits has continued for more than three decades. More recently, Danish statistician Bjørn Lomborg (2001) added fuel to this controversy with his copiously footnoted but heavily criticized book in which he portrayed a much more benign "real state of the world."

More than 30 years have passed since the MIT team initially startled a complacent world with its observations, and a quarter century has passed since the *Global 2000 Report* was presented to the president. A new millennium has dawned and it is timely to revisit the projections made and issues raised related to this human predicament. How accurate were these warnings? Have they been heeded and have the practices that led to these bleak scenarios changed? Or is it our destiny to continue to march in lemminglike formation over this projected cliff of self-destruction? Most important, how have perceptions of this projected predicament changed as more has been learned about these growth dynamics?

While it is now opportune to look back over the last three decades to see how well these research efforts anticipated changes in the human condition, it is much more important to learn from this research and experience. What can they tell us about the likely condition of the planet and its inhabitants over the next 30 years? What progress has been made in addressing the problems highlighted in these early warnings? What new challenges are on the horizon? Is life likely over the next three decades to become more secure for *Homo sapiens?* What could be done to make it more so?

These questions are addressed in the following chapters by experts who take a brief look backward at the evolution of crucial demographic, environmental, and resource trends. They then use this accumulated experience and knowledge to project forward and attempt to assess the changing nature of the human predicament in an era of accelerating globalization. Most important, the contributors suggest ways policy initiatives could help ameliorate some of the more serious emerging challenges to human well-being and that of the global ecosystem.

Beyond the Limits

The initial alarming projections of environmental scarcity, inadequate supplies of minerals to sustain industrialization, agricultural production too limited to meet the needs of a growing population, and environmental services inadequate to disperse increasing quantities of waste, have given way over time to a broader view of growing insecurity. As Matthias Ruth has observed in chapter 8, "While the debate about the adequacy of finite natural resources and the ability of technology to overcome limits continues to be waged, a set of new, global issues has shifted the debate from an emphasis on the sources of material wealth to the sinks for waste by-products." Another way of putting it is that thinking has moved beyond impending environmental limits to resource-intensive growth to more general concerns over future ecological security.

Ecological security is a more useful way of thinking about the many aspects of the predicament of humankind (Pirages 2004). The concept rests on empirical observations that for the foreseeable future, resource scarcity is likely to be a relatively minor source of human suffering. Rather, infectious disease now is clearly the primary cause of premature human deaths and disabilities, followed by conflict among peoples, starvation, and various kinds of environmental disasters.

Ecological security rests on preserving the following four interrelated dynamic equilibriums:

1. Between human populations living at higher consumption levels and the ability of nature to provide resources and services
2. Between human populations and pathogenic microorganisms
3. Between human populations and those of other plant and animal species
4. Among human populations

Insecurity increases whenever any of these equilibriums is disrupted either by changes in human behavior or in nature. The early perceptions of the human predicament forcefully called attention to growth in population and consumption as disturbing the equilibrium between people and nature. There was only a hint of the potential role of technological innovation in reestablishing equilibrium by expanding nature's capabilities. Moreover, there was only a brief mention of the other potential sources of disequilibrium.

In the early years of the twenty-first century there is still cause for concern over the nature of resource limits (Meadows, Randers, and Meadows 2004). But experience has shown that so far on a global scale there have been few natural-resource limits to growth. While the quest for resources may have caused environmental despoliation, they have ultimately been available. Energy crises have occurred, but so far they have not been the result of inadequate petroleum or natural gas reserves. And other minerals still seem to be in abundant supply. Malnutrition and famine persist as a cause of human misery, but globally food production has increased faster than population. On the other hand, however, infectious diseases, once thought to have been conquered, have made a comeback, and extinction of many species has become a serious problem.

Much has been accomplished in attempting to meet some of the most obvious challenges to future well-being identified in the 1970s, but much remains to be done. Population growth has been significantly slowed in many parts of the world through concerted efforts. But in many countries, declining fertility has led to a new set of problems associated with population "graying." The mass starvation once predicted has so far been avoided, largely because of innovations in agriculture, but pockets of starvation and considerable malnutrition persist. The world does not yet seem in danger of running out of petroleum and natural gas, due to increases in energy efficiency in industry and transportation, as well as to technological innovation in resource exploration and recovery. Indeed, production of petroleum and natural gas has not yet peaked, and reserves have slightly increased in recent years. But the world's remaining reserves are increasingly concentrated in the Middle East. And little progress has been made in dealing with the complex and costly problems associated with increased fossil-fuel use, greenhouse gas buildup and associated global warming.

Looking toward the next quarter century, challenges to ecological security are emerging that were not widely anticipated 25 years ago. Globalization is intensifying changes of all kinds and significantly altering the nature of the human predicament. There are a host of challenges to ecological security inherent in this intensification, as well as in the continuing spread of industrialization to densely populated poor countries. And innovations in transportation have dramatically increased the numbers of people and quantities of merchandise moving rapidly from place to place. Between 1950 and 1998, for example, the number of passenger-kilometers flown internationally grew from 28 billion to 2.6 trillion annually. During the same period, annual international air freight grew from 730 million to 9.9 billion ton-kilometers annually (French 2000, 6–7). Such huge numbers of people and massive quantities of merchandise and commodities in motion are facilitating the unintended and often-destructive spread of plants and pests into new environments and ecosystems that were once comfortably separated from each other by geographic and political barriers. And there is mounting evidence that this large-scale and rapid movement of people and goods is disturbing long-established equilibriums between people and pathogens by facilitating the rapid spread of new and resurgent diseases.

Demographic Challenges

Rapid demographic changes are destabilizing forces that can upset all the equilibriums defining ecological security. Rapid population growth, the so-called population bomb, has long been considered a source of evolutionary discontinuities and thought to be at the core of humankind's predicament (Ehrlich 1968). The *Global 2000* study understandably adopted a pessimistic tone about these increasing numbers and lamented that "rapid growth in world population will hardly have altered by 2000. The world's population will grow from 4 billion in 1975 to 6.35 billion in 2000, an increase of more than 50 percent. The rate of growth will slow only marginally, from 1.8 percent a year to 1.7 percent" (Barney 1980, 1). While the population projection of 6.35 billion by the year 2000 was not far off the mark, the projected population growth rate was. As of mid-2003, world population stood at 6.31 billion, still a bit short of the 6.35 billion projection for 2000. The population growth rate, however, had dropped much faster than expected to 1.3 percent (Population Reference Bureau, 2003).

The biggest demographic surprise has been the speed with which zero population growth (ZPG) has been achieved, or even surpassed, in many industrialized countries and in the Central and Eastern European countries that have been in political and economic transition. Twenty-one countries have now reached or dropped below ZPG, the United States being a big exception. Projections indicate that as many as thirty-six countries will have smaller populations in 2050 than they do now (Population Reference Bureau, 2002). In addition to the more than two dozen industrialized and transition countries that are expected to experience population decline, in the Western Hemisphere Cuba, Grenada, St. Vincent, Surinam, and Guyana are also expected to shrink. Three African countries, Zimbabwe, Botswana, and South Africa, are expected to have declining populations as well, but sadly this is not because of reduced fertility, but because of the devastating impact of HIV/AIDS.

This largely unanticipated demographic shock in the industrialized countries has accentuated a large gap in population growth rates between them and the poorer countries. For example, the population of Europe is currently declining by 0.2 percent yearly, while that of sub-Saharan Africa is growing at 2.4 percent (Population Reference Bureau, 2003). This differential is creating significant pressures to fill the relative vacuum in the North through increased migration from the South side of the demographic divide.

The problems associated with estimating population growth and its impacts are discussed in detail by Robert Engelman, Richard P. Cincotta,

Amy Coen, and Kali-Ahset Amen in chapter 2. Looking backward, they find that international assistance and policy interventions have played a major role in reducing population growth. The good news is that due to these changing circumstances the population bomb has been defused and fertility in many countries has dropped much faster than most demographers had projected. The bad news is that part of the decline in population growth is due to the grim mortality statistics in Africa because of HIV/AIDS, a disease that only came to public attention after the publication of the *Global 2000 Report.*

Looking ahead, Engelman and his colleagues see much more uncertainty in demographic projections for the next three decades than for the last three. This is at least partly because of a lack of follow-through on international financial commitments to family planning. The HIV/AIDS pandemic also introduces considerable uncertainty into projections, not only because of its likely devastating effects on African countries, but also because of its eventual impact on much more populous countries like India and China (National Intelligence Council, 2002).

But rapid population growth is only one kind of discontinuity that can create ecological insecurity. In chapter 3, Paul J. Runci and Chester L. Cooper focus on another socioeconomic challenge of demographic change that was not anticipated in the earlier studies. Declining fertility and greater longevity are creating new kinds of discontinuities that will only sharpen over the next 25 years. By 2030, one in four people in the industrialized world will be 65 years of age or older, up from one in seven at present (Peterson 1999b, 13). This reverse demographic shock could have serious consequences for innovation, economic growth, public and private pension systems, medical care, education, and immigration. And in only the slightly more distant future, both China and India, accounting for more than one-third of the world's population, could face similar or even more serious problems and challenges as their populations rapidly age in the face of woefully underfunded public and private pension systems.

Food and Water

The adequacy of the world's food supply to meet the demands of a growing population is not a new concern. Indeed, Thomas Malthus called attention to this potential problem at the end of the eighteenth century.

Worries about starvation and malnutrition increased along with the population explosion of the late 1960s and early 1970s. In 1967 William and Paul Paddock published their provocative book *Famine 1975!* Shortly thereafter Lester Brown (1974) began his repeated warnings of dramatic food shortages to come, and Garrett Hardin (1974) even suggested the need for lifeboat ethics and triage to deal with hunger problems in rapidly growing poor countries.

The *Global 2000 Report* considered the future of the world food supply to be a significant concern, even though it projected a steady increase of 2.2 percent yearly in food production over the 1970–2000 period (Barney 1980, 13). Worldwide, per capita consumption was to increase by 15 percent over the same period. But most of this increase was projected to take place in the wealthier countries. Food production in the less industrialized countries was expected to barely keep ahead of population growth (Barney 1980, 17). Land under cultivation would increase very little, with most production gains coming from technological innovation and greater use of energy-intensive inputs. Thus, people in many of the world's poorest countries could expect to see only modest improvements in per capita food availability (Barney 1980, 17).

In chapter 5, Marc J. Cohen finds that more progress has been made in increasing food production than was originally envisioned. Per capita food availability in the less industrialized countries has risen 26 percent over the last three decades. In contrast to pessimistic projections about rising food prices, between 1982 and 1997 world wheat prices dropped 28 percent, rice prices 29 percent, and maize prices 30 percent in real terms. However, few anticipated the current situation of shortages in the face of surpluses, a situation in which large numbers of people remain underfed because of poverty. At the same time, increasing numbers of people in the wealthier countries are overfed, suffering various maladies due to too much food consumption (Gardner and Halweil 2000).

Looking forward, Cohen expects the same economic disparities and trade barriers that have given rise to malnutrition in the past to persist into the future. With official development assistance steadily falling, less external help is available to poor countries to increase food production. Nor is it easy to develop domestic farming for export in the less industrialized countries. Agricultural production in industrial countries is still heavily subsidized and many barriers remain to agricultural imports from less developed countries. For example, the United States has a rigid import quota on sugar, one of the major export crops from poor countries, and gives cotton farmers an annual subsidy of $3 billion, which enables them to control more than 40 percent of global cotton exports (King, Samor, and Miller 2004). As a result, the poor and deeply indebted agrarian countries have limited capital with which to expand food production, little access to markets in the industrialized countries, and few sources of income with which to finance any essential food imports. Of greatest importance in fighting future starvation and malnutrition, Cohen argues, is the goal of making globalization work for the world's poor by opening up agricultural markets and reducing subsidies to agriculture in industrial countries. (The amount spent on subsidizing farmers in industrial countries is six times what these countries give in official development assistance.)

A more immediate concern related to many aspects of ecological security is an adequate supply of water for drinking, irrigation, and sanitation. The adequacy of future water supplies was of considerable concern in the *Global 2000 Report,* which projected that water requirements would double between 1970 and 2000 in the half of the world where population was expected to grow most rapidly (Barney 1980, 2). Ken Conca points out in chapter 5 that current worldwide water use is significantly lower than these projections anticipated. Even so, current annual water withdrawals amount to 54 percent of the total accessible runoff. More than 1 billion people still lack access to safe drinking water and 2 billion people lack access to basic sanitation services.

According to Conca, the adequacy of the future world water supply to meet growing needs is difficult to assess. Estimates of water withdrawals for the year 2025 range from 3,625 to 5,044 cubic kilometers. While obvious factors such as population growth, economic development, and technological innovation will be important in determining future water needs, there are three sets of sociopolitical variables that will also have a profound impact on freshwater use. These include the future course of international river diplomacy, stakeholder disagreements over water-supply infrastructure, and controversies over water financing and pricing. The adequacy of future world food and water supplies thus will be as much determined by political and economic decisions as by nature.

Energy and Warming

Whether the world's supply of fossil fuels can meet future energy needs has been a persistent concern over the last three decades. As the *Global 2000 Report* put it, "The projections point out that petroleum production capacity is not increasing as rapidly as demand. Furthermore, the rate at which petroleum reserves are being added per unit of exploratory effort appears to be falling. Engineering and geological considerations suggest that world petroleum production will peak before the end of the century" (Barney 1980, 27). While world reserves of coal are now more than adequate, those of cleaner burning petroleum and natural gas appear to be in much shorter supply relative to projected demand. The growing massive energy needs of an industrialized China and India add to future energy concerns. And the growing concentration of these reserves in the unstable Middle East and former Soviet Union raise geopolitical worries.

While these early fears of running out of petroleum and natural gas have proved to be premature, forecasting fossil-fuel adequacy for the next quarter century also is filled with uncertainties. But some things about the future market are clear. Petroleum now accounts for nearly 40 percent of measured energy consumption worldwide, and because much of it is used in the existing transportation infrastructure this is not likely to change much in the near future. Demand for oil (and natural gas) will be closely related to economic growth. If significant future industrialization occurs in China, India, and other densely populated poor countries, demand will rise significantly and reserves will be drawn down quickly. The future petroleum supply is more problematic. Experts differ considerably on prospects for additions to reserves. Geologists use physical models of reserves and production and tend to stress impending limits, while economists use shorter-term market models to come to more optimistic conclusions.

Geologist M. King Hubbert did some of the most respected work in projecting the future of petroleum production. Using his vast expertise in petroleum geology, in 1956 he constructed a curve that traced past and likely future production of petroleum in the United States. He forecast a peak in U.S. production to occur between 1965 and 1970. The peak actually occurred in 1970 and domestic production has been declining since then. Hubbert undertook a more ambitious exercise in 1979, forecasting a peak in world production. He estimated that world production would peak around the turn of the century and then begin to decline. While this appraisal proved somewhat pessimistic, some recent estimates foresee a production peak around 2010 (Deffeyes 2001).

Heather Conley and Warren Phillips comment on the changing nature of the world energy market in chapter 6. They observe that worries about running out of fossil fuels and other minerals expressed in *The Limits to Growth* and other literature from earlier decades missed the mark. Rather than being a period of increasing scarcity, the 1980s and 1990s were characterized by a glut of petroleum, as technological innovation played a key role in stretching petroleum reserves. Future issues will be geopolitical and economic in nature, with Middle Eastern oil being a crucial present and future security concern. Increased competition among larger and more diversified oil companies will make the market much more complex than in the past. With the possible exception of oil fields in the Caspian region, new oil fields outside of the Middle East are unlikely to provide significant additions to worldwide reserves. OPEC is likely to dominate the future oil market, because its share of the world oil supply could rise to 50 percent. In addition, demand growth in OPEC countries themselves, and continued industrialization in China and India, could substantially increase world petroleum consumption.

Gary Cook and Eldon Boes pick up at this point with an overview—in chapter 7—of the potential for replacing fossil fuels with renewable-energy resources. Renewable-energy resources are those that are continually replenished or are replaced after use through natural means. They include wind energy, solar energy, running water, and biomass. Cook and Boes point out that for many reasons—geopolitical, environmental, and so on—a rapid transition to renewable-energy resources would be desirable. Vast quantities of untapped renewables are available throughout the world. Using them would cause little pollution and create almost no greenhouse gases. They describe the technologies now available to make such a transition and demonstrate that they are becoming economically competitive with fossil-fuel energy. Yet these technologies still only account for less than 10 percent of world measured energy consumption. And most scenarios indicate rapid changes in their use will be unlikely.

There are few technological barriers to using renewables, and the reasons for the very slow pace of this transition to alternatives are socioeconomic and political. For example, the United States historically has been particularly well endowed with fossil fuels, and this legacy makes it politically difficult to legislate policies that would spur development of renewables. More important, energy price fluctuations have inhibited the worldwide development of the renewables industry. Major and minor energy crises have periodically caused petroleum and natural gas prices to soar, raising them to levels where renewables become economically attractive. But subsequent economic slowdowns have led to plunging fuel prices and have had a devastating impact on the renewables industry.

The most pressing constraint on future increases in fossil-fuel consumption and the strongest argument for embracing renewable-energy sources may be global warming. At the time of the release of the *Global 2000 Report,* climate change was considered little more than a scientific hypothesis. In fact, in the 1970s there was even some concern that future worldwide cooling could cause new famines (Bryson and Murray 1977). But much has happened over the last three decades to elevate global warming to the top of the global agenda. The 2001 report of The Intergovernmental Panel on Climate Change (IPCC) dispelled any lingering scientific doubts about the reality of global warming (Intergovernmental Panel on Climate Change, 2001a). But dealing resolutely with this issue requires changing the course of industrialization and unlearning old ways of defining progress.

The causes of global warming and potential policies to deal with them are taken up by Matthias Ruth in chapter 8. The evidence from the IPCC reports indicates that the buildup of greenhouse gases will lead to noticeable temperature increases over the next few decades, with more significant increases to follow in the latter part of the century. These higher temperatures will have a profound effect on all aspects of ecological security, because they will be accompanied by changes in precipitation patterns, snow and ice cover, and sea level. For Ruth, the most important questions are geopolitical in nature. Climate change will likely create winners and losers, thus complicating the problem of negotiating remedies. For example, low-lying Pacific islands are likely to suffer considerable damage from sea-level rise, or even disappear, while Siberian agriculture might well profit from warmer temperatures.

Ruth suggests a wide range of policies that could help ameliorate the impact of global warming. While a global response ultimately will be required to deal with this issue, there are many mitigation and adaptation strategies that would make sense even in the absence of global warming. After reviewing a series of policy options available to reduce greenhouse gas emissions and to adapt to climate change, he concludes with several recommendations for coping with this unprecedented challenge.

Jacob Park follows with his analysis of the evolution of the international politics of global warming and the likely future of climate-change agreements in chapter 9. Climate change raises important equity considerations in ongoing international negotiations. Many of the countries that produce the smallest greenhouse gas emissions are likely to suffer the worst effects from projected global warming. Because the interests of parties to these negotiations differ so greatly, Park sees little chance of a major breakthrough in the near future. In his view the Kyoto Protocol is at best a stopgap measure. He concludes that the crucial question for the international community is whether it has the vision and foresight to create crucial policy links between the present and the future.

Vanishing Forests and Species

The relationship between *Homo sapiens* and other species is a growing ecological-security concern. The *Global 2000 Report* stressed the importance of the impending loss of forests, particularly tropical forests in the less industrialized countries, which provide a habitat for millions of species. Deforestation was expected to be a continuing problem until 2020, when "virtually all of the physically accessible forest in the LDCs [less developed countries] is expected to be cut" (Barney 1980, 26). Prices of wood and wood products were expected to rise considerably as demand increased and supplies tightened. But as with the petroleum market, while the long-term prognosis has remained fairly grim, the projected increases in prices of wood and wood products have not yet materialized.

Patricia Marchak explores tropical-forest issues in chapter 10. Degradation of forests has been taking place since the beginning of human history, but she believes it has become a serious ecological and social problem only in the last 50 years. Tropical forests now supply only a small portion of total world forest products, but trade in wood products from these regions is growing rapidly as Northern countries can no longer meet their needs with domestic trees. The U.N. Food and Agricultural Organization (FAO) estimates that 15.4 million hectares of tropical forest have disappeared annually over the last two decades. Marchak points out that preserving these forests is especially important because of their role as carbon sinks. Their degradation releases carbon dioxide, thus contributing to the problem of global warming. She also points out that tropical forests are home to an estimated two-thirds of all the plants and animals so far identified by scientists.

The disappearance of tropical forests implies the loss of habitat for, and perhaps the extinction of, many of the world's species. There have been five previous large-scale species extinctions in the earth's history, but they have all been caused by natural catastrophes. There is a growing consensus that industrialization and globalization are leading to a sixth. One of the barriers to understanding the scope of biodiversity loss is that the total number of species in the contemporary world is unknown. A recent study estimated the number of existing species of all kinds to be 13.6 million. But of these, only about 1.8 million have been yet identified (UN Environment Programme, 1995). The UN Environment Programme (UNEP) estimates that 18 percent of mammals, 11 percent of birds, 8 percent of plants, and 5 percent of fish are now threatened (UN Environment Programme, 1995, 234).

David W. Inouye deals with these biodiversity issues in chapter 11. He points out that concern about the loss of biodiversity is fairly recent and that, aside from the loss of forests, it was not much stressed in the *Global 2000 Report*. The term *biodiversity* only came into use in 1985. Preserving biodiversity is of increasing concern for both utilitarian and nonutilitarian reasons. Preservation of greater diversity is important for future plant and animal breeding, but perhaps its greatest value is the life-supporting services that intact ecosystems provide.

Inouye projects the erosion of biodiversity to be a serious and growing threat to ecological security. At least one in eight plant species is already on the World Conservation Union's list of threatened species. While the causes of biodiversity loss are many, he claims that most of them can be traced to the activities of just one species—our own. As to the future, Inouye identifies global warming as a factor that may well accelerate the loss of diversity due to temperature increases, changes in precipitation patterns, and sea-level rise. He fears that as biological resources become more limited in the future, they could become an increasing cause of conflict.

Globalization and Ecological Security

The continuing spread of an industrial way of life to more densely populated countries such as China and India and the accelerating pace of globalization are changing the nature of many of these long-term problems, as well as raising new ones. The emergence of global commerce has ameliorated some problems but has created or exacerbated others. Along with the economic growth associated with an emerging worldwide division of labor come increasing challenges to ecological security. A growing flow of people, products, plants, pests, and pathogens through increasingly porous borders is threatening to upset delicate balances between people and nature and give rise to new problems, including bioinvasion and possibly future epidemics or even pandemics.

Bioinvasion refers to plants and animals moving from established habitats into new ecosystems, where they occasionally wreak havoc. The forces of nature have always driven a limited exchange of plants and animals among the world's diverse ecosystems. And species often have been moved intentionally, with occasionally destructive results. For example, the introduction of rabbits into Australia in 1859 was intended to enhance hunting experiences, but it has resulted in a bunny population explosion that has devoured Australian foliage. Now, however, the dynamics of globalization are increasing migration opportunities for countless organisms, and giving rise to long-distance migrations that were rare in the past (Bright 1998, 20). As travel and commerce have increased significantly, so has the unintended spread of species from one part of the world to another. And the likely acceleration of globalization over the next three decades will increase dramatically the unintended travels of plants and animals.

The extent of the total damage that has already been caused by bioinvasion is difficult to quantify, and there is likewise no good estimate of its likely future impact. A recent study of bioinvasion in the United States estimates a current annual figure of $138 billion for losses, damage, and control costs associated with invasive species (Pimental et al. 1999). The largest amount of direct damage is caused by the zebra mussel, which arrived in the United States from Eastern Europe ($3.1 billion); the fire ant, which has moved northward into the Southern United States and California ($2.0 billion); the Asian clam, which is now found in thirty-eight states ($1.0 billion); and the Formosan termite, which is destroying buildings and trees in Louisiana ($1.0 billion) (Licking 1999). It is much more difficult to estimate the current worldwide damage from bioinvasion, but Chris Bright (1998, 176) has roughly estimated the annual total world direct crop loss from nonindigenous pests to be between $55 and $248 billion.

The acceleration of travel and trade is also associated with growing threats from new and resurgent infectious diseases. Infectious disease was not considered likely to be to be a serious future problem in the 1970s. In fact, many public health officials assumed the battle against infectious disease had largely been won thanks to a new generation of pharmaceuticals. But there is now considerable evidence that a variety of pathogens are poised to launch attacks against people, plants, and animals on a global scale (Garrett 1994). Since 1973, twenty known diseases, including tuberculosis, malaria, and cholera, have strengthened and spread geographically. Furthermore, at least thirty previously unknown diseases have emerged during this period. Foremost among these is the deadly HIV/AIDS virus, which, although not easily transmitted, has moved steadily around the world for more than two decades. And the outbreak of the much more contagious SARS virus in 2003 could be a harbinger of new viruses to come.

There is much historical evidence that periods of increasing contact among previously separated peoples, characteristic of the current period of globalization, have been accompanied by disease outbreaks and epidemics. The expanding Roman Empire was beset with numerous strange maladies originating in the provinces. There were at least eleven disease disasters during Republican times (McNeill 1976, 115–117). As European commerce and contacts with distant parts of the world grew in the fourteenth century, the infamous Black Death was carried by rats and accompanying fleas from China to Europe in trade caravans. The disease spread across the continent killing between 30 and 40 percent of the European population in the first wave (Hobhouse 1990, 15). And in the Western Hemisphere the "discovery" of the Americas in the late fifteenth century resulted in the decimation of indigenous peoples by diseases, particularly smallpox, brought by the Europeans (McNeill 1976, 208).

Human immune systems have been honed by thousands of years of coevolution with a variety of pathogens, normally within the confines of relatively isolated ecosystems. Outbreaks and epidemics have occurred when people have encountered pathogens with which their immune systems have had no experience. In the contemporary world, people can become exposed in an increasing number of ways to pathogens against which their immune systems have only limited defenses. Because of increases in the speed of transportation, travelers can pick up diseases in one part of the world and spread them to others well before experiencing any symptoms. Presently more than 2 million people cross national borders each day (French 2000, 6). Disease outbreaks can also occur when people move into previously unsettled areas. Population growth in Latin America and Africa is pressuring people to move into remote areas where they can be exposed to new pathogens, such as the Ebola virus, that may have lurked in the tropical forest for a long time. Once liberated, these pathogens can quickly spread to more densely populated urban areas (Gibbons 1993). The same dynamics apply to the spread of pathogens that can adversely affect crops and livestock.

It is very difficult to make precise projections about the spread of infectious disease over the next three decades. It will be a function of the pace of globalization, innovations in biotechnology and medicine, better surveillance, and the extent to which governments in wealthy countries take the threat of disease seriously and devote more adequate resources to disease prevention at home and in poorer countries. At present, the continuing HIV/AIDS pandemic seems to pose the greatest future threat, although a new and more deadly form of influenza could quickly move around the world before a vaccine could be developed (Naik 2003). The HIV/AIDS pandemic is having an especially harsh impact on the poor in sub-Saharan African countries, where 27 million people are living with the virus (UN AIDS, 2003, 7). The most serious future threat is that the virus will spread in larger, more densely populated countries such as China, India, Russia, Nigeria, and Ethiopia. While there are presently about 39 million people with HIV/AIDS worldwide, it is estimated that the number of HIV/AIDS cases in these countries alone could grow from the present 14–23 million cases to 50–75 million by 2010 (National Intelligence Council, 2002).

From Limits to Sustainability

Much has happened over the last three decades to change perceptions of the human predicament. And much has been learned that will be useful in meeting the daunting challenges of the future. Perhaps the essence of the situation has been best summarized by the furry philosopher Pogo, who once succinctly pointed out that "we have met the enemy and he is us." While nature still sets constraints that human beings must live within, it has not been sudden changes in nature that have been responsible for increasing ecological insecurity. Rather, it is the persistence of values, institutions, and patterns of behavior that evolved during an era of resource abundance into a new era of much changed opportunities that is largely responsible for growing ecological insecurity. While technological innovation has played a crucial role in extending nature's limits to this point, it has now become essential that the socioeconomic, political, and ethical dimensions of these problems and issues be addressed.

People, their values, and their institutions are thus a cause of many of these pressing problems as well a potential source of solutions. The dynamics of globalization are bringing people closer together physically and psychologically in what could best be called an emerging global society. An increasing portion of the world's population is plugging into a growing telecommunications network. And an accelerating worldwide flow of people, images, and ideas is focusing attention on persistent technological, environmental, economic, educational, and demographic gaps among the various neighborhoods of the nascent global city. Just as issues of grave inequalities had to be addressed politically in the evolution of the industrial democracies, they now must be addressed globally. And just as mechanisms for wealth redistribution were required to maintain social peace within countries, some form of governance will be required to deal with distributional issues on a global scale.

The perceived predicament of humankind is thus now changing from one of population overshoot and environmental limits to growth to one of globalization, growing interdependence, increasing disequilibriums, and related distributional concerns. A population explosion has morphed into a set of discontinuities created by a birth dearth, differential growth rates, and growing pressures for migration. An expected global food shortage has not materialized, but issues of future food security and adequate purchasing power in poorer countries remain. Global warming has emerged as an impending challenge to all dimensions of ecological security. And an assumed victory over infectious disease has been transformed into fears of new epidemics due to changes in human behavior, increased global trade and transportation, and lack of adequate health care and surveillance in poor countries. Building a more sustainable global society now requires new forms of cooperation to create global public goods to redress the imbalances, disparities, and inequalities that are emerging in this era of increasing ecological insecurity (Kaul, Grunberg, and Stern 1999).

2

The Future Is Not What It Used to Be: World Population Trends

Robert Engelman, Richard P. Cincotta, Amy Coen, and Kali-Ahset Amen

Two projected growth trends—in human population and in per capita income—underlie many of the environmental projections that the *Global 2000 Report to the President* (Barney 1980) made for the world at the opening of the twenty-first century. And, of course, demographic changes are a crucial component of ecological security.

This chapter will consider global human population trends, with particular emphasis on what that report got right and what it got wrong. We describe the range of global and regional population projections generated by the *Global 2000* team of experts, with special attention to the projection that experts used throughout the report for modeling natural resource use and environmental impact. The chapter then contrasts this picture with the population dynamics that actually transpired in the following two decades. We speculate on why the experts' medium population projection for the year 2000 differed considerably from the reality, as illustrated in the United Nations Population Division's current assessment of year 2000 population.[1] Those differences illustrate some of the unforeseen changes in fundamental demographic trends that occurred during the last quarter of the twentieth century.

The world's demographic news is both good and bad. The good news—for those, like the authors of the *Global 2000 Report,* who see rapid population growth as a significant contributing factor in environmental degradation and ecological insecurity—is that fertility dropped in all of the world's regions faster than demographers had projected. These declines were especially dramatic in East and Southeast Asia. In several countries in these regions, falling fertility produced age structures that paved the way for unusually rapid national economic development.

Journalists dubbed these countries the "Asian Tigers" during the 1980s, and they became the focus of considerable economic and demographic research in the early to mid-1990s.

But this regional economic success story is only part of the story. By the turn of the new century, world population growth had slowed to about two-thirds of that described by the medium population projection featured in the *Global 2000 Report*. Population will thus peak considerably sooner than experts had predicted.

Nonetheless, there is bad news, as well. Crude death rates in Africa remain higher than the *Global 2000* experts expected. There was indeed progress in reducing mortality in the intervening years. The high death rates of the year 2000 reflect instead recent tragic reversals in trends in life expectancy in east and southern African countries due partly to resurgences in malaria and tuberculosis but mostly to the HIV/AIDS pandemic. Reflecting the perils of prediction, this disease—destined to become one of the most deadly epidemics known to humanity—first emerged to public view just after publication of the *Global 2000 Report*. The evolution of HIV/AIDS represents the kind of surprise development that no experts can possibly foresee in its specifics, but that prognosticators should allow for in general.

This chapter discusses these demographic changes, their causes, and the contributions of reproductive, maternal, and child health programs, investments in education, and other policies and programs to current trends in fertility and mortality. From our vantage point in the early years of the twenty-first century, it is a far easier task to identify effective development policies and programs, and to relate them to the slowing of population growth and the economic progress of nations, than it was when Gerald Barney oversaw production of the *Global 2000 Report*.

For the world of 2030, the UN's latest effort projects a population that, assuming low fertility, amounts to more than 7.5 billion people, with another 30 million born annually. A feasible upper boundary for fertility expectations also assumes continuing declines in fertility in the developing countries, yet would lead to a world of almost 8.8 billion in 2030. If the coming quarter century were to unfold as the last, world population would meander somewhere between these scenarios, dipping somewhat abruptly in the final decade. But just as the *Global 2000 Report* showed a limited ability to accurately predict world population twenty years in advance, we have no more assurance for being able to do so in 2005.

From the experience of the past twenty years, demographers and public health experts can now say with confidence that policies and investments that open greater access to quality reproductive health care and bring more girls into the classroom and more women into the workplace do indeed encourage smaller families and later pregnancies. These, in turn, powerfully slow population growth. Much about the future of world population thus depends on what citizens and policymakers do today to widen access to reproductive health care, to see that girls attend and stay in school, and to bring economic opportunities to women.

Projecting Population: A Primer

The *Global 2000 Report* opens with a rich discussion of the uncertainties that underlie all population projections. The demographers who contributed to the report knew all too well that only a small fraction of the scientists, analysts, and journalists who would use the projected populations and rates would actually understand how they were generated and how uncertain they might be. Human population grew markedly during the past 25 years, but the method of projection—called the *cohort component method* (CCM)—remained essentially the same.

Projectionists using CCM group national populations by sex and age-specific cohorts (usually 5-year groups). Each cohort is assigned age-specific rates of mortality, migration, and fertility. This last is applied for females of reproductive age, which demographers standardize as 15 to 44 or 49, depending on the projection. The cohorts are then "aged"—that is, advanced to the next interval, accounting for deaths and migrations that change the cohort's size. Births refresh the population in the 0- to 4-year cohort.

In projecting the demographic future, the challenge for demographers is to understand the complex and uneven trends in fertility, mortality, and migration and to consider to what extent they are likely to continue. As currently generated by the UN Population Division or the International Program Center of the U.S. Census Bureau, the two most frequently cited sources of population estimates and projections,[2] these projections are not statistically predictive. They are, rather, based on experts' educated guesses about future trends in the three basic drivers of population change: age-specific rates of fertility (the average number of live births per woman in an age group), of death, and of net migration (immigration minus emigration).

Once the time series of age-specific rates have been assumed for each country, they are applied to estimates of current national population numbers to project those populations into the future. In the *Global 2000 Report,* and in the most current UN biennial projection, three scenarios have been generated.[3] The medium scenario is often thought to represent the most likely outcome. It may be more appropriate to consider the band of projections generated by the high and low variants as the *expected range of probable outcomes,* without taking on the added task of assigning greater probability to any one scenario. In any case, the use of three scenarios helps illustrate the lack of statistical certainty that can be derived from this standard methodology.

When generating the three main projections, demographers vary their assumptions on how many children women will have in the future. These "fertility end points" are perhaps the most conspicuously unrealistic assumptions in current projection methodologies, because no country has exhibited stable fertility over long periods of time. For various reasons, demographers generally maintain consistent assumptions about death and (where applicable) migration rates across all the projections.

An important and often-overlooked assumption of present projection methods is that changes in fertility, mortality, and migration rates will occur gradually. While this may seem reasonable, demographers have found it often fails to conform to reality. Death rates have changed abruptly as a result of infectious disease. Migration rates can change explosively in the wake of conflicts and sudden changes in economic conditions or government policies. Finally, fertility rates have changed dramatically during the last 25 years. Modern contraception as well as educational and employment opportunities became increasingly available to young women in many developing countries, encouraging smaller average family size.

The Global 2000 Population Projections in Retrospect

Ultimately, the authors of the *Global 2000 Report* needed to settle on a single set of projected population data to support their environmental projections. They chose, appropriately enough, the medium scenario by the U.S. Census Bureau (1979), which was projected using 1975 population estimates. Today, we can see that this demographic scenario projected a larger population, faster growth, and higher fertility than the current 2000 world estimate (see table 2.1). In almost all regions, however, actual crude death rates fairly closely tracked the Census Bureau's projections.

There are important stories in the exceptions to these general statements. The most noteworthy are the population dynamics of North America and sub-Saharan Africa. Higher-than-expected migration to the United States was responsible for population growth that was more rapid than projected. Death rates in sub-Saharan Africa, though they declined rapidly throughout most of the latter half of the twentieth century, leveled off as AIDS mortality increased and infectious diseases, particularly malaria and tuberculosis, expanded throughout the continent.

In the year 2000, world population was growing at a bit less than 1.3 percent annually, a rate projected by the U.S. Census Bureau's lowest projections for 2000 (U.S. Census Bureau, 1979; Barney 1980). The annual growth is about four-fifths of the medium series projections (1.6 percent annually)—which the *Global 2000 Report* embraced as its own rate of projected world growth. This means that population momentum is weakening somewhat faster than expected. It may also mean that the peak of world population is approaching sooner than experts had imagined a quarter century ago.

Table 2.1
1975 Population projections and 2000 estimates

	2000 Population (billions)	2000 Population growth rate	2000 Fertility rate
1975 Projections			
High	6.80	2.0	3.9
Medium	6.35	1.6	3.3
Low	5.92	1.3	2.8
2000 Estimates	6.08	1.3	2.8

Some Lessons Learned

The fact that global population growth slowed surprisingly between 1981 and 2000 is striking, yet it is not the only trend that demographers and other experts failed to foresee two decades ago. First, today's world is demographically divided in unprecedented ways. More than two-fifths of the world's population lives in countries where fertility is close to or below replacement levels. Many of the world's wealthiest countries have total fertility rates so low that a continuation of the status quo would eventually result in substantial population declines in these countries, without major increases in net immigration. These are mostly countries in Europe, plus Japan, in which total fertility hovers between 1.2 and 1.6 children per woman.

However, this does not mean serious population decline will occur. Fertility rates could rise, or immigration to these countries could increase. It seems likely, at least, that the populations of many of the wealthiest nations will remain relatively constant or decline slightly in the coming decades. This has significant environmental implications for the nations involved and, given the geographic reach of their production and consumption patterns, for the world as a whole.

Even within the industrialized world, however, there is an important exception to the rule of relatively stable or slowly decreasing populations. The United States continues to grow rapidly, as noted above. In fact, the most recent census (2001) shows that the overall population growth rate of this nation is similar to that of the world as a whole, between 1.2 and 1.3 percent annually.

But the United States is an exception to the overall demographic trends of industrialized countries. On the other side of the global divide is a group of nations in which fertility remains quite high, exceeding five children per woman. Population growth continues in these countries at the relatively rapid pace of 2 to 3 percent a year, most of them in sub-Saharan Africa but also including several Middle Eastern and Asian nations. These nations show no clear sign of a population peak in the near future. As in 1981, it remains difficult to imagine how much longer these high growth rates can be sustained in countries where governments and other institutions tend to be weakest and most stressed by rapid change, and where critical natural resource bases are dangerously degraded. It would be hazardous to predict when these nations will experience their own population peaks, but it does seem safe to say that high proportions of their future populations may seek to migrate to countries in which population growth is proceeding more slowly.

A critical question on which few serious scholars have ventured to speculate is under what conditions further population growth might contribute to a slowing of population growth. Many projections of the future global environment (including The *Limits to Growth* (Meadows et al. 1972) and the *Global 2000 Report*) assume that human population could indeed reach levels at which key life-support systems are frayed so badly that increased death rates would inevitably result. Some argue that this has already occurred, and that high population densities in some ecosystems and natural resource bases are contributing to millions of deaths each year from diarrhea and other hazards.

The Demographic Impacts of HIV/AIDS

The world's population growth already is slowing, not only because women are giving birth to fewer babies than before, but because higher proportions of people are dying at younger ages. This is yet another surprise of contemporary population dynamics; today, both lower birth rates and higher death rates are slowing the pace of global population growth.

These increases in mortality rates are due primarily to HIV/AIDS in sub-Saharan Africa, and to alcoholism, stress, and other factors in Eastern Europe. Despite the scale of the human tragedy itself, HIV/AIDS' impact is currently *demographically* significant only in a few countries. Since the disease was first described in 1981, about 19 million people have died from causes related to HIV infection (UNAIDS, 2002). World population increased during the same period by 1.6 billion (United Nations, 2003).

What has caught the attention of demographers is not so much the present impact of the epidemic as the projected future. It appears that, by 2010, AIDS-related deaths could become the major factor in actual reversals of population growth in at least four African countries, by removing a substantial proportion of the core of these countries' age structure: those of productive as well as reproductive age. The countries so affected are Botswana, where about 39 percent of reproductive-age people are infected, Mozambique (13 percent), Swaziland (33 percent), and South

Africa (20 percent) (UNAIDS, 2002). A fifth country, Zimbabwe (34 percent), is projected to be on the very cusp of decline by 2010. Seen from the vantage point of the *Global 2000 Report,* this is truly a surprise: projections of rapid population growth presaging population declines.

However, enough scientific uncertainty remains about how easily HIV spreads that projections could be off in either direction. Overall accuracy of projections could also depend on how well experts forecast infection rates in China and India, where current HIV prevalence is relatively low (0.1 and 0.8 percent, respectively, among reproductive-age adults), but where there is scant information on AIDS mortality or the effectiveness of prevention programs (UNAIDS, 2002). Projections also assume that responses to the pandemic will be "business as usual," which, as we will see, is rarely realistic. In the case of HIV/AIDS (as with population growth as a whole), there is much that society can do to affect medium-and long-term outcomes. Based on current population estimates, lower birth rates contribute much more to slowing population growth than higher death rates do. These birthrate declines are overwhelmingly the product of a growing desire to have later childbirths and smaller families than previously, combined with improved family planning and related health-care services.

Yet the fact that increases in death rates are contributing to the slow-down of global population growth is hardly cause for celebration. The same is true of the troubling possibility that unintended infertility may also be slowing world population growth. Unintended infertility—the inability to conceive and bear a pregnancy to term—is extremely hard to quantify. Some health experts believe it is rising in many developing countries, probably due at least in part to increases in sexually transmitted infections, and particularly to HIV. Damage to human reproductive systems brought on by increased exposure to pollutants may also be a factor, though evidence so far is circumstantial. Clearly, a major goal of population policy should be that intended declines in fertility contribute more to future declines in population growth rates than either unintended fertility declines or tragic increases in death rates.

The Future, as Seen from Today

Where does this leave us in predicting the next few decades of human population growth? Bluntly, not very well off. As an old meteorologist's saying goes, "I'm not very comfortable with predictions, particularly when they're about the future." What matters most may be what we can say about the future by focusing on the *present* population. The momentum of past growth all but guarantees continued global growth for at least the next two or three decades. Only massive increases in deaths, or an equally dramatic crash in human fertility, could lead the world's population to peak before 2025.

Of course, neither of these can be ruled out, and after three decades in the future the crystal ball gets somewhat cloudy. The best guide is the UN Population Division (2003) projections to 2050, with its outer bounds (see figure 2.1) of a "statistically sound basis for what would be most likely to happen in a future without significant surprises" (Engelman 1997).

All projections by the UN Population Division continue to assume fertility declines in all developing regions of the world (see figure 2.2). Given the increasing participation in family-planning programs and the growing demand for contraception, particularly in most of Asia and Latin America, there is good reason to believe declines will continue in

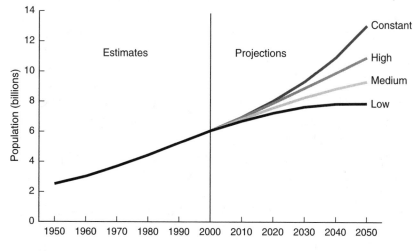

Figure 2.1
Estimated and projected population of the world, 1950–2050. *Source:* UN Population Division, *World Population Prospects: The 2000 Revision* (New York: United Nations, 2001).

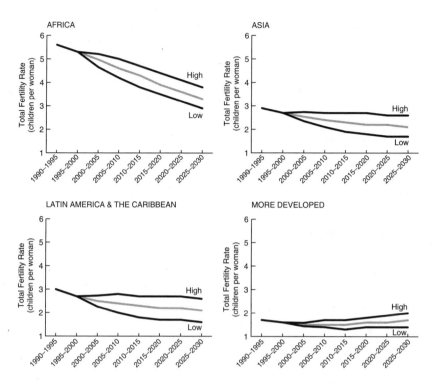

Figure 2.2
Fertility estimates and projections by region, 1990–2030. *Source:* UN Population Division, *World Population Prospects: The 2000 Revision* (New York: United Nations, 2001).

the coming decades. The United Nations estimates that worldwide some 62 percent (around 650 million) of the more than 1 billion married women of reproductive age (15 to 49 years) are currently using contraception (UN Population Division, 2003). In Africa, only 25 percent of married women are using contraception. In Asia, however, contraceptive use is high—66 percent among married women of reproductive age. And contraceptive use is higher still in Latin America and the Caribbean, at 69 percent. The global convergence of these trends, along with further delays in marriage and higher educational attainment among girls and women, could tilt regional fertility trends toward the UN's low scenarios.

According to the UN Population Division, Asia's large population (see figure 2.3) should continue to comprise roughly 60 percent of humanity well beyond 2030. Despite AIDS mortality, Africa's smaller population is projected to grow at the most rapid pace of any region during the next three decades. Even if Africa's population future matched the UN's low fertility scenario—which includes projections of AIDS mortality, and assumes an unprecedented decline in fertility across the continent— Africa would add another 65 percent, or nearly twice the current U.S. population, by 2030 (UN Population Division, 2003).

Thus, absent major surprises in death or birth rates, continued world population growth over the next 25 years is certain. Most of the people who will fuel that growth are already alive, and they are the most populous younger generation in history. Population pyramids (see figure 2.4)

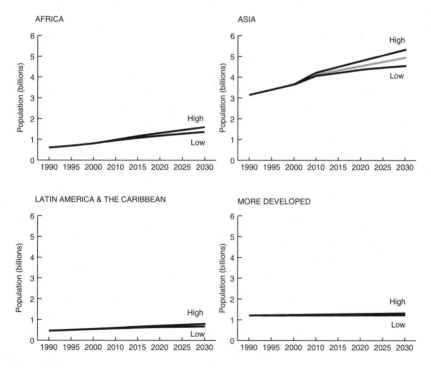

Figure 2.3
Population estimates and projections by region, 1990–2030. *Source:* UN Population Division, *World Population Prospects: The 2000 Revision* (New York: United Nations, 2001).

give us a sense of just what a challenge this generation presents in most of the world's developing nations. The issue is not simply that population growth is unlikely to end until they are well past their own childbearing years. It is that already strained societies in the least-developed countries will need to plan for and adapt to substantially larger numbers of young people who will need classrooms, health care, family-planning services, jobs, and housing as they move through their lives.

There are clear economic considerations here as well. With high proportions of young people, societies have high dependency ratios (defined as the ratio of children too young to work and older people too old to work, compared to the working-age population), even if the proportion of the elderly is low. Experience has shown that reductions in fertility can create a short-lived "demographic bonus" by reducing the proportion of the young before higher life expectancies can balance out the dependency ratio on the other end of life. Societies with sound institutions in a position to take advantage of this bonus, especially through investing in the health and education of their young populations, can make dramatic economic progress. The classic example is the Asian tigers in the 1980s and early 1990s (Bloom and Canning 2000; Asian Development Bank, 1997; Higgins and Williamson 1997). Societies with no demographic bonus stand to lose this opportunity, no matter how sound their institutions.

Pressures to migrate are likely to rise with the growing number of young people. If migration becomes less of an option, many young people will become vulnerable to the kind of hopelessness that feeds social disruption. Over the next decade the world will need to provide 460 million new jobs, more than twice as many as currently exist in the entire North American economy, to meet the demand for work stimulated by the population growth of the past two decades. Fully 97 percent of these new jobs will be needed in developing countries, two-thirds of them in Asia alone (International Labour Organization, 2001). To the extent that they are not provided, the unemployed and underemployed will seek to move to where they believe job availability is better, or they will seek opportunities outside of formal economic employment to give their lives meaning and to prove their worth.

Immigration to industrialized countries may become more welcome in those countries where natural increase is insufficient to keep labor

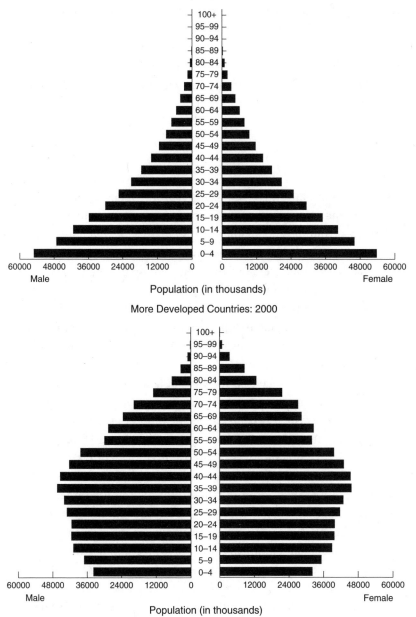

Figure 2.4
Age structure in the least and more developed regions, 2000. *Source:* UN
Population Division, *World Population Prospects: The 2000 Revision* (New
York: United Nations, 2001).

forces growing over the next 25 years, chiefly Japan and many European countries. But the same countries are already densely populated. Housing is expensive, transportation networks are challenged, and open space is at a premium. Would the demographic growth needed to preserve current ratios of workers to retirees be environmentally and socially sustainable? This question has yet to be raised in industrialized countries.

What Could Be

As the UN Population Division's low variant suggests, the surprising reality is that the world may not be very far—in time and in total numbers—from the epochal moment in history in which human numbers reach their all-time peak and then begin to recede gradually. If the lowest UN variants are close to reality, many people now alive will experience a decreasing world population, for the first time since Europe's Black Death in the fourteenth century. With good fortune, this coming downturn in global population will be much more the product of intended decreases in births than unintended factors related either to births or deaths.

The world's nations have been aware (at least since a key international population conference in 1994) of a strategy that will slow population growth, among several benefits, through voluntary reductions in births. At the International Conference on Population and Development in Cairo in 1994, representatives of almost all of the world's governments agreed to a Program of Action to refocus population policies and programs around the world on the quality of human life rather than the quantity of human lives. The objectives of the program were improved access to health care, better access to education for girls and improved economic, social, and political status for women. In particular, the 179 country delegations pledged to make access to information about and means to achieve family planning a reality for all who seek them by 2015, at an estimated cost of $17 billion a year by the year 2000. That cost would be shared roughly equally between the consumers of contraceptive services, developing-country governments themselves, and the governments of the industrialized countries, for which universal access is largely taken for granted.[5]

The Program of Action and the conference that articulated it mark a historic confluence of demographic research and the commitment of government policymakers, prodded by a movement of mostly women's nongovernmental organizations that may have been at its most vibrant in the mid-1990s. Research indeed confirms that the dramatic expansion of access to family-planning services in the last third of the twentieth century explains nearly half of the revolutionary drop in human fertility in that period (Bongaarts, Mauldin, and Phillips, 1990). Today's world population is probably smaller by about 700 million people than it would have been without organized family-planning programs. And that gap—between what is and what might have been—grows with time.

An even more important gap, however, will be between the health and demographic outcome that could result from full implementation of Cairo's Program of Action, and the outcome likely if nations renege on their commitment made in 1994. For the demographic evidence is also strong that when girls complete their schooling through at least secondary school they are more likely to have healthier babies—and fewer of them, later in their lives. Similar evidence is available for the influence of the economic empowerment of women. And experience and logic also lend credence to the hypothesis that underlies population policies in the twenty-first century. Worldwide, it is political will, funding, and widespread programs to help women make their lives what they want them to be that are the key to a healthier planet and an early peak in world population. The authors of the *Global 2000 Report* and the projections they relied on missed this point, which was much less well understood 20 years ago than it is today.

Today, there are no more excuses for missing the well-documented connection between women's well-being, the future of the world's population, and the connection of both to the global environment. Neither population nor the future itself can be forecast with perfection, much less controlled. But we can take action to influence both for the better, and the historical analysts of the future may salute the efforts we make, even if our foresight is far from perfect.

Notes

1. Unless otherwise noted, the data used are from the UN Population Division's 2002 revision of world population estimates and projections (Population Division, 2003).

2. The authors of the *Global 2000 Report*'s population section did, however, misconstrue the words *estimates* and *projections*. For demographers, estimates refer only to quantitative assessments of populations in the present day or in the past. These numbers cannot be known with precision, because current national censuses and past records tend to be flawed, out of date, or, in some countries, nonexistent. In discussions of future population numbers, the appropriate term is usually *projection*. This term refers to a mathematical calculation of how many people a population will include at a given time if certain specified assumptions about fertility and mortality—as well as migration, except when the number refers to the world as a whole—were to become a reality.

3. In the current UN biennial projections, another set of assumptions is used to generate a fourth scenario: the constant-fertility series projection. In these assumptions fertility is held constant while mortality and migration continue to change over time. The point of producing such an impossibly artificial scenario is simply to demonstrate the demographic importance of continued declines in fertility, for the constant-fertility projection produces the highest future populations of any scenario. The UN long-range projections (UN Population Division, 1999), which are issued less frequently than the biennial projections by the UN Population Division, consist of a set of seven scenarios: low, medium-low, medium, medium-high, high, constant fertility, and instant replacement. Medium-low and medium-high series are generated for long-term projections because, over the 150-year time frame of these projections, the assumptions for the low series produce absurdly low projections, and those for the high series produce absurdly high projections.

4. The least-developed countries, as defined by the United Nations General Assembly in 1998, include forty-eight countries: Afghanistan, Angola, Bangladesh, Benin, Bhutan, Burkina Faso, Burundi, Cambodia, Cape Verde, Central African Republic, Chad, Comoros, Democratic Republic of the Congo, Djibouti, Equatorial Guinea, Eritrea, Ethiopia, Gambia, Guinea, Guinea-Bissau, Haiti, Kiribati, Lao People's Democratic Republic, Lesotho, Liberia, Madagascar, Malawi, Maldives, Mali, Mauritania, Mozambique, Myanmar, Nepal, Niger, Rwanda, Samoa, São Tomé and Príncipe, Sierra Leone, Solomon Islands, Somalia, Sudan, Togo, Tuvalu, Uganda, United Republic of Tanzania, Vanuatu, Yemen, and Zambia. These countries are also included in the less developed regions.

5. *Access*, however, is a term much debated within the population and reproductive health communities. Most sides of the debate agree that it must mean more than the physical capacity to travel to a family-planning clinic and pay for a

contraceptive. It can also imply that services are appropriate for the individual needs of clients, that a variety of contraceptive options is provided, and even that clients have sufficient familial and social permission or approval to make use of the services offered. In the United States, where citizens presume that health-care services are among the best in the world, nearly half of all pregnancies are not intended, a clear indication that physical access to contraceptives is not all that matters to the intendedness of pregnancy (Institute of Medicine, 1995).

3

Reflections on an Aging Global Population

Paul J. Runci and Chester L. Cooper

When the *Global 2000 Report to the President* was published in 1980, population aging was far from the top of the national and global policy agendas. On the one hand, a decade of energy crises, stagflation, and global economic recession prompted many analysts and policymakers to focus their attention on the future of economic growth. On the other hand, the emergence in the early 1970s of the environmental movement and the publication of books such as *The Population Bomb* (Ehrlich 1968) and *Limits to Growth* (Meadows et al. 1972) prompted others to focus on the long-term implications of population growth trends for natural resource use and environmental quality. Few, if any, analysts, recognized the problem of population aging and decline as a serious possibility, let alone a consequential global trend.

Policymakers began to recognize the profound implications of population aging for societies around the world beginning in the 1990s, mainly due to growing financial burdens that those over 60 began to place on public social security and private pension plans, especially in the industrialized countries. As the baby boom generation approached retirement age, the possibility of an impending financial crisis drew more attention to the broader implications of population aging.

Since then, the aging trend has assumed a higher level of prominence as a policy concern. Panels, commissions, and analysts are now wrestling with the twin challenges of aging. First, the share of government budgets devoted to traditional government concerns such as national defense and infrastructure is gradually declining due to the growing demands of age-specific transfer programs such as social security. Second, the combination of greater longevity (table 3.1) and declining birthrates is leading to major changes in population age structure and to a steady decrease in the ratio of workers to retirees. In concert, these trends are expected to lead to a much larger share of GDP going toward programs for the elderly and, at the same time, to lower government revenues. This confluence of factors presents major and unprecedented challenges to fiscal policy planners in industrialized countries, who must ensure, with fewer available resources, that "traditional" government roles are fulfilled along with the growing new roles brought on by demographic change (Auerbach and Lee 2001, 1–6).

Table 3.1
Life expectancies at birth, 1995–2000 and 2045–2050 (projected), selected countries

	1995–2000	2045–2050
The world	65.6	76.0
Algeria	68.9	78.4
Belgium	77.9	83.8
Chile	74.9	80.1
Dominican Republic	67.3	72.5
Egypt	66.3	77.8
France	78.1	84.0
Greece	78.0	82.4
Hungary	70.7	79.4
Indonesia	65.1	77.4
Japan	80.5	88.0
Kenya	52.2	66.9
Lithuania	71.4	79.6
Malaysia	71.9	79.7
Norway	78.1	83.7
Oman	70.5	78.5
Peru	68.0	77.5
Qatar	68.9	78.3
Russian Federation	66.1	76.9
South Africa	56.7	66.4
Thailand	69.6	79.1
United States	76.5	82.6
Vietnam	67.2	78.2
Yemen	59.4	75.5
Zimbabwe	42.9	66.3

Source: United Nations, *The Aging of the World's Population* [Internet], UN Division for Social Policy and Development, 2000 [cited 2000]; available from www.un.org/esa/socdev/ageing/agewpop.htm.

Much less attention, however, has been paid to considerations (other than social security matters) that are implicit in lengthening life expectancies and life spans. These include the future of education, employment, intergenerational equity, immigration policy, national security, disease, and environmental quality, each of which will be affected by the demographic transitions now unfolding.

In this chapter, these and other issues will be addressed, on a global basis, and with regard to the situations in individual countries in the industrialized and developing worlds, over the course of the twenty-first century. The initial sections focus specifically on patterns and implications of aging and demographic change in the industrialized world. As mentioned earlier, some of the key challenges here relate to the management of public budgets in response to greater longevity and lower birthrates. The discussion also addresses the broader array of controversial issues raised by these trends, including the future of the workforce and the role of immigration. Subsequent sections focus on the question of aging and demographic change in the developing world, where, in many cases, different dynamics are at play. For example, in addition to the overall trend of aging and lower fertility, AIDS is now the most powerful driver of demographic change. In parts of Africa especially, aging and AIDS in tandem will likely heighten the misery of those already among the world's neediest. Having considered regional implications in previous sections, this chapter attempts to integrate the interplay of the global aging trend with other global ecological changes. In particular, it discusses ways aging and anticipated changes in the earth's climate might feed back to influence one another over the coming century. The concluding section of the chapter attempts to tie these trends together and summarize our argument.

Aging Trends in the Industrialized World

By 2030 the population of the industrialized world (i.e., the OECD countries) will be, on average, significantly older than it is today. The number of people over 60 is projected to increase by 50 percent. During this period, men and women over 75 years of age will be the fastest growing population cohort and will have doubled in number; one in four people will be at least 65 years old, compared with one in seven today (Peterson 1999a, 42).

Of the ten countries with the oldest populations in the year 2000, eight are currently "industrialized." Their median ages range from almost 39 years (Denmark) to slightly more than 41 years (Japan). Fifty years out, when many additional countries will be counted as "industrialized," the median age for these countries is projected to range from

Table 3.2
Ten countries with the oldest and youngest populations, 2000 and 2050 (UN medium variant)

2000		2050	
Country	Median age	Country	Median age
Oldest population			
1. Japan	41.2	1. Spain	55.2
2. Italy	40.2	2. Slovenia	54.1
3. Switzerland	40.2	3. Italy	54.1
4. Germany	40.1	4. Austria	53.7
5. Sweden	39.7	5. Armenia	53.4
6. Finland	39.4	6. Japan	53.1
7. Bulgaria	39.1	7. Czech Republic	52.4
8. Belgium	39.1	8. Greece	52.3
9. Greece	39.1	9. Switzerland	52.0
10. Denmark	38.7	10. China	51.9
Youngest population			
1. Yemen	15.0	1. Niger	20.4
2. Niger	15.1	2. Yemen	21.1
3. Uganda	15.4	3. Angola	21.2
4. Burkina Faso	15.6	4. Somalia	21.5
5. Democratic Republic of the Congo	15.6	5. Uganda	22.1
6. Angola	15.9	6. Burkina Faso	22.8
7. Somalia	16.0	7. Liberia	22.9
8. Burundi	16.0	8. Mali	22.9
9. Zambia	16.5	9. Burundi	23.2
10. Benin	16.6	10. Malawi	23.7
WORLD	26.5	WORLD	36.2

Source: United Nations, *The Aging of the World's Population* [Internet], UN Division for Social Policy and Development, 2000 [cited 2000]; available from www.un.org/esa/socdev/ageing/agewpop.htm.

almost 52 years (China) to just over 55 years (Spain). For the world as a whole, the median age in 2000 was estimated at 26.5 years, while projections for 2050 suggest a median of 36.2. Table 3.2 illustrates some likely changes in the age profile of the world's populations over the next 50 years.

These projections, it is important to note, are based on baseline projections of population change. They do not take account of ongoing progress in biotechnology and medicine, as well as lifestyle changes that may extend life expectancies even further. Moreover, as some scientists now predict, within 50 years, medical science and technology may be successful in extending life spans well beyond the currently accepted maximum of 120 years (Bulkley 2000).

Because of low fertility rates in virtually every Organization for Economic Cooperation and Development (OECD) country, the size of the workforce will almost certainly decrease. Tables 3.3 and 3.4, showing current and projected age structures in selected OECD countries, illustrate the trend.

Note that all of these countries have a current fertility rate of less than 2.1, the rate at which a population can replace itself. Only one (the United States) barely creeps up to replacement rate by 2050. The trends are clear both for these countries and for the developed world generally: there will be fewer young people, fewer middle-aged people, significantly more older people, smaller workforces, and more pensioners. These

Table 3.3

Age composition in 2000 and 2050, selected OECD countries

	2000 age cohorts			2050 age cohorts		
	0–14	15–59	60+	0–14	15–59	60+
France	18.7%	60.7%	20.5%	16.0%	51.3%	32.7%
Germany	15.5	61.2	23.2	12.4	49.5	38.1
Japan	14.7	62.1	23.2	12.5	45.2	42.3
U.K.	19.0	60.4	20.6	15.0	51.1	34.0
U.S.	21.7	62.1	16.1	18.5	54.6	26.9

Source: United Nations, *The Aging of the World's Population* [Internet], UN Division for Social Policy and Development, 2000 [cited 2000]; available from www.un.org/esa/socdev/ageing/agewpop.htm.

Table 3.4
Fertility rates in 2045–2050, selected OECD countries

	Current	2045–2050
France	1.73	1.90
Germany	1.33	1.61
Japan	1.41	1.75
U.K.	1.70	1.91
U.S.	2.04	2.10

Source: United Nations, *The Aging of the World's Population* [Internet], UN Division for Social Policy and Development, 2000 [cited 2000]; available from www.un.org/esa/socdev/ageing/agewpop.htm.

significant changes in population age structures raise the possibility of increasing intergenerational conflicts within societies. As smaller, younger age cohorts are asked to shoulder an ever-increasing share of the financial burden of the elderly, for example, a new form of class conflict may start to simmer. A new fault line between young and old could emerge similar to those that have divided economic classes in the past. The possibility of this type of conflict in industrialized countries, such as the United States, seems especially strong considering the political and financial clout of the "gray lobby" in the political system. The former American Association of Retired Persons (now known simply as AARP) currently has over 33 million members, 1,700 paid employees, and an annual budget of more than $5.5 billion (Peterson 1999a, 52–53). Intergenerational tensions might be expected to rise along with growth in the perception that the elderly wield disproportionate political and economic influence.

The pressures and incentives for resettling the global population will grow stronger in upcoming decades. Considering that the developing world will account for an expanding share of the world's population and that economic opportunities will be greater in OECD countries, international migration will be an increasingly important factor in the world economy. Immigration could play a major role in the economic health of recipient countries and could help to reshape population age structures to forestall the fiscal impacts of aging (Alvarado and Creedy 1998, 46–50). This, of course, assumes that there will be no political backlash against policies encouraging immigration.

With respect to the United States, the United Kingdom, Denmark, and Sweden, for example, the past two decades have already seen a major inflow of workers from developing countries. The fact that immigrant populations tend to have higher fertility rates than indigenous groups in host countries helps to explain why fertility rates are noticeably higher in these countries than in others, such as Germany and Japan, where immigration rates are lower (see Raffelshausen 2001, 202–207). This trend appears likely to change, however, especially in Europe (Alvarado and Creedy 1998, 55). A German parliamentarian, for example, has been quoted as saying that the country needs "demographic development in the face of a declining birth rate. That means reconsidering immigration" (Peel 2001, 2). The economic implications of a steadily shrinking workforce in the industrialized countries due to population aging and low fertility appear poised to force the immigration issue to the top of the policy agenda in the coming decades.

The "migration solution" to the workforce shortage, however, is often a controversial matter considering its potentially high social, economic, and political costs. The processes of receiving new immigrant populations often place large burdens on the public treasury, and the social and political challenges of assimilation can be great. Xenophobic violence has flared up with increasing frequency in recent years in many European countries, including the United Kingdom, France, and Germany, where immigrants have been perceived as threats to cultural identity and economic welfare, and as the source of a host of other social problems. Since 1989, anti-immigrant political parties have gained seats in almost every European parliament and, in Austria, have even attained the office of prime minister. Thus, policymakers in OECD countries will face difficult choices with regard to immigration. Immigration's potential alleviation of problems associated with a shrinking workforce will have to be balanced against its real and perceived consequences for social and political institutions (Alvarado and Creedy 1998, 55–60).

Aging Trends in Developing and Postcommunist Societies

The demographic picture in much of the developing world is, in many respects, an improving one. Improvements in access to health care and medicine in many countries over the past few decades have helped to extend the aging and declining fertility trends in the developing world, as figure 3.1 shows.

Surprisingly, the populations in many developing countries have been aging even faster than those in the OECD countries. The success of public health programs in the developing world raises as wide an array of policy issues as it does in the OECD countries. Since virtually all growth in the world's population over the next several decades will occur in the developing world, the policy challenges assume even greater complexity and urgency. Table 3.5 shows the growth rates of several developing countries.

Considering this diversity of demographic situations in countries across the developing world, it would be misleading to combine them to create a composite picture of demographic trends there. However, since these trends, like those in the OECD countries, do add up to a cumulative set of planetary impacts, there is an argument to be made in favor of aggregate analysis, such as that presented here. Countries with the lowest life expectancies in 2000 are all in southern Africa, in large part due to the

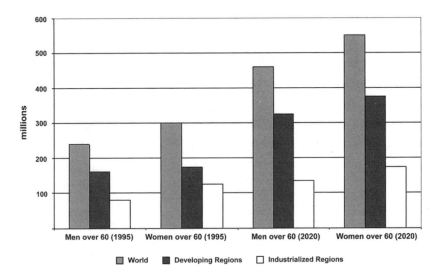

Figure 3.1
The aging of the global population, 1995–2020. *Source:* United Nations, *The Aging of the World's Population* [Internet], UN Division for Social Policy and Development, 2000 [cited 2000]. Available from www.un.org/esa/socdev/ageing/agewpop.htm.

Table 3.5
Population growth in selected developing countries, 2000–2050

Country	Population 2000 (millions)	Population 2050 (millions)
Algeria	30	51
Bangladesh	137	265
Brazil	170	247
Egypt	68	114
Ethiopia	63	186
Indonesia	212	311
Iran	70	121
Kenya	31	55
Mexico	99	147
Pakistan	141	344
Vietnam	78	123
Yemen	18	102
WORLD	6,056	9,322

Source: United Nations, *The Aging of the World's Population* [Internet], UN Division for Social Policy and Development, 2000 [cited 2000]; available from www.un.org/esa/socdev/ageing/agewpop.htm.

impact of AIDS. Countries with the highest current and projected fertility rates are virtually all in Africa or the Middle East. Countries with the lowest fertility are predominantly postcommunist states (of thirty-nine countries in which population is expected to decline by 2050, twenty-one are former members of the Soviet Union or the Warsaw Pact). Several Western European countries will lead the world in low fertility.

The sociopolitical and economic implications here pose some difficult issues for the politicians and policymakers of societies faced with population decline, especially since the smaller populations will, in almost every case, consist of a significantly larger cohort of older people. Thus, it is estimated that the Russian Federation will have 28 percent fewer people in 2050 than at present, and more than 37 percent of the population will be over 60, compared with 18.5 percent now. For Ukraine, a loss of almost 40 percent is projected. Of this 2050 population, 38 percent will be at least 60 years old, compared with 20.5 percent in 2000. For the Czech Republic the outlook is also bleak—a population loss of 18 percent with 40 percent of the 2050 total projected to be at least 60 years old (more than doubling that age cohort).

Since many of the countries of the former Soviet Union have experienced more than a decade of acute economic contraction, the aging and low fertility trends threaten to intensify existing economic and fiscal crises. Government revenues are already insufficient for the provision of adequate program funds in key areas such as public health, education, and social security, due in part to the sluggish growth of the private sector. While recent growth in the Russian economy is a promising sign, it will have to be a robust and prolonged phenomenon if it is to overcome the momentum of the country's demographically constrained fiscal reality ("Russia and the WTO: Shaping Up for the Club," 2001).

Like population growth, however, population decline also has far-reaching political implications. For instance, analysts anticipate that the shrinking of Russia's population will negatively affect the prospects for long-term political stability. Currently, 50 percent of Russia's population lives in twenty major population centers; elections are won largely in the ten largest centers, a factor that is being reinforced by extensive internal migration to these urban areas. Thus, some analysts anticipate that the declining electoral weight of groups in peripheral regions could prompt backlashes of ethnic and religious nationalism by those seeking a stronger political voice and greater self-determination (Herd 2001). As table 3.6 shows, population decline is likely to occur in several countries in Europe and the former Soviet Union during the next century.

The Demographic Impact of AIDS in the Developing World

Of the forty-five countries most affected by AIDS, thirty-five are in Africa, four are in Asia, and six are in Latin America. All are considered "developing" countries, and most are among the poorest of the world's poor. The demographic implications of the AIDS epidemic are starkly revealed in table 3.7, which shows life expectancies in a dozen affected countries over a period of 20 years.

Although Botswana, Ethiopia, Kenya, Mozambique, and South Africa are among the extreme cases, they illustrate a general demographic picture of staggering dimensions. As table 3.7 shows, for example, the difference in life expectancy with and without AIDS in 2020 for the population of Botswana differs by 30 years; for Kenya, the difference is almost 20 years, while for South Africa, it is more than 17 years. The cost of the

Table 3.6
Percent expected population decline in selected countries, 2000–2050

Country	%
Estonia	46.1
Bulgaria	43.0
Ukraine	39.6
Russian Federation	28.3
Italy	25.3
Spain	21.6
Romania	19.1
Japan	14.1
Germany	13.7
Poland	13.6
Sweden	2.1
United Kingdom	0.8

Source: United Nations, *The Aging of the World's Population* [Internet], UN Division for Social Policy and Development, 2000 [cited 2000]; available from www.un.org/esa/socdev/ageing/agewpop.htm.

AIDS pandemic in the mortality of young and old, in quality of life, and in economic growth defies measure. What is certain is that scarce funds otherwise available for overall health services, education, environmental protection, and infrastructure will continue to be diverted to meet some of the insatiable demands of AIDS care.

Since AIDS takes its toll primarily on people in their reproductive years, AIDS effectively contributes to the aging of populations as a whole and the contraction of the workforce by assaulting the younger and middle-aged cohorts of the population. The disease is literally consuming the middle-aged cohorts of many countries.

The impact of AIDS in the developing world is cruel and ironic for many reasons, and especially because of the progress being made on another important health front. Oral rehydration therapy (ORT), developed in the past decade, is a simple, inexpensive treatment for diarrhea, a disease responsible worldwide for more infant mortality and childhood illness than any other. But in many of the world's poorest countries, limitations on government revenues, institutions, and infrastructure in conjunction with the demands of AIDS treatment place severe constraints on

Table 3.7
Life expectancy at birth with and without AIDS, 1995 and 2015

	2000		2015	
	With AIDS	Without AIDS	With AIDS	Without AIDS
Angola	44.6	46.5	49.0	52.5
Botswana	44.4	67.6	43.0	73.0
Cambodia	56.5	58.0	59.2	64.8
Dominican Republic	67.3	68.2	66.1	71.9
Ethiopia	44.5	50.6	46.9	58.1
Ghana	56.3	60.0	61.5	66.8
Honduras	65.6	67.1	67.7	69.7
Kenya	52.2	63.6	51.5	69.8
Liberia	48.1	51.8	60.7	63.6
Mozambique	40.6	47.0	41.0	53.0
Nigeria	51.3	55.6	55.9	63.1
South Africa	56.7	63.3	42.0	69.6

Source: United Nations, *The Aging of the World's Population* [Internet], UN Division for Social Policy and Development, 2000 [cited 2000]; available from www.un.org/esa/socdev/ageing/agewpop.htm.

the availability of even simple and inexpensive medical treatments for the majority of the population. The oldest age cohorts, whose care requirements are the largest, experience the most significant lack of care as a consequence (HelpAge International, 1999, 65–66).

A ray of hope has emerged for societies struggling to deal with AIDS. In response to demands from major developing countries, particularly Brazil and South Africa, some major pharmaceutical companies have agreed to provide key AIDS drugs at affordable rates or to waive patent restrictions on the manufacture of generic equivalent drugs in the developing world. The wider availability of these treatments could have a major impact on life expectancies.

A recent U.S. study also offers hope that the cost of AIDS treatment might be reduced by half using a new method of intermittent drug therapy. By cutting the cost per patient to as little as $125 annually, this new method could soon extend millions of lives in the developing world and alter the population age structures of many countries significantly in coming decades. The promise of further medical breakthroughs in

AIDS prevention and treatment offers further hope that the current dire demographic projections—based on extrapolations of current trends— might turn out to be overstated (Recer 2001).

The Population Giants

Of the more than 6.4 billion people in the world today, about one-third live in India and China. By 2050 the world population is expected to reach 9 billion, of which India and China will still account for one-third. Since they are likely to account for a larger share of the global economy and a growing portion of global energy and resource use, demographic change in these countries merits special attention.

While these anticipated demographic changes in India and China are significant, ongoing trends in the two population giants become even more impressive if one looks backward as well as forward. For example, in 1950, the population of China was 555 million (about half its current population, and one-third of that projected for 2050), while that of India was 358 million (one-third its current level and approximately one-fifth of its projected 2050 size) (see World Resources Institute, 1994, chaps. 4 and 5).

Population growth rates in both China and India are slowing, however. China's growth rate has declined slightly, to 1.4 percent, due in part to its implementation of a strict one-child-per-family policy enforced by high fines and, in some cases, forced sterilization for violators. Despite such aggressive policies, however, population growth in rural areas far from government oversight has remained higher than that in urban centers (Tien 1992, 38–39; World Resources Institute, 1994, 62). Similarly, declining fertility in India is reducing the population growth rate there. India has been relatively successful in increasing the social acceptability of contraceptive technologies. After several decades of extensive government-sponsored education programs, family planning, in conjunction with social and economic improvements since the 1970s, has been a key factor in India's fertility decline (World Resources Institute, 1994, 86–87).

With its rapidly growing middle class (estimated now at around 400 million), India is progressing through the demographic transition, whereby improvements in living standards and quality of life foster both greater longevity and lower fertility. In fact, reductions in the incidence of infectious and chronic diseases and improvements in overall health have contributed to the rapid growth of India's elderly population. Since 1950, for example, the percentage of India's over-60 population has grown by approximately 25 percent each decade (Gokhale et al. 1999, 76).

The expanding elderly populations of large developing countries such as India and China present great social and economic policy challenges. For instance, while the elderly have historically lived in multigenerational homes with their families, industrialization and urbanization in these countries often disrupt traditional family structure. Increasingly, the economic and overall well-being of the elderly is declining, with the gradual erosion of family and community. As the megacities of the developing world swell with newcomers from the countryside seeking economic opportunity, rural areas suffer the social and cultural consequences of strained family and household structures. The lot of the elderly in the developing world is slowly coming to resemble that of the elderly in the Western world (Gokhale et al. 1999, 161–165).

Aging and Ecological Security

In thinking about the societal challenges associated with demographic change, it is important to put these issues into an ecological-security context. Recognizing that human affairs and human systems are linked inextricably to those of the natural environment and earth systems in general, the implications of major demographic change grow in scope and become more uncertain. Demographic changes do not unfold in isolation from ecological changes, but interact with them in a complex and nonlinear system of causes, outcomes, and feedbacks. Scholars have referred to this intricate interplay of human-made and natural systems as the "man-milieu relationship" (Sprout and Sprout 1965, 9–10).

To address global population aging in the broader ecological-security framework, this section discusses reciprocal relationships between population graying and other likely changes in the global ecosystem. It first considers ongoing changes in the global environment and climate, then focuses on advancements in medicine and biotechnology.

Although humans have altered their environments throughout history, the scale of anthropogenic environmental change grew significantly during the twentieth century. Through the sheer growth in human numbers, the inexorable increase in fossil-energy use, the clearing of forestlands, and the impacts of technology, humans have come to threaten the long-term viability of ecosystems on a global scale for the first time in history. Obviously, these changes have implications for an increasingly vulnerable aging global population.

Future impacts from climate change are likely to be most severe in those parts of the developing world, particularly in Asia and Africa (e.g., Bangladesh, Egypt), where large populations live on densely populated, low-lying coastal lands. Likewise, shifts in global precipitation patterns associated with climate change are expected to alter both the quantity and quality of freshwater resources available in many areas, raising the health risks associated with inadequate freshwater and diminishing the productivity of large tracts of agricultural lands. While decreases in precipitation are expected to be most severe in already-arid areas such as the Sahel, reduced rainfall in temperate regions such as Europe and North America are also likely. Thus, the human and ecosystem health impacts of climate change are likely to be broadly felt (Intergovernmental Panel on Climate Change, 2001; Pan 2001).

Emerging changes in the global environment raise a variety of questions with respect to population aging. For example, it is unclear how environmental health effects and demographic changes might interact with one another as climates change and populations age. Considering that the very young and the very old are the population cohorts most susceptible to illness and infectious disease, future environmental changes likely will present many public health challenges and uncertainties for the future. The developing world, where populations are aging most rapidly, could be particularly vulnerable as a consequence of generally lower levels of health services and more limited institutional infrastructures (HelpAge International, 1999, 64–66).

Political responses to future environmental change are also made more complex by the changing perceptions of the natural world on the part of older populations—another integral aspect of the human-milieu relationship. Attitudes toward environmental protection and quality might be expected to evolve in response to demographic changes such as population aging, although the direction of that evolution is still a matter of speculation. For example, older populations might place less value on conservation and environmental protection because their interactions with the natural world are likely to be more limited and their immediate needs more urgent. Direct trade-offs, either real or perceived, between public expenditures on social security or environmental protection might figure more prominently in future policy debates.

On the other hand, as people come to expect longer and healthier lives, there could be an increasing sensitivity to and policy priority for environmental stewardship and sustainability. However, even under this more optimistic scenario for environmental protection, the fiscal challenge of environmental protection is likely to be difficult. Since public spending on pensions in the industrialized countries is expected to more than double by 2050 (amounting to 17 percent of gross domestic product), government revenues available for such social and economic programs as environmental protection could be more meager in the future (World Bank, 1994, 7).

Innovation and Technological Change

The major innovations and technological changes that have occurred over the past 50 years probably exceed the sum of innovations in previous human history. Indeed, the greatest innovation of the late nineteenth and early twentieth centuries may well have been the institutionalization of the process of innovation. It was this, after all, that spawned the ever-accelerating pace of technological change that has improved living standards and quality of life for much of humanity (Mowery and Rosenberg 1998, 2).

Technological advances in health and medicine are typical of the major strides that occurred during the twentieth century. Innovations in public health, such as immunization and disease eradication, *doubled* the life expectancy of U.S. males between 1900 and 1990 (World Resources Institute, 1996, 195). More recent advances in medicine that have routinized surgical procedures such as joint and organ replacements and cataract removal have improved the quality of life for millions and have resulted in billions of dollars of avoided health-care costs. Thus, to a large extent, the ongoing aging trend reflects the stream of technological successes that began in the last century.

Foreseeable breakthroughs in genetics and biotechnology are likely to spark revolutionary changes in society, especially, as may be the case, if they occur suddenly. The prospect of a sudden, step-level change—rather than incremental increases—in future life expectancy and life span brought about by a technological breakthrough, could present an array of difficult policy challenges (Bulkley 2000). How economically tenable, for example, would a society be in which the majority of citizens spent more than half their lives in retirement? Since labor forces in many countries are already shrinking and the number of retirees growing, further acceleration in the pace of medical and biological advances will make social and economic policy adjustments, and competition for public revenues, even more difficult and urgent. If more people live longer and healthier lives, policymakers may be forced to raise the minimum retirement age and provide additional incentives to keep people in the workforce longer.

That said, advances in other high-technology fields, such as information and telecommunications, could facilitate a softer economic landing for aging societies. As many economies become increasingly based on knowledge, services, and information, rather than on manufactured goods and physical labor, opportunities may also grow for older people to remain in the work force (Nye and Owens 1996, 20–36).

The extent to which people work beyond what is now considered retirement age may, in turn, depend on the extent to which educational and retraining opportunities are available. Societies with aging populations and technology-based economies will face the challenge of providing citizens with continuing education and fostering lifelong learning. In the United States, the average individual is expected to have three distinct careers over the course of a lifetime. With increasing life expectancies, growing elderly populations, and ever-accelerating technological change, industrialized societies will need to restructure their educational systems accordingly. Since most industrialized countries already face impending pension and social security crises, enabling older citizens to remain professionally active longer in a technology-based economy may hold the keys both to fiscal solvency and to future economic growth.

Moreover, the knowledge-based economy could have an important role to play in reducing the environmental impacts associated with population growth and aging. To the extent that technology reduces the resource intensity of the global economy, it could also lighten the burden placed on the earth's ecosystems by the larger populations of the future. In short, the older population of tomorrow bears the possibility—even if not the likelihood—of treading lighter on the planet than the younger and smaller populations preceding it.

Conclusion

In virtually every industrialized country and most developing countries, declining fertility rates and greater longevity will continue to characterize the planet's demographic scene for decades to come. As a consequence, the global population in 2050 will be, on average, significantly older than it is today.

The global population will also continue to increase, largely because fertility rates in most developing countries will remain above the replacement level during this period. Nonetheless, during the middle decades of this century, the global population is likely to grow at a decreasing rate largely because fertility rates, overall, will probably continue on their gradual trajectory toward stabilization (United Nations, 2000).

The trend toward a stabilized and older population in developed countries and toward increasing and aging populations in the developing world will also influence, directly and indirectly, political, economic, social, and ethical developments at every level of governance. For example, the needs of aging populations will play a role in increasing pressures for migration from developing to developed countries. On the other hand, rapidly aging populations in many developing countries (combined with AIDS-induced mortality among younger cohorts) may eventually reduce the pool of would-be migrants.

Smaller, older populations also raise security concerns in several aging countries including Russia, Ukraine, Japan, Germany, Italy, and even the United States. Aging presents a manpower challenge to the militaries of industrialized countries. Of course, the continuous development of (and reliance on) ever more sophisticated weapons, in conjunction with the evolution of warfare itself, could reduce the need to deploy large armies in the future.

Thus, the aging of the global population has important and uncertain implications for virtually every dimension of human society. In addition to the issues discussed here, many other direct and indirect effects of aging warrant the attention of government policymakers, economic advisors, national security analysts, and academic experts. However, at the moment most attention seems to have been captured by the AIDS epidemic raging in many countries of the developing world, and by the viability of public and private pension systems in most of the industrialized world. This focus, although surely warranted, is obviously much too narrow.

Our aim here has been to call attention to a wide array of potential problems awaiting policymakers and society in general in the coming decades as demographic trends now evident continue to unfold. While policymakers can never be prepared for every eventuality, they should have their eyes open to a broad set of contingencies and, in response, seek to enhance the resiliency of institutions and of society itself in the face of impending change.

4

Global Water Prospects

Ken Conca

Unlike such obviously global problems as climate change, destruction of the ozone layer, or the loss of biological diversity, water is often thought of as primarily a local concern, played out in individual watersheds and regional or national water policies. When water has been a topic of international discussion, most of the emphasis has gone to a few obviously transnational issues: border-crossing rivers demand cooperation among neighboring countries; building water infrastructure in poor countries requires international development assistance and foreign capital investment.

Nor is it easy to draw a comprehensive global picture of water availability, water use, and water quality, for several reasons. Water availability can vary greatly across seasonal, annual, and other time scales—making it impossible to develop simple global generalizations about water-supply or water-quality issues (Shiklomanov 1998). Projecting global water use has also proven difficult. Models based on simple drivers such as population growth or changes in world output have proven inadequate—partly because those key inputs to the model are themselves hard to project, and partly because they are clearly not the only determinants of water supply and demand.

Yet there is a pressing need to think about water futures carefully, because water looms as one of the great global challenges of the next few decades. Any meaningful notion of long-term sustainability must include both human and "in-stream" water needs—that is, providing an adequate supply of water for meeting basic human needs while safeguarding critical ecological services. Neither of these linked tasks is adequately accomplished by current practices. On the one hand, more than a billion people around the world lack clean drinking water and more than 2 billion lack adequate sanitation services. As a direct result, waterborne diseases remain the single greatest public health threat to most of the world's poorest people.

At the same time, ecologists warn us that current levels of water diversion and withdrawal are already pushing many of the world's freshwater ecosystems to (or beyond) the breaking point. The consequences of manipulating water—including intervention in the water cycle, impacts on freshwater biodiversity, altered land-use patterns, and the transformation of critical ecosystems—accumulate in ways that add up to genuinely global ramifications. Freshwater ecosystems are home to most of the world's endangered fish species. Although covering only 1 percent of the earth's surface, freshwater habitats are home to more than 40 percent of known fish species and 12 percent of known animal species (World Resources Institute, 1998, 190). The global rate of freshwater-fish-species extinction is five times that of saltwater species, with dams, channelization, and other forms of river manipulation the chief factors in their precarious status (World Water Commission, 2000, 14). Water trapped behind the world's dams has inundated almost 500,000 square kilometers, an area roughly the size of France, Kenya, or Ukraine. That volume of water has been sufficient to produce a small but measurable change in the earth's orbit (Chao 1995).

Another reason to take a global look at water is that the social determinants of water supply and demand are themselves increasingly transnationalized. Processes of marketization and privatization are converting water from the prototypical public good provided by the state to a marketed commodity that generates a return on private capital—much of it transnational. Activism against current water-related practices is also increasingly transnationalized, be it opposition to large dams and forced resettlement or resistance to the privatization of public water supplies. Environmentalists, human rights groups, indigenous activists, and local groups of affected people are forging denser links among previously isolated struggles. As a result, actors on all sides of "local" water controversies increasingly call on an array of transnational allies.

This chapter undertakes three central tasks. First is an overview of past efforts to gauge global water futures, with particular attention to how the *Global 2000 Report* and other projections from that era fared in anticipating today's global water picture. Reviewing these efforts cautions us to pay careful attention not only to population growth and technological change, but also to critical social variables that may be difficult to capture in simple models. The chapter then turns to look at a few general indicators of the current global water situation, stressing in particular the scale, scope, and location of water vulnerabilities and the challenges of expanding water availability for basic human needs, balancing the growing intersectoral competition for water and the need to protect the world's besieged freshwater ecosystems. The chapter concludes by pointing to a few critical sociopolitical or institutional variables likely to shape global water futures.

Global 2000, Then and Now

As discussed in chapter 1 of this volume, the *Global 2000 Report* involved an unprecedented effort to look at the various dimensions and determinants of natural resource use trajectories. The central water-related finding of *Global 2000* matched the report's theme for other natural resource sectors, stressing burgeoning demand and growing scarcity. Thus regional water shortages would become more severe:

In the 1970–2000 period population growth alone will cause requirements for water to double in nearly half the world. Still greater increases would be needed to improve standards of living. In many (less-developed countries), water supplies will become increasingly erratic by 2000 as a result of extensive deforestation. Development of new water supplies will become more costly virtually everywhere. (Barney 1980, 2)

Interestingly, *Global 2000* did not independently estimate global water withdrawals in the year 2000, but relied on a 1971 projection of the Food and Agriculture Organization that world water use would almost triple from 1967 to 2000, reaching approximately 5,450 cubic kilometers (Barney 1980, 150). As with most projections of that era, this proved to be substantially higher than the actual figure for the year 2000. Gleick has compiled several efforts to project year 2000 global water withdrawals (presented in figure 4.1). There is a striking pattern of systematic overestimation, with repeated downward adjustments to the conventional wisdom as the target year approached.

What accounts for this pattern? Most of the projections were based on crude models that assumed close links to population and economic growth, did not allow for adjustments to demand related to price

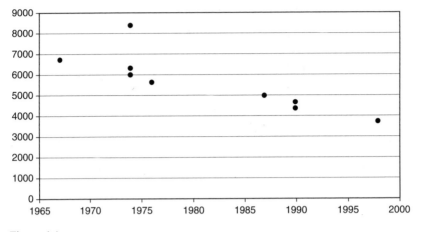

Figure 4.1
Projected global water withdrawals in year 2000 (cubic km), by year of forecast.
Source: Compiled from data in Peter H. Gleick, *The World's Water 2000–2001*
(Washington, DC: Island Press, 2000), table 3.15, p. 59.

changes, and incorporated little detail beyond a few highly aggregated sectoral components of global demand. Instead, population growth proved to be somewhat lower than projected; some types of demand proved to be substantially more price sensitive than anticipated. Technological change also led to increasing efficiency of water use. However, it should be stressed that prognosticators also missed the mark because of an implicit assumption that the unmet needs of the world's poor would in fact be met through public policies and capital investment. This assumption, as discussed below, proved to be unwarranted.

Nevertheless, several of the report's qualitative observations have withstood the test of time reasonably well. In an observation that anticipated the growing marketization, privatization, and commodification of water-supply systems and water itself, the report suggested that "the notion of water as a free good available in essentially limitless quantities will have disappeared throughout much of the world" (Barney 1980, 157). *Global 2000* also underscored the importance of sectoral analysis of water demand as opposed to crude projections based on population and economic growth. Finally, the report warned of growing interstate tensions, anticipating the "water-war" scenarios that several water analysts have flagged in recent years:

As pressures on water resources increase, conflicts among nations with shared water resources are likely to intensify. Interstate disputes between upstream and downstream users of multinational river basins are particularly apt to occur over questions of water rights and priorities. Long-standing quarrels could easily worsen as pressures become critical. (Barney 1980, 159)

Thus, the report provides both a cautionary tale for current efforts to assess future prospects and a suggestion of the direction such assessments must take. Even if it were possible to gauge accurately the trajectory of drivers such as population growth, economic output, and rates of technological innovation, these are unlikely to be the sole determinants of global water futures; enormous uncertainties remain in socioeconomic and political spheres. At the same time, the report's emphasis on key sociopolitical variables, such as interstate water conflict and the privatization/marketization trend, suggests the direction in which analysis must head. These circumstances force us to shift our focus from projecting a single water future to envisioning a range of possible futures.

Current Measures of the World Water Situation

Water is a basic human need, a critical ecosystem constituent, and a valuable resource for an array of agricultural, industrial, and municipal uses. Currently world water withdrawals for agriculture, industry, and municipal use, as well as reservoir losses, represent slightly more than 10 percent of the total available annual runoff in the global water cycle. About half of withdrawals are consumed directly, with the rest returned to streams and aquifers (and often degraded in quality on return). If "in-stream" uses of water (e.g., dilution of pollution or the dissipation of waste heat) are included, human appropriation rises to about 17 percent of annual runoff. However, much of the untapped global runoff either consists of uncontrollable floodwaters or occurs in remote regions, making human use infeasible. A more accurate baseline is the subset of global runoff judged to be available for physical capture, also known as the "accessible runoff." Estimates suggest that current withdrawals and in-stream uses combine to appropriate an astonishing 54 percent of the accessible runoff (Jackson et al. 2001).

Irrigation constitutes nearly 70 percent of total withdrawals, with flood irrigation consuming an estimated 30–40 percent (via evaporation and plant growth), and the rest returned for reuse or to recharge streams and aquifers. Drip irrigation, in contrast, has a use efficiency on the order of 90 percent, thereby requiring less water to be withdrawn (Cosgrove and Rijsberman 2000, 7–8).

Although agricultural use predominates, industrial and municipal uses are growing rapidly. Global water withdrawals for agriculture increased an estimated 500 percent during the twentieth century, while corresponding figures for industry and municipalities were 1,875 percent and 1,750 percent, respectively.

Such projections suggest difficult future challenges. As the UN Commission on Sustainable Development has pointed out, various scenarios for industrial, agricultural, and urban water demand typically assume strong growth in coming decades, in isolation from projections for other water-using sectors. Thus, for example, the UN Industrial Organization projects that current trends will lead to more than a doubling of 1995 industrial water use (and a more than fourfold increase in industrial pollutant loading) by 2025, while projections of the amount of water required to provide a healthy diet for the world's growing population typically envision a 50 to 100 percent increase in agricultural use (UN Commission on Sustainable Development, 1997). These projections beg some important questions: Is it economically or ecologically feasible to expand global water withdrawals to the level implied by the sum of these projections? If not, what market-based or policy-based mechanisms will allocate water across competing sectoral demands?

Human Needs and Water Insecurity

Water-related human insecurities remain vast at the start of the new millennium. The UN Commission on Sustainable Development (1997) estimates that 20 percent of the world's people lack access to a safe supply of clean water and that 50 percent lack access to adequate sanitation. The World Health Organization (WHO) estimates that more than 5 million people die each year from diseases caused directly by unsafe drinking water and inadequate sanitation, including more than 2 million children (UN Commission on Sustainable Development, 1997; Cosgrove and Rijsberman 2000, xx). According to the World Resources Institute's (WRI) Pilot Analysis of Global Ecosystems (PAGE), 2.3 billion people (more than 40 percent of the world population in 1995) lived under conditions of "water stress" (defined as water availability of less than 1,700 cubic meters per person per year), with 1.7 billion living in "highly stressed" river basins (water availability of less than 1,000 cubic meters per person per year) (World Resources Institute, 2000, 107).

These water-related insecurities are not distributed evenly, geographically, or socioeconomically. Not surprisingly, the most vulnerable are concentrated in the global South. The UN Development Program (UNDP) estimates that 28 percent of the population of "developing" countries lack access to safe water supplies. Disaggregated by region, the proportion of the population lacking safe water ranges from an estimated 17 percent across the Arab world to an estimated 46 percent in Sub-Saharan Africa (see table 4.1).

Data on water use provide another perspective on water-related insecurities. The WHO has established the figure of 50 liters of water per day as an estimate of the minimum adequate supply for basic human needs. Table 4.2 indicates that a very large number of countries, with a combined population of 3.8 billion people, have per capita water consumption levels in the vicinity of this figure (and in many cases, well below it).

Although crudely useful in capturing the scope of the problem, these country-level figures can mask as much as they reveal. As I have argued elsewhere, the "myth of the average citizen" reflected in national per

Table 4.1

Percentage of the population lacking access to safe water, by world region

World region	Population proportion lacking access to safe water
All developing countries	28
Arab states	17
East Asia	32
excluding China	8
Latin America and the Caribbean	22
South Asia	18
excluding India	15
Southeast Asia and the Pacific	29
Sub-Saharan Africa	46
Least developed countries	36

Source: UN Development Programme, *Human Development Report* (New York: Oxford University Press, 2000).

Table 4.2
Per capita domestic water use

Per capita domestic water use (liters per person per day)	Countries at this level or lower	Population of countries at this level or lower	Largest countries in group
<25	39	738 million	Nigeria, Bangladesh, Ethiopia, Democratic Republic of the Congo
<50	62	2.2 billion	Above plus India, Indonesia
<100	81	3.8 billion	Above plus China, Pakistan

Source: Compiled from Peter H. Gleick, *The World's Water 2000–2001: The Biennial Report on Freshwater Resources.* (Washington, Island Press, 2000).

capita figures can distort our understanding of power relations and structural inequality, both within and across societies (Conca 2000). Large dams and irrigation projects can have enormous distributive consequences within a country, providing water to some regions and classes while denying others livelihoods by flooding settlements or disrupting downstream ecosystems.

Gender is another dimension of water-related inequality that can be masked. In poor families, both the task of water provisioning and the harmful consequences of water insecurities tend to fall disproportionately on the shoulders of women. The lack of access to clean water sustains the "feminization of poverty" and inhibits efforts to empower women by undercutting family health, denying girls the opportunity to go to school, and draining time that might be spent in education, job training, and employment (World Water Council, 2000; van Wijk, de Lange, and Saunders 1998).

Progress on clean water has been sluggish at best in recent decades. In 1977, the United Nations designated the 1980s as the International Drinking Water Supply and Sanitation Decade. At the end of that decade, according to the WHO, 1.3 billion people around the world lacked access to safe drinking water and 2.6 billion lacked adequate sanitation services (Gleick 1998a, 40). A report to the eighth session of the UN Commission on Sustainable Development in 2000, assessing progress during the

1990s, underscored the entrenched character of the problem, estimating that at the turn of the millennium some 1.1 billion people remained unserved in terms of drinking-water supplies and almost 2.5 billion regarding sanitation. In other words, expanded access to safe water barely kept pace with world population growth during the 1990s.

The Richness and Fragility of Freshwater Ecosystems

Freshwater ecosystems—lakes, rivers, wetlands, floodplains, estuaries, and deltas—provide human societies with several critical natural resource goods and ecosystem-based services. Goods include drinking and irrigation water, fish, hydroelectricity, and genetic resources; services include buffering of the timing and volume of water flow, dilution and removal of wastes, cycling of nutrients and movement of sediments, maintenance of biological diversity, and provision of aquatic habitat (World Resources Institute, 2000, 9). Efforts to assess the relative value of different types of ecosystems as sources of natural capital and critical ecological services have identified freshwater ecosystems as among the most valuable on a per hectare basis (Costanza et al. 1997). Freshwater ecosystems are also associated with a few notable "bads" such as flooding and harboring disease-bearing pests.

The world's freshwater ecosystems have been subjected to stresses from a variety of sources. Most observers agree that the biggest stress has been large-scale manipulation of watercourses, such as damming rivers and diverting water flows for hydroelectric supply, irrigation, flood control, or navigation. According to the WRI,

Freshwater systems have been altered since historical times; however, the pace of change accelerated markedly in the early 20th century. Rivers and lakes have been modified by altering waterways, draining wetlands, constructing dams and irrigation channels, and establishing connections between water basins, such as canals and pipelines, to transfer water. Although these changes have brought increased farm output, flood control, and hydropower, they have also radically changed the natural hydrological cycle in most of the world's water basins. (World Resources Institute, 2000, 103)

Estimates suggest that there may be as many as 800,000 dams on the world's rivers, including more than 40,000 "large dams" (15 meters or more in height) and more than 300 "major dams," such as Aswan on the Nile, Hoover and Glen Canyon on the Colorado, and Itaipu on the Parana.[1]

These dams have been built for a range of purposes, including hydropower, irrigation, and flood control. Damming disrupts riverine ecosystems by inhibiting the movement of water, sediment, nutrients, and living organisms. The WRI's PAGE analysis examined the world's 227 largest rivers (with size defined in terms of average annual flow volume). The PAGE assessment concluded that 60 percent of these rivers, accounting for almost 90 percent of the total volume of water flowing in these basins, are "strongly" or "moderately" affected by fragmentation and altered flows.[2] The assessment also determined that "the only remaining large free-flowing rivers in the world are found in the tundra regions of North America and Russia, and in smaller basins in Africa and Latin America" (World Resources Institute, 2000, 106).

Damming also imposes stark upstream/downstream differentiation on riverine ecosystems. Upstream, river valleys are transformed into reservoirs by flooding often-vast expanses of land. Downstream, in addition to dramatically changing the volume and rates of water flow, dams also reduce sediment loads and change erosion rates—reducing the input of nutrients to ecosystems downstream. Finally, dams can have major impacts on the physical and chemical properties of river water, altering temperature, turbidity, dissolved oxygen levels, and mineral and nutrient concentrations.

According to the World Commission on Dams (2000, 6), half of all the world's large dams were built for irrigation; dams feed 30–40 percent of the world's 271 million hectares of irrigated cropland, amounting to only 17 percent of world cropland but generating an estimated 40 percent of world food output (UN Commission on Sustainable Development, 1997). Virtually all projections of future water use assume that irrigation will be increasingly important to expanding the world food supply.

A second major source of stress has been landscape and land-use changes through deforestation, draining wetlands, and agricultural conversion. Revenga et al. (1998) estimate that almost a third of the world's watersheds have lost more than 75 percent of their original forest cover and that seventeen of these—including the Indus, Niger, Nile, Seine, Tigris and Euphrates, and Volta—have lost more than 90 percent. Deforestation alters local water, nutrient, and energy cycles, because forests play a major role in shaping local processes of runoff, soil stabilization, soil moisture, evapotranspiration, and microclimatic energy flows.

Wetland losses have also taken a major toll. Estimates of the global value of various ecosystem services typically identify wetlands as among the ecosystem types with the very highest "value added" for human well-being. Global data on the extent of wetlands are not available, making it impossible to estimate rates of loss with any precision. One often-cited estimate, made by ecologist Norman Myers (1997), is that the world lost half of its expanse of wetlands during the twentieth century. A 1992 investigation on 344 wetlands sites listed under the Ramsar Convention, the international treaty on wetlands, found that 84 percent were either "threatened" or "experiencing ecological changes" (Dugan and Jones 1993).

Along with large-scale manipulation of watercourses and aggressive landscape alteration, a third major source of stress is water pollution. Leading problems include dumping inadequately treated sewage and excessive nutrients such as phosphorous and nitrogen, which accelerates algae growth in rivers and lakes, reducing oxygen content and leading to eutrophication. In its *Comprehensive Assessment of the Freshwater Resources of the World*, the UN Commission on Sustainable Development (1997) highlighted leading sources of regional water pollution, including the discharge of raw sewage and industrial waste in Latin America and West Africa, irrigation-induced salinity in Western Asia, high sediment loading in the Asia-Pacific region, and acid deposition in North America and Europe. One estimate has suggested that to clean the world's freshwater supplies through dilution would require a volume of water equal to two-thirds of the reliable annual global runoff (Wallensteen and Swain 1997).

A final, related source of stress has been the growth of human settlements in and around freshwater ecosystems. Approximately 1.6 billion people live in the world's ten most populous watersheds, with densities exceeding 300 persons per square kilometer—a concentration comparable to the average population density of Denmark or Poland (World Resources Institute, 2000, 105).[3]

As previously mentioned, the WRI's PAGE analysis drew an alarming picture of the health of the world's freshwater ecosystems, with regard to four critical clusters of goods and services: food and fiber production, water quality, water quantity, and biological diversity. The picture on food production is mixed. Habitat degradation and overharvesting have undercut the ability of freshwater ecosystems to support wild fish stocks, but freshwater aquaculture has grown rapidly and is now thought to exceed the annual freshwater catch from wild stocks. With regard to water quality, water quantity, and biodiversity, however, the capacity of freshwater systems to provide these vital goods and services is uniformly decreasing. Outside of the United States and Western Europe, "water quality appears to be degraded in almost all regions" as a by-product of agricultural intensification, urbanization, chemical contamination, and the loss of wetlands' filtering and purification services. If current consumption patterns continue, the assessment projected that roughly half the world's population will live in conditions of "high water stress" by 2025 (World Resources Institute, 2000, 107). On biodiversity, the assessment concluded that "of all the ecosystems examined in this report, freshwater systems are by far in the worst condition from the standpoint of their ability to support biological diversity—on a global level" (World Resources Institute, 2000, 118).

Toward Water-Related Sustainability

Perhaps cautioned by past failures, current efforts to project global water futures tend toward scenarios as opposed to authoritative predictions. Table 4.3 summarizes several recently published scenarios for the year 2025, including both business-as-usual scenarios, in which few major policy adaptations take hold, and visions that stress lower growth and more efficient use stimulated by a range of policy and market reforms. Given the range between the high-end and low-end figures in table 4.3, it becomes clear that global water futures are less a matter of guesses than of guidance. A set of three contrasting water futures spun out by the Global Water Partnership (GWP) illustrate the extent to which social, economic, and political variables will dictate future trends (table 4.4).

Given the wide variability across these and other scenarios, what are the critical social, economic, and political variables that will guide global society along one or another of these paths? Certain general factors cited in (or omitted from) the *Global 2000 Report* are still relevant today: rates of global population and economic growth, as well as technological change. Technology presents the greatest uncertainties—a vast array of

Table 4.3
Projected water withdrawals in the year 2025

2025 Scenarios	Projected withdrawal (km³ per year)
Raskin "reference"	5,044
Seckler "business as usual"	4,569
Gleick "vision"	4,270
World Water Council "vision"	4,200
Raskin "reform"	4,054
Seckler "efficiency"	3,625

Source: Compiled from Peter H. Gleick, *The World's Water 2000–2001: The Biennial Report on Freshwater Resources.* (Washington, Island Press, 2000).

innovations (both high-tech and low-tech) promise more efficient water use, yet the rates at which such practices will be adopted and spread can only be estimated.

Beyond such blunt drivers as population, technology, and economic growth, what factors can we identify as potential turning points? In the following section I discuss three sociopolitical variables likely to have a profound impact on patterns of future freshwater use. These include (1) the efficacy of international river diplomacy, (2) whether and how stakeholder controversies around water-supply infrastructure are resolved, and (3) trends and controversies in water financing and pricing.

International River Diplomacy

Nearly all of the world's largest rivers cross national borders—a recent survey identified 263 internationally shared watercourses. The basins through which these run cover about 45 percent of the Earth's land surface area; some 145 countries have some portion of their territory in an international basin. Of these, almost two-thirds (92 states) have at least half of their national territory lying in an international basin, and more than a third (50 states) have 80 percent or more of their national territory in an international basin (Wolf et al. 1999).

These facts, combined with mounting stresses on water supply and water quality almost everywhere, have led to sometimes-dire predictions of "water wars" between upstream and downstream states. In 1995 the World Bank's Vice President for Environmentally Sustainable Development, Ismail

Table 4.4
World Water Council's global water scenarios

"Business-as-usual"	• Current water-resource management policies continue. Population growth, economic development, and technological change remain in line with UN-family predictions.
	• Today's problem (low access to water supply and sanitation), tomorrow's problem (insufficient food production), and the long-term problem (environmental degradation) do not get resolved.
	• The limits of natural and socioeconomic systems are reached by 2025. Increasing scarcity of renewable and accessible water resources and diminishing water quality further narrow the resource base of healthy ecosystems. At best this leads to chronic problems, but catastrophes may trigger regional and even global crises.
"Technology, economics, and the private sector"	• Water is priced and water rights are made tradable in order to improve equity, efficiency, and sustainability.
	• The water sector expands and higher prices lead to increased investments, accelerated R&D, and an increasing role for the private sector.
	• Social and ethical debates about the use of new technologies are resolved. Biotechnology, information technology, desalination, and improved water management increase water productivity. Irrigated areas are expanded, storage is increased, and human water use goes up considerably.
	• International institutions remain unchanged; poor countries and poor groups within countries risk being left out of globalization. Absolute poverty decreases but income inequalities grow. The environment suffers.
"Values and lifestyles"	• Education is a key pathway to developing sustainable values and lifestyles. Emphasis is on changing institutions and management, nationally and internationally.
	• Community-level action drives watershed management as well as rainwater harvesting and focuses on increasing mean yield levels in irrigated and rainfed areas. Decision making in the water sector is transparent and involves all stakeholders.
	• Ecological functions are recognized and maintained. Human water use is made sustainable.

Source: Gilberto C. Gallopin and Frank Rijsberman, "Three Global Water Scenarios," in William J. Cosgrove and Frank R. Rijsberman for the World Water Council, *World Water Vision: Making Water Everybody's Business* (Paris: World Water Council, 2000); CD-ROM edition.

Serageldin, stated that "the wars of the next century will be over water" (Wolf 1999, 2). The influential British publication *The Economist* has warned that water shortages would constitute "the stuff of future wars . . . conditions are ripe for a century of water conflicts" ("Water Fights," 2000). Researchers looking into the prospects for "environmentally induced" violent conflict have pointed to shared water resources as the single most likely route by which environmental change might trigger interstate hostilities (Homer-Dixon 1991, 1994).

Yet the centrality of shared rivers also suggests that effective international river diplomacy could be an important entry point for responding to the world's water challenges. Hamner and Wolf (1997) have identified 145 treaties since 1814 that deal with some nonnavigational aspect of international water issues in a particular river or lake basin. In 1997, the UN General Assembly passed a framework convention on the Law of the Non-Navigational Uses of Internationally Shared Watercourses to serve as a blueprint for basin-level agreements among coriparian states. That convention was the outgrowth of nearly three decades of efforts to develop a framework of globally applicable legal principles for the governance of international rivers (McCaffrey 2001). The convention articulates general principles for the content of basin-specific accords, the process by which such accords should be negotiated, and the standing to be accorded to states within a shared river basin or lake basin. The convention also contains explicit, albeit highly general, statements of a state's environmental responsibilities, including ecosystem protection and preservation, pollution reduction, controlling alien species, and protecting and preserving affiliated marine environments such as estuaries.

The patchwork of current basin-level international agreements falls far short of the ideals of the Watercourses Convention. Of 263 international river basins, the Transboundary Freshwater Disputes Database identifies less than one out of five that are covered by a modern, ratified international agreement. Content analysis indicates that most fall far short of the shared-governance ideals of the UN convention: few incorporate all states within the basin to which they apply; few make even rudimentary issue linkages to land-use practices, environmental management, or watershed protection; few contain significant enforcement mechanisms, monitoring provisions, or requirements for regular information exchange (Hamner and Wolf 1997).

Nor has the international community given an unambiguous endorsement to the convention's principles. The Watercourses Convention passed in the General Assembly on a vote of 103 in favor and 3 opposed, with 27 abstentions, including several important river states such as Egypt, Ethiopia, France, India, and Pakistan. Two of the negative votes came from upstream states in major river controversies: Turkey on the Tigris/Euphrates and China on the Mekong. Large-scale water-development schemes in both Turkey's Eastern Anatolia project and China's Three Gorges project have been strongly criticized by environmental and human rights activists. By the convention's closure date (May 20, 2000), only six states had ratified (Finland, Jordan, Lebanon, Norway, South Africa, and Syria); seven more had signed, but had not yet ratified it through domestic legislative processes (Côte d'Ivoire, Germany, Hungary, Luxembourg, Paraguay, Portugal, and Venezuela).

To be sure, most of the world's rivers do not cross borders, and many threatened watersheds are not international. But the large number of countries and the vast amounts of national territory encompassed in international basins suggest the importance of interstate water diplomacy as an entry point for global responses. Norms of shared governance and sustainable watershed management that take root around international rivers might "swim upstream" in the sense of having broader domestic reverberations for national water policy and practice.

Stakeholder Controversies around Water-Supply Infrastructure

If the problem were simply one of expanding national water supplies while managing the flow of harmful effects across borders, diplomatic initiatives and basin-scale accords might be sufficient. But rivers are part and parcel of the watersheds through which they flow, key constituents of ecosystems, and critical components of the global hydrologic cycle. Rivers are also important sources of livelihood, anchors of culture and community, and key components of national economic-development strategies. In other words, rivers must be understood as elements of broader and more complex socioecological systems. Conflicting demands such as basic human need, agroindustrial growth, and in-stream ecosystem uses generate ecological and socioeconomic controversies that spill far beyond the confines of river basins and sovereign diplomacy.

The most common form of international water conflict today is not the interstate "water war" foreseen by many prognosticators, but rather the increasingly transnationalized "local" conflicts between river developers and their opponents. These are triggered by the enormous financial, social, and ecological costs of large water-infrastructure projects, the often highly skewed distribution of benefits, the tendency of river-development advocates to oversell benefits and understate costs, and the trail of victims such projects often leave in their wake. On one side, typically, is an array of local beneficiaries, national-government organs, and the transnational builders and financiers of large-scale water projects. On the other side are opponents from affected local communities and their supporters from sympathetic international environmental or human rights organizations (Donahue and Johnston 1998).

The resulting social conflicts are extensively—and increasingly—transnationalized. The push to manipulate rivers has always had a strong transnational dimension, given the role of international funding and the participation of multinational firms in the construction and operation of major projects. A more recent development has been the transnationalization of opposition, through growing linkages among local affected peoples' organizations, environmentalists, human rights activists, and indigenous peoples' groups (McCully 2001; Keck and Sikkink 1998). As a result, many basins and watersheds lying beyond the formal reach of international law and interstate diplomacy are nevertheless subject to intense, conflicting transnational pressures.

Some critics of the antidams movement have charged it with inhibiting the ability of governments in poor countries to provide needy people with access to water. As figure 4.2 indicates, the rate of construction of major dams has slowed appreciably over the past few decades. One consequence is that the amount of irrigated land, which increased by 50 percent from 1960 to 1980, grew at only half that rate from 1980 to 2000. The one regional exception to this trend is Asia, where the governments of China and India have forged ahead despite flagging support from international capital and aid agencies.

Several factors have contributed to this slowdown: cost overruns and financial riskiness, few good remaining sites, and the increasing cost competitiveness and greater flexibility of small gas-fired turbines. However, one of the principal forces in slowing large dam construction has been

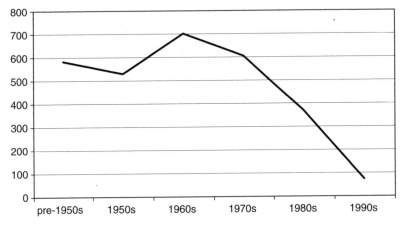

Figure 4.2
Construction of large reservoirs over time. *Source:* Compiled from data in Peter
H. Gleick, *The World's Water 2000–2001*, (Washington, DC: Island Press, 2000),
table 16, p. 272.

social opposition by environmentalists, human rights advocates, indigenous peoples' groups, and local organizing and advocacy by negatively
affected communities. These increasingly dense and transnationalized
networks have transformed previously isolated, local struggles into
global controversies.

   Water-infrastructure projects face a much tougher gauntlet of social-
movement activism, public doubt, and financial-market skittishness than
they did in decades past. These factors may have eliminated some necessary and appropriately designed projects, even as they have screened out
bad ones. But far from representing know-nothing opposition to social
progress, these challenges must be understood in the context of what Peter
Gleick (1998b, 9) has described as a changing global water paradigm:

The twentieth-century water-development paradigm, driven by an ethic of
growth, has now stalled as social values and political and economic conditions
have changed. More people now place a high value on maintaining the integrity of
water resources and the flora, fauna, and human societies that have developed
around them. There are growing calls for the costs and benefits of water management and development to be distributed in a more fair and prudent manner and
for unmet basic human needs to be addressed. And more and more, efforts are
being made to understand and meet the diverse interests and needs of all affected
stakeholders.

A central element in the new thinking to which Gleick alludes is the idea of integrated water resource management (IWRM). The framework typically stresses three key themes: the multiplicity of social, economic, and ecological uses; the resulting importance of "cross-sectoral" management; and the importance of multilevel management, coordinating local, regional, national, and transnational practices and institutions (Global Water Partnership, n.d., 5).

The result of this process was the World Commission on Dams (WCD), an unusual mixed-membership body that took an unprecedented, broadly encompassing look at the costs and benefits of large dams. The commission's findings emphasized the frequent failure of large dams to meet economic targets, the highly uneven social distribution of costs and benefits, and a systematic failure to anticipate or deal adequately with ecological and social consequences. Its recommendations emphasized the need to shift the focus away from dams as ends in themselves and toward comprehensive options assessments for water and energy needs, and to establish "core values" of equity, efficiency, participatory decision making, sustainability, and accountability in all decisions related to dams and their alternatives.

In general terms, dam critics have been more pleased than proponents (Dubash et al. 2001). Many activist groups have pressed for the commission's recommendations to become binding. Southern governments have been divided in their response, with many expressing skepticism that the recommendations could be implemented as strict policy guidelines. The International Commission on Large Dams (ICOLD), the international dam-industry umbrella group, has rejected the report as flawed and inadequate. On the other hand, some donor governments have indicated that they will be guided by WCD recommendations in making future decisions on whether to support dam projects. The World Bank has only committed itself to considering the recommendations in a nonbinding manner, despite being a key catalyst for the stakeholder dialogue that culminated in the WCD process.

The WCD exercise seems likely to have a twofold legacy: first, it has set a new standard for global water governance, in terms of both participatory procedures and substantive comprehensiveness; second, the WCD experience illustrates the direction in which global water dialogue must move—away from interstate bargaining and narrow sectoral considerations in development assistance, and toward broader and more participatory stakeholder dialogue. There are presently *several* bitter non-dam-related controversies in the water arena: property rights, pricing mechanisms, trade in water, investment patterns, and privatization. The dams debate shows that water elites cannot ignore dissenting voices on these matters. The ability of the international water community to foster effective stakeholder dialogue around such controversies will therefore be critical to shaping global water futures.

Water Pricing and Marketization Controversies

In a meeting with nongovernmental organizations at the Second World Water Forum in 2000, the World Bank's Vice President for Sustainable Development Ismail Serageldin identified two critical social controversies to be resolved if the "world water vision" presented at that event were to become a reality. One was resistance to water infrastructure projects, as sketched above. The other was the linked set of controversies around water pricing, water property rights, bulk water exports, privatization, and foreign ownership in the water sector.

Acknowledging the economic value of water identifies but does not resolve the central tension in water marketization—the quest for price-induced efficiency versus the fear that the price mechanism is inadequate to meet basic human needs affordably. Unresolved is the question of how to reconcile the contradictions between the dominant means of providing efficiency (pricing and market mechanisms) and the elements of equity, voice, and participation that underpin the idea of community.

One strand in the marketization controversies involves the looming prospect of bulk water exports, linking water to the larger trade-and-environment debate. The global push for neoliberal structural adjustment and the hyperliberalization of trade arrived relatively late to the water sector. The North American Free Trade Agreement (NAFTA) and the World Trade Organization (WTO) have created a foundation for accelerated international water marketization. NAFTA defines freshwater as a tradable good subject to NAFTA free-trade provisions. NAFTA's provisions for national treatment, proportional sharing, and enhanced legal standing for foreign corporations have raised Canadian fears that U.S. firms will lay claim to Canada's rich water resources for export to the

South, with local communities in Canada powerless to stop them (Barlow 2001). Indeed, when the provincial government of British Columbia banned bulk water exports in 1998, an American company filed suit against the Canadian national government under Chapter 11 of NAFTA, seeking to hold the national government liable for profits lost due to the provincial government's actions (Chalecki 2000).

Emerging in parallel with trade-related water controversies has been the push to privatize water-supply services, typically by attracting foreign owners, as a way of expanding capital investment. The WTO also recognizes water as a tradable commodity, and its General Agreement on Trade in Services (GATS) extends the transnationalization of water to water-supply services. Some see enhanced international private-sector investment as the only practical way to keep pace with expanding water-supply needs. In this view, guaranteed profits linked to "full-cost" pricing schemes are simply the cost of doing business. According to the GWP, public-sector funds (including both government spending and "international public finance" or development assistance) will barely keep pace with current investment levels, meaning that virtually all future increases will have to come from the private sector. One way of reading the privatization push, therefore, is as an effort to raise rates of return and reduce risk sufficiently to attract that private capital.

One example of the conflict potential surrounding the role of foreign capital in the water sector was seen in Cochabamba, Bolivia, in the spring of 2000 (Schultz 2000). Late in 1999 the government entered into a $200 million contract giving control of the city's municipal water-supply system to a consortium of foreign investors. The new owners promptly implemented a system of "full-cost" pricing in which even the poorest residents, including families living on the minimum salary of less than $100 per month, were required to pay prices reportedly as high as $20 per month or more. The result was massive popular mobilization in opposition to the price hikes and foreign control of the water-supply system. The government responded with force—shutting down or seizing local media, implementing martial law, and repelling protesters with tear gas and riot police. The protests persisted and the government eventually conceded, withdrawing from the agreement.

One emerging approach that seeks to counter marketization involves the recognition of water as a fundamental human right. As Gleick (1998b, 490) has pointed out, there is already a strong basis for asserting a human right to water in existing international human rights law, covenants, and declarations, particularly in the sense of water rights as "an implicit part of the right to food, health, human well-being and life." In 1998 a group of prominent international figures led by former Portuguese president Mario Soares issued "The Water Manifesto," in which they called for water to be recognized as the common property of all Earth's inhabitants and for the recognition of water as "an inalienable individual and collective right" (Global Committee for the Water Contract, 1998). A related idea is the notion of a "social charter" or "social contract" for water, in which the basic water rights of all people are articulated even as the need to move toward more efficient pricing systems is acknowledged (Académie de l'Eau, 1999). For example, South Africa's innovative 1998 national water law begins with the establishment of water as a natural resource that belongs to all of the South African people and establishes the government as the "public trustee of the nation's water resources." The national government is thus "ultimately responsible to ensure that water is allocated equitably and used beneficially in the public interest, while promoting environmental values." Rights of ownership are distinct from rights of use, and the national government retains the power to "regulate the use, flow and control of all water in the Republic" (Republic of South Africa, 1998).

The social-contract and human rights approaches do not in and of themselves define a proper balance between efficiency and equity. Water transactions are replete with externalities (positive as well as negative) that make it exceedingly difficult to specify exactly what constitutes "full-cost" pricing or "efficient" resource allocations in practice (even if gross inefficiencies are readily spotted). But they do seek to place considerations of efficiency within the confines of a more fundamental commitment to some minimally necessary levels of social equity.

Conclusion: The Four Capitals of Water Sustainability

In recent years the World Bank has grown fond of referring to the four "capitals" of sustainability: *economic capital,* in the form of money and the stock of capital goods generated by its investment; *natural capital,* in the form of nature's endowment of critical resource goods and ecological services; *human capital,* in the form of skills and energies of people; and *social capital,* in the form of institutions and practices that link individuals, provide public goods, and overcome barriers to cooperation for social gain. Although the Bank has not always heeded its own wisdom in paying attention to the noneconomic forms of capital, this list nevertheless provides a useful framework through which to view global water futures.

The challenge of sustainability is clear—to find the right mix of economic, natural, human, and social capital to meet basic human needs, to reconcile competing sectoral claims to water supplies, and to protect and preserve crucial freshwater ecosystems and life-sustaining natural processes. The key to meeting this challenge will be to move away from a vision in which technological innovation and new supplies are expected to outrace growing consumption. Instead, we need a vision in which instream ecological uses take their place along side economic extractive uses; in which water pricing and allocation systems internalize both the true value of water and the true cost of denying it to so many; and in which we generate a sufficient measure of global social capital to address increasingly transnationalized water controversies that spill outside the confines of traditional diplomacy.

Notes

1. According to Oud and Muir (1997), the International Commission on Large Dams defines a large dam as a dam at least 15 meters high, or a dam of 10–15 meters in height if it has a crest length over 500 meters, a spillway discharge of 2,000 cubic meters, or a reservoir volume of more than 1 million cubic meters. "Major dam projects" are defined as those meeting one or more of the following criteria: dam height of more than 150 meters, dam volume of more than 15 million cubic meters, reservoir volume of more than 25 billion cubic meters, or installed electric generating capacity of more than 1,000 megawatts.

2. According to the assessment, "'Strongly affected' systems include those with less than one-quarter of their main channel left without dams, as well as rivers whose annual discharge has decreased substantially. 'Unaffected rivers' are those without dams in the main channel and, if tributaries have been dammed, river discharge has declined by no more than 2 percent" (World Resources Institute, 2000, 106).

3. The watersheds included in this estimate are the Amazon, Congo, Mississippi, Nile, Ob, Parana, Yenisey, Lake Chad, Lena, and Niger. "Largest" in this context refers to the land area of the watershed.

5

Food Policy: Underfed or Overfed?

Marc J. Cohen

At the beginning of the twenty-first century, humanity faces a glaring contradiction: the persistence of food insecurity amidst plenty. Without significant changes in both developed- and developing-country policies, over the next two decades hundreds of millions of people will remain food-insecure, millions of children will die each year from malnutrition, and environmental degradation will continue unchecked. This is the devastating prospect in spite of projected gains in food availability. However, there is nothing inevitable about such a disturbing scenario. If governments, international agencies, nongovernmental organizations (NGOs), business and industry, and individuals are willing to back their words with action and resources, accelerated progress toward sustainable food security is possible without harming the environment.

An adequate supply of food is a critical component of ecological security. Without it, people die prematurely or become susceptible to disease. As defined at the 1996 World Food Summit, *food security* exists when all people, at all times, have physical and economic access to sufficient, safe, and nutritious food to meet their dietary needs and food preferences for an active and healthy life (UN Food and Agriculture Organization, 1996b). As of 1998, 777 million people in the developing countries lived in food insecurity (UN Food and Agriculture Organization, 2001b). This is nearly three times the population of the United States. The world has made progress—albeit too slowly and very unevenly—in reducing hunger over the last three decades. Since 1970, the absolute number of food-insecure people has declined by nearly 20 percent, or from 37 to 17 percent (UN Food and Agriculture Organization, 2000a, 2001c).

In the late 1960s and early 1970s, much of Asia was considered "a basket case." It was feared that the world faced a Malthusian nightmare of too many people and not enough food (Brown 1974). The threat of famine gripped West and Central Africa, Ethiopia, and Bangladesh, while the popular press in the industrialized countries turned out tomes on "lifeboat ethics" and "triage" (Paddock and Paddock 1967; Hardin 1974).

In fact, food availability in the developing world has improved dramatically over the past three decades, rising 26 percent. In 1970, daily per capita calorie supplies in developing countries were 2,140 (below the minimum requirement of 2,350). By 1997, the average was 2,667, or more than enough to meet minimum requirements if supplies were distributed according to need (see figure 5.1). Nevertheless, per-person food availability in Sub-Saharan Africa and South Asia lagged behind the developing world as a whole (UN Food and Agriculture Organization, 1996b; Rosegrant et al. 2001).

Between 1967 and 1997, per capita cereal production in the developing world increased 28 percent, contradicting Malthusian predictions. This resulted from technological innovation and the related widespread

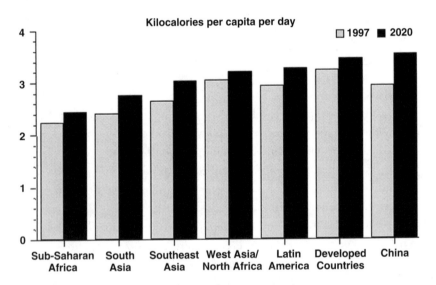

Figure 5.1
Daily per capita calorie consumption by region, 1997 and 2020. *Source:* Mark W. Rosegrant, Michael S. Paisner, Siet Meijer, and Julie Witcover, *Global Food Projections to 2020: Emerging Trends and Alternative Futures* (Washington, DC: International Food Policy Research Institute, 2001).

adoption of "Green-Revolution" high-yield varieties, complemented by increased irrigation and fertilizer use. Production expanded broadly in the developing world (especially in Asia), though sub-Saharan Africa lagged behind. Increased output created nonfarm rural employment opportunities. Yield gains have slowed since the mid-1970s, but from 1982 to 1997, world wheat prices dropped 28 percent in real terms, rice prices 29 percent, and maize prices 30 percent (Rosegrant et al. 2001). Lower food prices benefited nonfarm consumers and poor farmers who were net purchasers of food. Farmers who produced more than they consumed gained because technical advances reduced production costs (Kerr and Kolavalli 1999).

Yield gains attributable to the Green Revolution are estimated to have preserved over 300 million hectares (more than all farmland in the United States, Canada, and Brazil combined) of forests and grasslands, including considerable wildlife habitat, conserving biodiversity and reducing carbon releases. However, in some instances widespread planting of high-yield varieties contributed to ecological insecurity through increased soil salinity and lowered water tables, health problems due to pesticide use, and degradation of water, air, and soil from excessive chemical use (Rosegrant et al. 2001; Cohen and Pinstrup-Andersen 2001; Consultative Group on International Agricultural Research, 2001a, 2001b; McNeely and Scherr 2001).

At present, the vast majority of food-insecure people (64 percent, or 497 million people) live in the greater Asia-Pacific region, with 61 percent of the regional total found in South Asia. Though the proportion of food-insecurity in this region represented a drop from 41 percent in 1970 to 16 percent in 1998 (UN Food and Agriculture Organization, 2000a), high population growth rates have meant that the absolute number of food-insecure South Asians actually rose 14 percent over the same period. Trends in sub-Saharan Africa have been particularly discouraging, where food insecurity remained unchanged between 1970 and 1998, at 34 percent—the highest of any region. The number of food-insecure Africans has more than doubled over this period, from 88 million to 194 million. Together, South Asia and sub-Saharan Africa are home to over three-fifths of all undernourished people.

Food insecurity also exists in higher-income countries. In 1998, there were 27 million food-insecure people in countries in transition from centrally planned to market economies, and 11 million in industrialized countries (UN Food and Agriculture Organization, 2001c). The U.S. Department of Agriculture estimates that in 2000, 33 million Americans lived in households that were too poor to afford all the food they needed on a regular basis (Nord et al. 2002). Still, food insecurity in developing countries generally is more severe, and affects a far larger proportion of the population.

Child Malnutrition

Malnutrition among preschoolers in developing countries is of particular concern. In 1997, 166 million children under the age of 5 were malnourished in the developing world (31 percent, compared to 46 percent in 1970) (see figure 5.2) (Rosegrant et al. 2001). Inadequate nutrition is a factor in 5 million developing-country child deaths each year (ten times

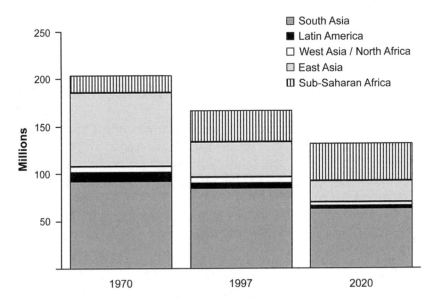

Figure 5.2
Number of malnourished children by region, 1970, 1997, and 2020. *Source:* Mark W. Rosegrant, Michael S. Paisner, Siet Meijer, and Julie Witcover, *Global Food Projections to 2020: Emerging Trends and Alternative Futures* (Washington, DC: International Food Policy Research Institute, 2001).

the number of U.S. cancer deaths), and those who survive face impaired physical and mental development (World Health Organization, 2001). This scourge compromises future health, productivity, and thus ecological security, and accounts for 20–25 percent of the economic impact of childhood diseases in developing countries (World Health Organization, 2001; Flores and Gillespie 2001). It impedes both economic growth and equity, robbing the world of future artists, scientists, community leaders, policymakers, and productive workers. Between 1970 and 1995, the number of malnourished preschoolers in the developing world declined by 37 percent. At the 1990 World Summit for Children, the international community pledged concerted action to halve moderate and severe child malnutrition by 2000 (UNICEF, 2001), but the actual reduction between 1990 and 1997 was a mere 6 percent.

Birth weights of less than 2.5 kilograms are a major factor leading to child malnutrition. These usually result from poor maternal nutrition both before conception and during pregnancy, and affect 25 percent of developing-country newborns. In effect, malnutrition is passed from one generation to the next (UN Administrative Committee on Coordination, Sub-Committee on Nutrition/International Food Policy Research Institute, 2000).

Nutritionists generally agree that if a person takes in enough calories, she or he will also get the necessary protein. But caloric sufficiency does not guarantee adequate micronutrients—vitamins, minerals, and trace elements. Two billion people suffer from anemia, due mainly to iron-deficient diets, including 56 percent of pregnant developing-country women and 76 percent of pregnant South Asians. Half of all anemic women live in South Asia. Anemic women have a 23 percent greater risk of maternal mortality; their babies are more likely to be born prematurely, have low birth weights, and die as newborns. Anemic preschoolers face impaired health and development and limited learning capacity. Anemia can impair immune systems of all age groups. Even when iron deficiency does not progress to anemia, it can reduce work performance. Meat and fish are the best sources of iron, but poor people often cannot afford them or avoid them for religious and cultural reasons. Iron deficiency causes annual economic losses of nearly 2 percent of gross domestic product in Bangladesh, over 1 percent in Pakistan, and nearly 1 percent in India, for a total of $5 billion per year. Nevertheless, high levels of iron-deficiency anemia have persisted over the past two decades, and there are few high-priority public health programs to tackle this problem (UN Administrative Committee on Coordination, Sub-Committee on Nutrition, 1997; UN Administrative Committee on Coordination, Sub-Committee on Nutrition/International Food Policy Research Institute, 2000; Gillespie and Haddad 2000; World Health Organization, 2001).

Vitamin A deficiency is the leading cause of preventable blindness in children and raises the risk of disease and death from severe infections. It affects 100–140 million children, mainly in sub-Saharan Africa and South Asia. One-quarter to one-half million go blind each year, and half of them die within 12 months of losing their sight. Pregnant vitamin A– deficient women face night blindness and increased risk of mortality and mother-to-child HIV transmission. Although trends in the incidence of clinical eye disorders due to vitamin A deficiency are encouraging, inadequate vitamin A intake remains a serious developing-country public health problem (World Health Organization, 2001; UN Administrative Committee on Coordination, Sub-Committee on Nutrition/International Food Policy Research Institute, 2000).

Ironically, although obesity is quite common in developed countries (Gardner and Halweil 2000), it is also found in developing countries. Although only limited data are available, it seems to be rising in Latin America, in the Middle East, and in urban areas of other regions. In Mexico, it is emerging as a marker of poverty, rather than affluence. In China, obesity in men tripled to 14.1 percent between 1989 and 1997, and doubled for women to 20.7 percent, with increased consumption of pork, oil, and other sources of fat. Overweight is associated with increased prevalence of cardiovascular risk factors and chronic illnesses such as diabetes. Some countries with high levels of obesity still report significant rates of child malnutrition, and there are instances of undernourished children in households with overweight mothers (Flores and Gillespie 2001; Gillespie and Haddad 2000).

Causes of Food Insecurity

Poverty is the principal cause of food insecurity. Hunger endures amidst adequate food supplies because food-insecure people cannot access the food that is available. Globally, 1.2 billion people (20 percent of the world's population) live on the equivalent of less than $1 a day (see table 5.1) and are unable to afford food and other necessities. About 70 percent of the world's poor people live in South Asia and Sub-Saharan Africa (World Bank, 2001a). Despite rapid developing-country urbanization, 75 percent of poor people live in rural areas (International Fund for Agricultural Development, 2001). Surveys in several developing countries have found that child malnutrition rates for the poorest 20 percent of households significantly exceed those of the wealthiest 20 percent (World Bank, 2001a).

Poor people frequently lack access to land and other productive resources, and so cannot produce food for themselves. Owners of even marginal landholdings tend to have higher incomes and consume more food than landless people. Landless rural people are more vulnerable to famine and have higher infant mortality rates (International Fund for Agricultural Development, 2001).

In urban areas of the developing world, poor people often lack formal economic opportunities. They frequently have inadequate access to social-assistance programs, although these are generally better targeted in urban areas than in the countryside. Urban poor people usually have fewer opportunities to grow their own food, though urban agriculture is widely practiced (Garrett and Ruel 2000).

In mid-2002, UN humanitarian agencies reported that 27 million people were in need of food and other emergency aid as a result of violent conflicts and their aftermath. This figure included 14.6 million people in sub-Saharan Africa and another 7.5 million in Afghanistan (OCHA, 2002; World Food Programme, 2002b). Not only does violent conflict cause hunger, but hunger can also contribute to conflict, especially when resources are scarce and perceptions of economic injustice are widespread, as in Rwanda in 1994 or Central America in the 1970s and 1980s. Even after conflict ends, the costly reconstruction burden may leave many people food-insecure for years (Messer, Cohen, and D'Costa 1998; Messer, Cohen, and Marchione 2001).

Policies and cultural practices that marginalize people on the basis of gender, age, race, and ethnicity also contribute to food insecurity. Food-insecure people are disproportionately female and either very young or elderly. In rural Guatemala, indigenous children are more likely to be malnourished than others; in India, tribal peoples and members of low-status castes face a higher risk of poverty (World Bank, 2000b).

Table 5.1
People living on less than $1 per day (millions)

	1990 (%)		1998 (%)		2015 (Optimistic) (%)		2015 (Pessimistic) (%)	
Developing world	1,300	29	1,200	23	777	13	1,000	16
Sub-Saharan Africa	242	48	302	48	361	40	462	47
East and Southeast Asia	452	28	267	15	65	3	101	5
South Asia	495	44	522	40	297	18	426	25
Latin America and the Caribbean	74	17	61	12	43	7	58	9
West Asia and North Africa	6	2	6	2	5	1	6	2

Source: World Bank, *World Development Indicators* (Washington, DC: World Bank, 2001).

In many parts of the developing world, gender discrimination negatively affects health, nutrition, and household income and assets. In sub-Saharan Africa, women farmers have less access to education, labor, and farming inputs than men, and often face limitations on their right to own or control land. In both Africa and Latin America, extension services focus primarily on male farmers, though women play significant roles in both food and cash-crop production throughout the developing world. In South Asia, because brides' families must pay dowries, girls tend to receive less care, food, and education than boys, and have higher mortality rates (Quisumbing et al. 1995; Meinzen-Dick et al. 1997; International Food Policy Research Institute, 2000).

In many developing countries, poverty, low agricultural productivity, and environmental degradation interact to increase ecological insecurity in a vicious downward spiral. This is especially true in resource-poor areas with fragile soils, irregular rainfall, relatively high population concentration and growth rates, and stagnant agricultural productivity. Such areas are home to hundreds of millions of food-insecure people. Nearly two-thirds of the rural population of developing countries (1.8 billion people) live in such areas, including marginal agricultural areas, woodlands, and arid zones. These are characterized by low agricultural productivity, severe land degradation, exceedingly low yields, widespread deforestation, overgrazing, soil erosion, and soil nutrient depletion. The threat of famine is severe. Failure to address natural resource issues effectively will result in greater food insecurity (Hazell 1999; Pender and Hazell 2000).

Some resource degradation in agricultural areas has been caused by misuse of modern farming inputs, such as pesticides, fertilizers, and irrigation. But a great deal of environmental degradation, particularly soil degradation and deforestation, is concentrated in resource-poor areas that have not adopted modern technology, where yield gains have failed to keep up with population growth. Rural poor people often cannot afford to invest in land improvements. Degradation and lack of access to high-quality land frequently push poor people into clearing forests and pastures for cultivation at the expense of wildlife habitat and park land, contributing to further degradation, productivity losses, and reduced biodiversity. Since 1980, 20–30 percent of forestland has been converted to agricultural use. Farming practices have also led to aquifer depletion and pollution from farm-chemical runoff (Wilson 2001; Wood, Sebastian, and Scherr 2001; Rosegrant et al. 2001; Rosegrant and Hazell 2000; Pender and Hazell 2000; Scherr 1999).

Finally, losses to pests are estimated to reduce potential farm output value by 50 percent; in developing countries, losses greatly exceed agricultural assistance. Developing countries' share of the global pesticide market is expected to increase significantly during the early twenty-first century. Insecticides currently used in developing countries are often older and acutely toxic, and are banned in many developed countries except for export (Yudelman, Ratta, and Nygaard 1998).

Factors in Future Food Security

Many factors will influence the prospects for sustainable food security in the coming years. Globalization offers developing countries significant new opportunities for broad-based economic growth and poverty alleviation, but also presents significant risks. These include the short-term inability of many developing-country industries to compete, potential destabilizing effects of short-term capital flows, increased price risk exposure, and worsening inequality within and between nations. Continued protection and subsidization of domestic agriculture and increasing food-safety concerns in industrialized countries may limit developing countries' market access. The most critical issues are how globalization can be guided so that it benefits low-income people (particularly in their food and nutrition situation), and does not have an adverse impact on natural resources.

In response to the 1994 Uruguay Round trade agreements and structural adjustment programs, many developing countries have liberalized food and agricultural trade. Yet, developed countries have not reciprocated, instead maintaining barriers to high-value imports from developing countries such as beef, sugar, peanuts, dairy products, and processed goods. Some developed countries continue to subsidize agricultural exports; many developing countries lack the administrative, technical, and infrastructural capacities to comply with global trade rules (Diaz-Bonilla and Robinson 1999; Pinstrup-Andersen, Pandya-Lorch, and Rosegrant 1997, 1999).

Forty-five of the poorest countries (thirty in Africa) owe $235 billion to external creditors, mainly governments and international financial institutions. Most of these highly indebted poor countries cannot afford to make payments, due to low prices for their primary exports (Catholic Relief Services, 2001; Pettifor 2000). Many of these indebted countries suffer from high levels of food insecurity (UN Food and Agriculture Organization, 2001c). To repay their debts, poor-country governments delay investments in schools, clinics, and roads. They also seek to boost exports to earn the hard currency to make payments, and so may encourage production of exports, such as flowers for developed-country markets, instead of domestic staple food crops (Catholic Relief Services, 2001; Pettifor 2000).

With the end of the Cold War, official development assistance (ODA) became a much lower priority for industrialized-country governments. Aid from the principal donor countries fell 21 percent in real terms from 1992 to 1997. Since then, ODA levels have increased somewhat, but the aid provided in 2000 was still 8 percent less than in 1992. In the wake of September 11, major donors (including the United States) have indicated that they will increase aid. However, it is unclear to what extent donors will target funds to sustainable development in the poorest countries, as opposed to merely providing cash transfers to countries deemed strategic.

New technological advances in molecular biology and information and communications offer potential benefits for poor people that may advance food security and sustainable natural resource management. However, there are serious concerns about what amounts to scientific and technological apartheid, wherein technological progress focuses primarily or even exclusively on industrialized countries (Serageldin 1999). Past agricultural research tailored to solving problems of small-scale farmers and low-income consumers in developing countries helped to expand productivity, protect the environment, and increase food security. The financing, management, and organization of agricultural research may require new policies to ensure that low-income people benefit. The private sector accounts for a growing share of global agricultural R&D, subjecting both products and research processes to intellectual-property-rights protection. This raises concern about whether future R&D will actually help to eliminate hunger (Alston, Pardey, and Taylor 2001). Appropriate polices and institutions are needed to ensure that biological and communications technologies contribute to advancing sustainable food security (Thussu 2001; Pinstrup-Andersen and Cohen 2001; Mohan 2000).

A global health crisis is afflicting the impoverished and impoverishing those affected. The tragic pandemic of HIV/AIDS, persistent threats of malaria, tuberculosis (TB), and a variety of chronic diseases compromise food and nutrition security in many developing countries. African preschoolers account for 90 percent of malaria deaths; because malaria often strikes during harvest time, it threatens food security. Hungry children are likely to miss school due to illness and diet-related diseases—perhaps linked to undernutrition in utero—reducing the workforce and absorbing resources from primary health services. The interaction of inadequate dietary intake and disease leads to malnutrition, disability, and death. Insufficient access to food, inadequate health services, low status of women, and poverty also play catalytic roles (Flores and Gillespie 2000).

Most of the population increase in coming years will occur in the cities and towns of developing countries; by 2020, a majority of the developing world's population will live in urban areas. This will present new challenges to provide employment, education, health care, and food. While current efforts must continue to focus on the rural areas where the majority of poor and food-insecure people reside, future policies must pay

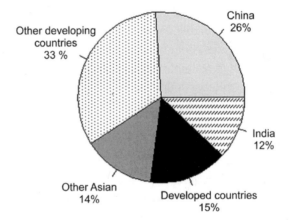

Figure 5.3
Share of cereal demand increase, 1997–2020. *Source:* Mark W. Rosegrant, Michael S. Paisner, Siet Meijer, and Julie Witcover, *Global Food Projections to 2020: Emerging Trends and Alternative Futures* (Washington, DC: International Food Policy Research Institute, 2001).

increasing attention to growing urban poverty, food insecurity, and malnutrition (Garrett and Ruel 2000).

A number of factors such as an aging farm population, the feminization of agriculture, and the decreasing cost of capital relative to labor are resulting in rapid changes to the structure of farming in many developing countries. These emerging issues call for new and innovative approaches to agricultural policy and rural institutions. Small-scale family farms, traditionally the backbone of much of developing-country agriculture, are under threat from labor scarcity caused by out-migration and disease. Globalization and domestic investment in infrastructure improves markets and makes capital available for larger production units (International Food Policy Research Institute, 2001).

Projections of Future Food Security

Income growth, population growth, urbanization, and associated changes in dietary preferences all affect food demand. The International Food Policy Research Institute's (IFPRI) International Model for Policy Analysis of Agricultural Commodities and Trade (IMPACT)[1] has been used to project several alternative global food futures. In the most likely, food availability will increase in all regions by 2020. Even in sub-Saharan Africa, per capita availability will exceed minimum requirements, though African food availability will continue to lag behind that of other regions (Rosegrant et al., 2001).

IMPACT projects income growth in all regions over 1997–2020, with the slowest growth in sub-Saharan Africa. Urban population in developing countries is expected to double between 2000 and 2020 (UN Population Division, 2000b, 2001). When people move to cities, they tend to shift consumption to foods requiring less preparation time (e.g., from coarse grains and root crops to rice and wheat), and to more meat, milk, fruit, vegetables, and processed foods (Garrett and Ruel 2000).

In the most likely scenario, IMPACT forecasts a 49 percent increase in developing-country cereal demand between 1997 and 2020, with Asia (led by China) accounting for 52 percent of the increase (see figure 5.3). Maize will overtake rice and wheat, accounting for 30 percent of total cereal demand, compared to 26 percent in 1997. Most increased maize demand will be for animal feed, due to rising meat consumption, expected to increase 57 percent globally and 92 percent in developing countries, again led by China (see figure 5.4). Cereal production will grow 1.3 percent annually over 1997–2020. Yield gains will account for 85 percent of increased developing-country cereal production, but yields will grow less than 1 percent per year globally. Slowing rates of yield growth will result from increasing input requirements to sustain Asian yield gains and slowed public investment in agricultural research and irrigation. U.S. and European Union (EU) exports will fill the gap between developing-country cereal production and demand (Rosegrant et al. 2001).

IMPACT also projects declining real cereal prices over 1997–2020, but at a slower rate than in the 1980s and 1990s. Wheat prices will decline 8 percent, rice will drop 13 percent, with maize prices remaining flat. Prices will only begin to decline significantly after 2010, after remaining fairly stable during 1997–2010 (Rosegrant et al. 2001).

Without significant changes in national and international policies, IMPACT projects that by 2020, the number of malnourished preschoolers in developing countries will decline only 21 percent from the 1997

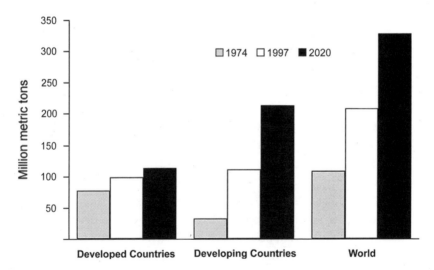

Figure 5.4
Total meat demand by region, 1974, 1997, 2020. *Source:* Mark W. Rosegrant, Michael S. Paisner, Siet Meijer, and Julie Witcover, *Global Food Projections to 2020: Emerging Trends and Alternative Futures* (Washington, DC: International Food Policy Research Institute, 2001).

level, to 132 million (see figure 5.2). Although South Asia will reduce child malnutrition more rapidly than the developing world as whole, it will remain home to nearly half of all malnourished preschoolers. The number of malnourished sub-Saharan African children is expected to *rise* by 26 percent (Rosegrant et al. 2001).

Food Security and Development

If developing and developed countries alike implement appropriate policies and establish appropriate institutions, progress against food insecurity and child malnutrition could accelerate substantially. Given the rural center of gravity of poverty, broad-based agricultural and rural development is essential to ensure food security in developing countries. For every new dollar of farm income earned in developing countries, the national income as a whole rises by up to $2.60, as growing farm demand generates employment and income (Delgado, Hopkins, and Kelly 1998).

Well-functioning and well-integrated markets for agricultural inputs, commodities, and processed goods can contribute enormously to poverty alleviation, food security, and overall quality of life. Market performance improves when governments no longer monopolize trade, but guarantee contract enforcement, enact and implement food quality standards, maintain public safety and health, and provide a favorable environment for savings and investment (Kherallah et al., 2000).

Nevertheless, markets alone cannot ensure equity. Good public policies and strong institutions are needed to guarantee that small farmers have access to land, water, credit, and extension services, as well as yield-increasing and environment-friendly technologies. They must also have the opportunity to participate in export-crop production. In addition, trade, macroeconomic, and sectoral policies must not discriminate against agriculture and must be favorable to poverty reduction and food security. Respect for human rights and conflict resolution are essential for sustainable agricultural and rural development. (Tweeten and McClelland 1997; Drèze and Sen 1989; Sen 1999). Programs must engage low-income people as active participants, enabling them to gain economic and political empowerment and strategic alliances with non-poor people (Kherallah et al. n.d.; Delgado 1997; Pinstrup-Andersen 1993; Cohen 1994).

ODA donors must also reverse the precipitous decline in agricultural aid, which in 1998 was 8 percent below 1990 levels. Reducing ODA to agriculture is shortsighted, because such aid is not only effective in promoting sustainable development and poverty alleviation, but leads to increased export opportunities for developed countries, spurring general economic growth and demand (Pinstrup-Andersen and Cohen 1998).

Agricultural Research Is Vital

Public investment in agricultural research that can improve small farmers' productivity in developing countries is especially important for food security. It can boost productivity, furthering broad-based income growth and lowering food-production costs. Such research should focus on small-scale farms, staple food crops, livestock, fisheries, and agroforestry, as well as high-value cash crops (Pinstrup-Andersen and Cohen 2001).

The benefits attributed to the Green Revolution stemmed in large part from the efforts of international agricultural research centers and national agricultural research systems in developing countries. The private sector is unlikely to undertake such research, because expected profits are not likely to cover investment costs. Though gains to society and the poor are high, these returns can only be obtained through public investment (Alston et al. 2000).

Modern agricultural biotechnology has the potential to advance food security. Whether it will do so depends on the relevance of R&D to poor people, the policy environment, and the nature of the property rights governing the technology. Biotechnology could increase productivity by introducing pest resistance and developing cereals capable of capturing nitrogen from air, increasing tolerance to adverse weather and poor soil quality, enhancing durability during harvesting and shipping, and developing more nutritious varieties. However, except for limited work on rice and cassava, little transgenic crop research currently focuses on the productivity and nutrition of poor people. In 2001, North America accounted for 74 percent of transgenic crop plantings, with 68 percent in the United States (James 2001). Additional public and philanthropic resources will be needed to support appropriate research.

Successful adaptation of genetically modified (GM) crop technology to benefit poor farmers and consumers in developing countries will require effective legislation to balance intellectual property rights with farmers' rights to save, reuse, and exchange seed. Food and biosafety regulations should reflect both international agreements and a society's acceptable risk levels, including those associated with *not* using biotechnology. Poor people should be included directly in decision making about technological change. Unless developing countries have such policies in place, there is a risk that the introduction of agricultural biotechnology will increase inequality, as larger farmers capture most of the benefits through early adoption.

The outcome of global agricultural trade negotiations could also bear on developing countries' risks related to biotechnology. Some warn that if the "precautionary principle" becomes the basis for animal and plant health standards and technical barriers to trade, then the European Union and Japan could discriminate against GM crop exporters without scientific evidence of harm (Paarlberg 2000). Low-income developing countries may choose to differentiate and label GM and non-GM foods, and to the extent that they can manage such a system, they would be able to capture the benefits from modern agricultural biotechnology for domestic consumption while maintaining export markets for GM-free foods. In view of the importance of agricultural productivity increases, most low-income countries will want to use appropriate biotechnology once effective biosafety regulations are in place. Rejection of GM crops in Europe and Japan may make such crops cheaper for developing-country importers.

Sustainable Management of Natural Resources

A high degree of complementarity among agricultural development, poverty reduction, and environmental sustainability is more likely when agricultural development is broad based, market driven, participatory, decentralized, and driven by technological change that enhances productivity without degrading natural resources. Failure to replenish soil nutrients must be rectified through efficient and timely use of organic and inorganic fertilizers and improved soil management. Chemical fertilizer use should be reduced where heavy application causes environmental harm; subsidies that encourage excessive use should be removed, though some may remain necessary for less favored areas where current use and soil fertility are low. Policies should aim to raise the value of forests and pastures, offer incentives for sound management, and help create non-farm employment opportunities (Pinstrup-Andersen, Pandya-Lorch, and Rosegrant 1997, 1999; Hazell 1999; Scherr 1999).

Until recently, developing-country governments and aid donors encouraged the use of synthetic pesticides. Now, consensus is emerging on integrated pest management (IPM), which emphasizes greater reliance on alternative means of pest control, such as natural predators, biological pesticides, crop rotations, and pest-resistant crop varieties (Yudelman, Ratta, and Nygaard 1998).

More efficient use can save a large share of the water needed to meet increased demand through 2020. Comprehensive water-policy reform can help save water, improve use efficiency, and boost per-unit crop output. Such reforms are difficult, due to widespread practices and norms that treat water as a free good, and vested interests that benefit from current arrangements. Devolving irrigation infrastructure and management to user associations, combined with secure access to water, will provide incentives for efficient use (Rosegrant and Ringler 2000; Pinstrup-Andersen, Pandya-Lorch, and Rosegrant 1997, 1999; Rosegrant 1997).

Tackling Malnutrition

The IFPRI has also examined the factors behind the substantial reduction in child malnutrition between 1970 and 1995. Improvements in women's education accounted for 43 percent of the reduction, followed by improvements in per capita food availability (26 percent), improvements in the health environment (19 percent), and improvements in women's status, as measured by the female-to-male life expectancy ratio (12 percent) (Smith and Haddad 2000). Empowering women reduces the proportion of the population below the poverty line; assets in women's hands also increase education's share of household expenditures. Training poor mothers in child-feeding practices and preventive health care greatly improves child nutrition. However, it is necessary to change social programs, as well as property rights and divorce laws, to give women equal access to resources and opportunities (International Food Policy Research Institute, 2000).

Food fortification and supplementation are cost-effective approaches to reducing micronutrient malnutrition. Promotion of dietary diversity has great promise for improving iron and vitamin A intakes. Development of iron-and vitamin A–rich staple crops through both conventional breeding and biotechnology is another potentially effective approach, and requires only a one-time investment. Such strategies should be viewed as complementary, not either-or choices (Bouis 2000; World Health Organization, 2001).

Developing-country governments, with support from aid donors, need to devise appropriate policy responses and programs for growing urban food insecurity. These should improve livelihoods and employment among urban poor people, support environmentally sound urban agriculture, and promote healthy physical environments and adequate care and feeding practices (Garrett and Ruel 2000).

Making Globalization Work for Poor People

Developing countries must participate effectively in global agricultural trade negotiations, and pursue better access to developed-country markets. Coalitions with some higher-income countries may help improve bargaining positions—the developing world cannot be expected to endorse one-sided agricultural trade liberalization ad infinitum. If industrialized countries want developing countries to continue to open their markets, they must open their own, too, and reduce trade-distorting farm subsidies. Global agricultural subsidies currently total $360 billion, with 80 percent provided by developed-country governments—subsidies amount to nearly six times the amount of all ODA.

However, without appropriate domestic economic and agricultural policies, developing countries will not fully capture the potential benefits of trade liberalization. Because the distribution of benefits depends on the distribution of productive assets, countries should enact reforms that remove biases against small farmers and poor people, while facilitating access to the benefits of freer trade. With technical and financial support from industrialized countries, developing countries must develop strong animal and plant health standards appropriate for developed-country markets. Food aid donors should provide assistance on a multiyear basis, targeted in ways that do not displace domestic production in low-income countries.

Meeting Health Challenges

Governments and international agencies should address health risks as key to their food-security strategies. Integrated solutions can achieve multiple benefits and be more cost-effective. Food supplements for nutritionally vulnerable pregnant women may be linked to community-based prenatal-care programs to reduce low birth weights; micronutrient supplementation can also reduce malnutrition and low birth weight. Drip irrigation, which reduces water waste, also reduces the habitat of malaria-spreading mosquitoes. Food-based micronutrient programs should be integrated into agricultural development efforts (Flores and Gillespie 2001).

Food and agriculture programs must also integrate efforts to prevent and mitigate the spread of HIV/AIDS. As labor supplies decline, it may be necessary to develop new technologies and crop varieties that rely less on labor. Farmer field schools can facilitate transfer of knowledge within and between generations. Encouraging agricultural research centers to become more client focused may help natural resource management to remain effective in the face of weakened social capital and property rights (Flores and Gillespie 2001).

Conclusions

Implementing the policy changes outlined in this chapter will be expensive and will require difficult political choices. But the task is far from impossible. The "business-as-usual" scenario, in which the number of malnourished children falls from 166 to 132 million during 1997–2020, assumes investments of $579 billion in irrigation, rural roads, agricultural research, clean-water provision, and education. IMPACT projects that an investment of $802 billion would reduce the number of malnourished preschoolers to 94 million, a substantial step toward true food security. If total expenditures by developing-country governments stayed constant at 1997 levels, the investments needed to achieve the more favorable outcome would amount to just 4.9 percent of total developing-country government spending from 1997 to 2020. On an annual basis, this represents only 5 percent of conventional military security spending in low- and middle-income developing countries, clearly a very positive trade-off (Rosegrant et al. 2001; World Bank, 2001b).

Over the next few decades, if governments are unwilling to take the steps to achieve food security for all, they must be held accountable by their own citizens and in the court of international public opinion. Civil-society groups, including organizations of food-insecure people themselves, are critical to persuading governments and public international organizations to make poverty reduction, food security, and sustainable natural resource management higher policy priorities. Failing to take the appropriate steps will mean continued low economic growth and rapidly increasing food insecurity and malnutrition in many low-income developing countries, as well as environmental deterioration, forgone trade, widespread conflict, and a more ecologically insecure world for all.

Notes

1. IMPACT generates scenarios for global food demand, supply, and trade, as well as child malnutrition. It covers thirty-six countries and regions that account for the bulk of global food production and consumption, and covers sixteen major agricultural commodities. IMPACT is a partial equilibrium model of the global food economy, specified as a set of country or regional submodels, within each of which supply, demand, and prices for agricultural commodities are determined. The submodels are linked through trade. The model uses a system of supply-and-demand elasticities, incorporated into a series of linear and nonlinear equations, to approximate the underlying production and demand functions. FAO base data for 1996–1998 are used for figures on supply, demand, and prices. Projected numbers of malnourished children are derived from the estimated relationship between the percentage of malnourished children and average per capita calorie consumption, the percentage of females with access to secondary education, the quality of maternal and child care (as measured by the ratio of female-to-male life expectancy at birth), and health and sanitation (measured by the percentage of the population with access to clean water). Since each of the thirty-six country groups produces and/or consumes at least some of each commodity, thousands of supply-and-demand parameters are specified (income, price, and cross-price elasticities of demand; production parameters including crop area and yield growth trends; price-response parameters; trade-distribution parameters; and so forth). Parameter estimates are drawn from econometric analysis, assessment of past and changing trends, expert judgments, and synthesis of the existing literature. IMPACT projections cited in this chapter are from June 2001 and reported in Rosegrant et al. 2001, which also provides a detailed description of the model.

6

Energy, Security, and Cooperation over the Next Quarter Century

Heather Conley and Warren Phillips

In the early 1970s the *Limits to Growth,* a report of the Club of Rome's project on the predicament of humankind, produced a set of conclusions that were stunning to the international community (Meadows et al. 1972). It was ultimately published in 30 languages and sold over 30 million copies. According to the study, the world would ultimately run out of many key resources, including fossil fuels. The prediction that shortages of energy and other natural resources would soon become widespread in the face of growing demand has now been recognized as an error. The 1980s and 1990s revealed that this neo-Malthusian type of thinking missed the mark and that there was actually a glut of oil and gas. The price of such fossil fuels actually experienced a significant decline. But as we entered the twenty-first century, particularly in 2004, energy prices seemed to soar and the questions of what the future would bring seemed once again to be very relevant.

Energy is a critical component of ecological security, but when projecting forward over the next 25 years, our thoughts are most likely informed by equal parts of outdated assumptions and entirely new and diffuse ideas and concepts. Today, energy policy is at a transition point—we have just begun to move beyond the tired concepts of the twentieth century, yet we do not have a firm grasp on a new set of variables that will inevitably alter current energy and security futures.

As we peer into this foggy energy future, we do know that, barring the sudden discovery of a low-cost "super technology" that will dramatically reduce our enormous appetite for fossil fuels, the availability and hence the security of a sufficient supply of fossil fuels will be an imperative for developed economies, and certainly essential for developing economies such as China and India. Several trends appear relevant to the discussion of sustaining a substantial energy supply and ensuring its security for the next 25 years.

Contemporary energy availability is now more determined by technology, efficiency gains, environmental imperatives, and competition than in previous decades. New forms of integration and strategic alliances are emerging. Privatization and deregulation in the energy industry have accelerated this process. Responsibility for managing national assets has become paramount, in light of an overall trend toward consolidation, with increasingly large corporations holding greater known reserves.

The new market forces have begun to render obsolete the supply management techniques that oil producers used so effectively in the past. The ability to see oil prices on a screen and trade oil and its products 24 hours each day have introduced global price transparency, such that short-term price swings even out over time, while reductions in operating costs since the stock-market crash of 1986 have already changed the relationship between oil suppliers and consumers. This new paradigm means that transportation costs and foreign-supply diversification are becoming more important. And the issues are becoming those of supply concentration and immediate energy security, not the absolute availability of fossil fuels.

Growing Energy Demand

There are a number of important changes taking place in the energy marketplace, in particular, the rise of natural gas as the fuel of choice for power generation and the development of renewable energy as an important additional source of supply.[1] Yet, far from being relegated to the sidelines, the role of crude oil continues to be one of the most interesting and critical stories for the future. It is not simply supply that dominates discussions; issues of energy-distribution costs are now beginning to emerge as critical to future energy security over the next 30 years.

Regional consumption patterns (see figure 6.1) suggest that energy availability, the cost of recovery, the cost of transportation, and returns on investment are the most important issues that will face the international community in the near future. The recent shift to natural gas for power generation and the emergence of a liquefied natural gas (LNG)

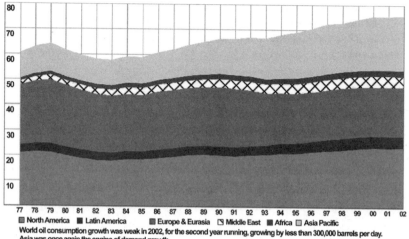

Figure 6.1
2002 regional energy use by source (million barrels daily). *Source:* BP AMOCO Alive, *BP Amoco Statistical Review of World Energy 2003: BP Amoco Alive* [Internet]. BP Amoco, 2003 [cited May 2004]. Available from www.bp. com/worldenergy.

trading market are important elements in domestic energy strategies. These regional patterns of use suggest that the mix of coal, crude oil, and gas in regional demand is undergoing change. Environmental and social considerations now play a much more meaningful global role than in the past because of international concerns over greenhouse gas emissions and because cleaner fuel and conservation technologies are becoming more available.

While these issues are important, the key concern for policymakers is not predicting the specific movements of the future fossil-fuel market, but grasping the importance, and the potential disruptive impact, of those markets on national and international interests, be they of an economic, political, or even a security nature. The concept of energy security is fast becoming a major topic of discussion in international relations. The Nautilus Institute (2004) defines the concept as follows:

Energy security stresses the need to take measures to reduce vulnerability to energy supply disruption, especially foreign oil. Such measures include diversifying energy fuels, developing fuels and technologies which enhance environmental health and build regional confidence, strengthening demand-side management, and engaging in preventative diplomacy along vital sea lanes. The energy security framework is especially salient in Japan, which is highly dependent on foreign energy sources.

The nature of the world in the twenty first century is vastly different in terms of predicting energy demand than it was in the last century, so much so that it is difficult to grasp the very concept of energy security. In 1970 the world population totaled 3.4 billion: 1.2 billion were living in the "more developed" countries and 2.2 billion resided in "less developed" countries. The rich poor split was 35–65. Three decades later, the world's total population is 6.4 billion (Simmons 2000). The split is now 20–80! It is anticipated that this wealth gap is likely to expand to greater magnitudes as the century plays out. More importantly, the list of large, heavily populated countries is changing. For instance, China and India alone are, today, the size of the entire less developed population of the globe 20 years ago.

What will happen as developing countries, such as China and India, industrialize and vastly increase their energy appetites? Perhaps by 2030, either or both countries could become the next Japanese economic miracle. If, for example, China grows from its present per capita energy consumption to the lowest level of OECD-country energy consumption, then China's energy consumption would grow more than sixfold to over 100 million BOE (barrels of oil equivalent) per day, or in stark terms two-thirds of the entire world's energy use today. In China's case, 75 percent of its current energy mix comes from coal. If it develops along these lines, its coal usage would increase to a level 50 percent greater than all the coal now consumed by the entire world. The greenhouse gas implications of this development are enormous (Zhou 2000). The projected share of northeast Asia's global fossil-fuel use and its share of world carbon dioxide emissions are already expected to continue to rise precipitously. Nearly a third of the growth in annual carbon-dioxide emissions through 2010 is projected to come from this region. Such dramatic growth in energy use has the potential to exacerbate global environmental concerns, including climate change and marine pollution (von Hippel 2000). It also has the potential to put great pressure on supplies of petroleum and natural gas.

New Sources Of Oil

As shown in figure 6.2, oil of Middle Eastern origin will clearly continue to be the major source for the future. While the states of the Former Soviet Union (FSU), Africa, and Latin America show significant volumes of proven reserves, they pale in comparison. This simply points out the extreme reliance on the Middle East to relieve the projected growth in world demand.[2] It also highlights the need to establish more proven reserves. It is important to look at these new reserves in perspective. For example, most estimates of the significance of Caspian basin oil deposits suggest that, while certainly significant, the total impact on proven reserves would be between 3 and 5 percent. This is not earth shattering, to say the least. While a worldwide shortage over the next 30 years is not likely, there will be significant dislocations and there are no easy solutions to the demand problem. The worldwide reserve base is not likely to see great expansion from new finds (Deffeyes 2001). The cost of extraction from newer fields should increase rapidly, because they are mostly found

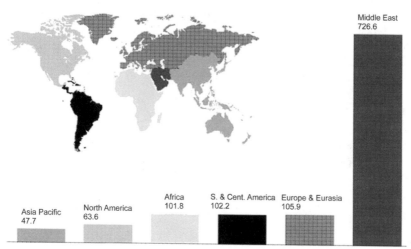

Figure 6.2
2002 Proven oil reserves (thousand million barrels). *Source:* BP AMOCO Alive, *BP Amoco Statistical Review of World Energy 2003: BP Amoco Alive* [Internet]. BP Amoco, 2003 [cited May 2004]. Available from www.bp.com/worldenergy.

in difficult locations. Transportation costs for oil and gas will increase, making transit costs more important in the future. However, when all is said and done, the real issues are market-driven issues of the need for capital to develop and distribute energy resources and the identification of future key energy actors, be they nations or corporations.

Certainly, world oil demand will not remain at current levels. However, according to a recent study, at current rates of consumption, world oil reserves will be depleted at a much faster rate than new discoveries are being made. The Geneva-based IHS Energy Group stated in its annual research report that there are sufficient oil reserves to ensure a supply for the next 40 years ("New World Oil Reserves Lag Growing Consumption," 2001). The clamor for oil is growing ever louder, and efforts to reduce dependence on hydrocarbon fuels remain, unfortunately, modest at best.

Dependence on foreign oil means that consumer countries will not want the price to rise too much as demand soars, so new sources will have to come into play while old sources continue producing. All this oil will have to come from somewhere, and exploration is booming more in the Caspian region and Siberia than it is anywhere else in the world. This said, however, it needs to be remembered that the Caspian and Sakhalin Island fields in the Russian Far East will take many years to be fully developed depending on the rise and fall of oil prices over the years.[3] The problems associated with developing these new fields are typical of those to be confronted in the future.

New Supplies: Caspian Sea Development

The debate over the route of a main export pipeline (MEP) out of the Caspian basin began several years ago, after the Azerbaijan International Operating Company (AIOC), the working arm of a thirteen-member consortium that is developing three offshore deposits in the Azerbaijan sector of the Caspian Sea, began looking for a way to send its main output to world markets. The consortium partners decided to enlarge an existing trunk pipeline that ran from Baku, Azerbaijan, to the Russian oil terminal of Novorossiisk via Chechnya, and either construct a new high-capacity pipe from Baku to Supsa on the Georgian Black Sea coast or build a new line from Baku to Ceyhan via Georgia and eastern Turkey.

The U.S. government has in the past been reluctant to throw its support behind any one of proposed export route, saying instead that it hoped to see multiple pipelines built in the region to avoid transport monopolies in Russia and Iran. But during the Clinton administration, the U.S. government, citing the need to have an alternative export route to a Russian pipeline for Caspian oil and the need to keep any pipeline from going through Iran, became active in supporting a Baku—Tbilisi—Ceyhan (BTC) route. This pipeline is supported by the Turkish government, which sees a need to minimize the flow through the Bosporus due to environmental and security concerns.

Onshore deposits of oil at Tengiz, Kazakhstan, will probably have the most immediate impact on oil availability and environmental demands from the Caspian region. As the largest commercial shareholder, ChevronTexaco plays a leading role in the consortium developing the Tengiz field. The Caspian Pipeline Consortium (CPC) has built a pipeline from Tengiz to Novorossiisk on the Black Sea to ship this crude to the Black Sea and off to market. The main problem is that most of this new oil will not be able to transit the Bosporus because of the narrow, winding nature of the straits. The current throughput in the Bosporus is about 35 million tons per annum (MTA). It can handle a maximum of 50 MTA. The CPC oil may amount to as much as 50 MTA alone. This and other new oil coming into the Black Sea via Georgia is projected to exceed the capacity of the Bosporus by more than 100 MTA by 2010. Thus pressure is building on having a western bypass for the Bosporus as well as the BTC route from Baku to Ceyhan.

Another new cartel has formed to develop the Kashagan field offshore in Kazakhstan. This field is reported to be one of the biggest finds in Central Asia with a projected 13 billion barrel yield. There is as yet no final plan for exporting its oil although the Kazakhstan government has expressed interest in diverting the route to China or to Iran. Commercial entities would like to use the CPC or BTC export routes. Currently the leader in this consortium is ENI, the Italian company, and AGIP. Due to the size of this field, the exit routes that the consortium chooses will have a tremendous impact on the financial returns on all caspian energy projects.

Together the three regimes (AIOC, Tengiz, and Kashagan) will have a tremendous impact on the availability and delivery of new oil and gas.

The issue is where the oil will be sold to maximize profits for the oil companies and to facilitate supply stability. Most of this oil will not be sold in the Mediterranean as that market is well supplied. It also is not likely to supply refineries in Eastern Europe, because those refine Urals crude blend and cannot handle the heavier blends coming from the Caspian without major refurbishing of the refineries. Such refurbishment is quite expensive with few companies seeking this type of capital expense. Therefore, Caspian oil is most likely destined for European and U.S. markets and the transit costs are only competitive if the oil is shipped in supertankers (VLCCs—very large crude containers, 200,000–319,000 tons).

The interplay between the U.S. government's focus on strategic interests and the oil companies' focus on commercial interests has many people wondering just who will pay for the pipelines and which will actually be built. Several major oil companies have refused to support the BTC pipeline because the construction costs are not yet justified in the export quantities identified by exploration. Yet strategically the U.S. government as well as other western governments see many benefits to having a variety of export routes from the region.

New Supply: Sakhalin Island

In 1977, the first oil deposit was discovered to the northeast of Sakhalin Island, and during the last two decades five offshore reserves holding an estimated 273 million metric tons of oil, 878 billion cubic meters of gas, and 64 million metric tons of condensate have been discovered. Unexplored offshore reserves are estimated to contain an additional 450 million metric tons of oil and 700 billion cubic meters of gas. Extraction of the hydrocarbon resources in the Sea of Okhotsk is constrained by severe climatic conditions, including an icing period of up to 9 months a year and ice thickness reaching 1.5–2 meters. The depth of the sea in drilling areas can reach 30–50 meters. Moreover, the area is one of high seismic activity.

Unable to start development of the offshore Sakhalin reserves due to the lack of necessary technology and funds, the Russian Federation issued several tenders between 1991 and 1993 inviting participation by foreign oil companies experienced at drilling in Arctic conditions. As a result, three separate tenders—Sakhalin-1, Sakhalin-2, and Sakhalin-3—were won by various leading oil companies: Exxon, Marathon, McDermott,

Shell, Mobil, Mitsui, Mitsubishi, and Texaco. The projects are being developed under production-sharing agreements (PSAs) designed to split oil revenues with the Russian authorities in exchange for tax and legal stability. The attraction of the PSA model, developed with the support of the World Bank, was that it offered substantial revenues up front to the Russians, who made no investment but received "royalties" on oil and gas sales of 6 percent, rising as high as 50 percent if a return on investment of 17 percent is reached in the future. Agreements have already been signed for two projects, Sakhalin-1 and Sakhalin-2.

But now the Russian government has argued that they do not need PSAs anymore. With the growth in the price of crude oil and in the Russian economy, the Russian government is at best ambivalent about this form of foreign investment. The victim of bureaucratic delays in Moscow, the heads of the two projects have decided to withhold royalty payments to the Russian government to compensate for VAT that was levied in contravention of the PSA. This set of conflicts could mean real setbacks in terms of fossil-fuel supply to the growing markets in the Far East. More importantly, it signals the struggle for control of revenues between multinationals and Russia.

If one charts the dialogue at international conferences on oil development in Russia over the last 10 years, it is easy to see these shifts. With oil prices being quite low, the Russians were actively trying to push PSAs. Oil and gas companies support PSAs as a means of accessing Russian and other FSU oil and gas assets. Extremely large investments are needed to develop fields in Siberia or the Urals and get the fuels to markets. To recoup these investments, PSAs were seen as a safe bet. As the price of oil rose, the Russians began to be more concerned about the size of the equity opportunity they were losing in the PSA arrangements, and the whole process has slowed down. The Russian move to privatization of the oil companies such as LUKOIL, YUKOS,* and SlavNeft was a first step. They have attempted to attract stock investment, private bank loans, and equity investment at various times over the last 10 years. In the last 2 years of conferences they have talked much more about issuing bonds or developing mutual funds to support development. This is a

---

*At the time of publication, a major push was underway by the Russian government to exert greater control over the future of YUKOS.

much more controlled approach to sharing profits from the extraction of oil and gas and shows increasing sophistication on the part of the oil-rich developing countries in their efforts to control their own assets. It is consistent with growing national concerns about control over local natural resources and demands for a greater share of the returns from extraction.

These two new sources of oil point out two very different burdens corporations and countries face in maintaining enough supply of product to meet demand. The first is the political issues of dealing with newly emerging regions in both their domestic difficulties with their governments, and their lack of understanding of the financial, environmental, and political issues arising from access to great wealth in regions of a country that may have been the poorest in the past. Other issues concern who should get these supplies, and who should benefit from the transit revenues for transportation.

Natural Gas Demand

Recent global energy-consumption patterns amply demonstrate that gas is becoming the major new energy source. World gas consumption rose by 2.4 percent in 1999, significantly higher than the 1.7 percent average of the past 10 years. Over the past 10 years, annual gas production has increased by 16 percent. Experts contend that, without any new discoveries, there is approximately 64 years of gas available, assuming current patterns of consumption ("New World Oil Reserves Lag Growing Consumption," 2001). The African region saw the fastest rate of growth in use of natural gas, 7.2 percent (BP AMOCO Alive, 2004). Europe and the FSU also exceeded their 10-year averages. In Portugal and Greece, for example, consumption more than doubled in 1999. Despite the increase in consumption, the world's two largest producers—Russia and the United States—produced the same amount in 1999 as they had in 1998.

Natural gas as a source of power appears set to expand dramatically in the future. In the United States the energy crisis in California in 2002 highlighted the need for gas and the growing likelihood of both spot shortages of gas and power plants to produce electricity. In Europe, the major projects for gas distribution are the Yamal pipeline from Northeast Russia to Germany and the Baltic pipeline system. As Figure 6.3 shows, Europe will

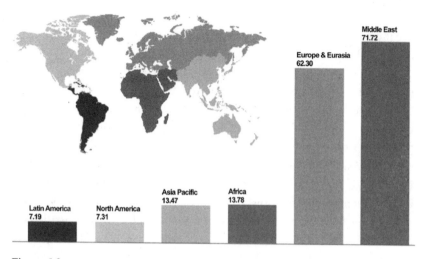

Figure 6.3
2003 Proven natural gas reserves (trillion cubic meters). *Source:* BP AMOCO Alive. 2004. *BP Amoco Statistical Review of World Energy 2003: BP Amoco Alive* [Internet]. BP Amoco, 2003 [cited May 2004]. Available from www.bp.com/worldenergy.

play a leading role in the use of gas. The Asia-Pacific region has myriad gas needs, including the need for gas pipelines. Improved gasification technology using coal, petroleum coke, orimulsion, and residual fuel oil will further develop gas-fired power in this region.

In the Middle East gas is viewed as an export commodity. Iran is becoming a more important exporter as the development of the South Pars Field and construction of a gas pipeline into Turkey are realized. Qatar, which has the third largest reserves globally, has taken substantial measures to develop its 8.5 billion cubic meters of reserves by coinvesting in LNG technology with foreign partners, notably Japan. It plans to supply the states along the southern Arabian Gulf in the future as their needs become greater. Oman is also expected to become a prominent gas exporter by building an underwater pipeline to Pakistan for the South Asian market (Fusaro 2002). BP has announced the construction of a new gas pipeline from its field in the Caspian to Turkey. Blue Stream, the pipeline proposed to go under the Black Sea to supply gas to Turkey from Russia, will also add to the distribution system for gas in this region.

The Future of Coal

We must not lose sight of the importance of coal in the developing countries. Coal is an important source of energy in both Asia and Africa, and contributes 30 to 40 percent of both continents' domestic energy requirements. While there are variations from region to region, and/or country to country, in the mix of fossil fuels consumed, it is essential to examine both growing and diminishing demand. Coal accounts for about one-quarter of the world's total energy consumption.[4] It is primarily used as a source of energy in Asia. The Chinese have been most active in using coal to produce electricity. If coal retains its current importance, absent some revolutionary improvement in the emissions it produces, the world's future atmosphere will obviously be very different than it is today. Unfortunately, world coal consumption has been increasing in recent years. It increased by 19 percent between 1993 and 2003. The increase was modest in the industrialized countries, but significant in the developing areas. Coal consumption increased by only 2.5 percent in North America, but by 10 percent in the Asia Pacific region. Consumption in China leveled off in the late 1990s, but it increased dramatically (15 percent) in 2003. This increase is linked to China's rapid pace of industrial growth and the related demand for electricity. China is also increasing petroleum imports.

Look at the trends across the three primary fossil-fuel resources (figure 6.4). While all three are rising slowly, gas seems to be the only one that has shown major increases in the 1990s. Consumption of coal is hopefully leveling off.

Technological Innovation

Oil recovery costs are defined as the per-barrel cost of exploration, production, and development. These costs declined in the 1980s, but they have shown significant increases since 1995. Cost increases are associated with drilling, acreage acquisition, equipment leasing, and other overhead costs. Other associated costs are due to a major change in technology. Increased reliance on remote sensing and three-dimensional seismic-data acquisition and interpretation adds costs specifically related to information acquisition, storage, and analysis. Thus far such information technology costs have been absorbed by the industry and are expected to level

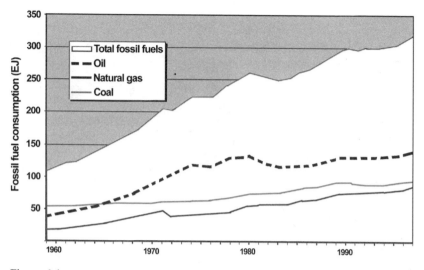

Figure 6.4
Fossil-fuel consumption. *Source:* BP AMOCO Alive. 2004. *BP Amoco Statistical Review of World Energy 2003: BP Amoco Alive* [Internet]. BP Amoco, 2003 [cited May 2004]. Available from www.bp.com/worldenergy.

off in the future. The advances gained in recognizing new finds and proving reserves have been dramatic, however.

The application of these information technologies and other technologies such as horizontal drilling, three-phase pumps, subsea completions and separation, and coiled tubing should have a still more pronounced impact on the exploration success rate. In fact, many of these advances mean that much of the new oil in the short run will be derived from rehabilitation of existing wells and oil fields. This is a trend with major implications for a jump in prices, once existing fields become depleted, however.

The United States and Western Europe will have to replace falling domestic production, and both distance and cost are critical. Figure 6.5 shows 319 million tons of oil moving from the Middle East and Persian Gulf to Northern Europe and the Americas. But as previously mentioned, much of this oil will also need to flow toward the East as Asian development leads to an increased demand for energy. Oil from Siberia will also be expected to flow to Asia to satisfy growing demand.

The key to understanding the likely flows lies in the distance and cost of transport between the Mediterranean and the Gulf to specific destinations. The European and American markets will want to replace Persian

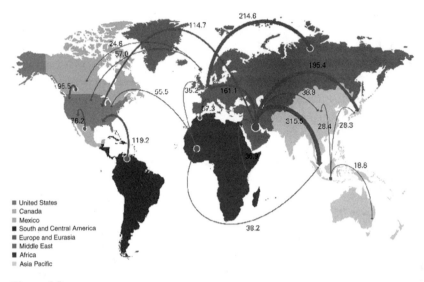

Figure 6.5
Major oil flows (million tons). *Source:* BP AMOCO Alive. 2004. *BP Amoco Statistical Review of World Energy 2003: BP Amoco Alive* [Internet]. BP Amoco, 2003 [cited May 2004]. Available from www.bp.com/worldenergy.

Gulf oil, if they can find oil that is cheaper to ship to market. It will probably come from the Caspian area. Much of the technology debate centers on how big a tanker can be used to supply what market. These issues are becoming more important. The Bosporus, for instance, cannot accept tankers (fully loaded) of the size needed to ship from the Mediterranean to most major ports (the United States, Northern Europe, or Asia). The cost of transit requires VLCCs at least. This means that most of the oil coming into the Black Sea cannot be supplied to major markets unless it comes through Baku, Azerbaijan or Vellore, Bulgaria, the only two ports in the Mediterranean that can handle such large ships.

Increasing Competition

In the early days of the post-1973 energy market, Western oil companies did quite well. They operated the fields, bought the crude oil, refined it into gasoline and other products, and passed along any price increases. However, as the new national oil companies developed, the *value-added* concept began to rule the economies of oil. The national oil companies began building petrochemical plants, fertilizer plants, and refineries to make more profit from their natural resources. Petroleum engineering schools in the West began to swell with students from around the world who sought insight into how the profits could be made and reinvested. There is now a sense of great risk and uncertainty because the large traditional oil companies hold legal claims to only a tiny fraction of the reserves they need to stay in business ("Worldwide Report," 2000).

Measured in reserve base (the number of barrels of oil owned in the ground), Exxon Mobil is the world's twelfth largest oil company. It is just behind Brazil's national oil company, Petroleos Brasileiro and just ahead of Russia's LUKOIL (Langenkamp 2000). ChevronTexaco—the world's fourth largest publicly held U.S. oil company—ranks just behind Pertamina (Indonesia). The aggregate reserves of the top ten U.S. companies are less than those of Mexico's Pemex alone and less than 4 percent of the world's top ten companies (Langenkamp 2000). We are all aware of the importance of OPEC and the national oil companies of giant exporting countries, but there is now a new group of players on the field. The Chinese National Oil Company has reserves two and a half times those of Exxon Mobil. India's Oil and Natural Gas Company has reserves larger than those of ChevronTexaco. Japan, Australia, Taiwan, Malaysia, Egypt, Italy, Turkey, Spain, and Norway are all aggressively seeking reserves throughout the world.

As U.S. oil companies scramble to develop the necessary reserves to stay in business, they find themselves contending not only with their traditional Western competitors, but also with a host of large national companies, some of which represent countries as hungry for crude oil as the United States is. Even the traditional U.S. dominance of gasoline marketing in this country is threatened by the entry of companies such as Venezuela's PVCSA (Citgo) and Russia's LUKOIL, which purchased Getty with its 1,300 service stations in 2002 (Langenkamp 2000).

Western companies are now seeking fossil fuel overseas in increasingly difficult environments and in competition with new, overseas competitors. The costs and risks are substantial and even the largest companies cannot afford to go it alone. Exxon Mobil lost out on the management control of the new Kashagan oil field off the Kazakhstan coastline in the Caspian to ENI, the Italian oil company. In part this was due to the

Government of Kazakhstan's desire not to rest too much power in the hands of American companies, particularly noting ChevronTexaco's substantial involvement in the Tengiz project on shore in Kazakhstan. Oil is being sought in great depths in the Caspian Sea, off the west coast of Africa, in the South China Sea, in the frigid waters of the North Sea, in deep waters off the Canadian East Coast, and in the jungles of South America.

Mergers and Acquisitions

In the mid- to late 1990s, there was a dramatic scramble for the identification and exploration of new energy reserves by the international oil and gas industry. Newspaper headlines announcing one merger and acquisition after another became almost routine as oil and gas firms consolidated, restructured, and took other steps to increase their reserves and ensure global geographic diversity. The prevalence of low oil prices during this time was also a driving factor for the frenzied merger environment. British Petroleum bought ARCO and AMOCO, Exxon bought Mobil, and Chevron acquired Texaco. There are several reasons for these moves. Much of the logic stems from the need to control proven reserves and the international refinery and delivery system. It also suggests the necessity of extremely large amounts of capital and equity to make the energy system of the new millennium work more efficiently. The short-term result: very large multinational firms became even larger with the ability to withstand the ever-changing crude-oil market climate. While the regulatory communities in both the United States and Europe required some divestiture of localized assets by the multinational oil firms (primarily in the downstream sector) in order to avoid monopolizing any given market, all the mergers thus far have been approved.

The merger environment of the 1990s has led to another trend whereby many international oil and gas companies have become so large and have reserves so significant that they now have the necessary capital and political muscle to alter the economic and political landscape of many countries. Certainly, the annual incomes of these firms far exceed the gross domestic product of many developing nations. Moreover, the discovery of hitherto-unknown quantities of fossil fuel can play the role of "king maker," or perhaps more accurately, "state maker." For example, the economic and political viability of newly independent East Timor is made all the more secure by a lucrative agreement with Australia for recoverable reserves in the Timor Gap. The economic and political independence of many states in Central Asia and the trans-Caucasus, such as Azerbaijan and Kazakhstan, may rest on the fact that these countries possess significant natural resources and are able to transport them to energy-hungry markets.

As the giant Western oil companies look to expand their profit base they have turned to Eastern Europe to find small acquisitions in order to secure long-term supply deals. Three of the largest companies in Central Europe—OMV of Austria, PKN of Poland, and MOL of Hungary—are maneuvering defensively to protect themselves from outside predators (Buchan 2001). Shell and British Petroleum have both acquired refineries and gas stations in Poland, Austria, Hungary, and the Czech Republic. LUKOIL, from Russia, is looking to do the same. Long-term supply deals are usually the major object of this form of smaller expansion.

Growing OPEC Power

Much of the merger and acquisition activity discussed above is in response to OPEC pricing policies. OPEC's eleven members collectively supply about 40 percent of the world's oil output, and possess more than three-quarters of the world's total proven crude oil reserves.

Oil revenues are vital for the economic development of the OPEC nations, and these nations aim to bring stability and harmony to the oil market by adjusting their oil output to help ensure a balance between supply and demand. Twice a year, or more frequently if required, the oil and energy ministers of OPEC countries meet to decide on the organization's output level, and consider whether any action to adjust output is necessary in light of recent and anticipated oil-market developments.

Representatives of OPEC member countries (heads of delegation) meet at the OPEC conference to coordinate and unify their petroleum policies in order to promote price stability and commercial harmony in the oil market. They are supported in this by the OPEC secretariat, directed by the board of governors and run by the secretary general, and by various bodies including the Economic Commission and the Ministerial

Monitoring Committee. The member countries consider the current situation and forecasts of market fundamentals, such as economic growth rates and petroleum demand-and-supply scenarios. They then consider what, if any, changes they might make in their petroleum policies.

When oil prices begin to climb, it is almost routine for the U.S. Secretary of Energy to travel to the capitals of friendly OPEC nations to seek increased production in order to reduce prices. U.S. diplomats implore their counterparts in Riyadh, Kuwait City, and Abu Dhabi to increase production, notwithstanding the demands of their OPEC partners. With limited hope now that OPEC will support future U.S. efforts to dampen worldwide crude-oil prices, increasingly U.S. policymakers have turned their attention to non-OPEC members, such as Russia. Yet production in the most important non-OPEC source, the North Sea, has peaked and is expected to decline over the next 10 years. Moreover, no other production source seems likely to replace the North Sea in the short term. While there had been much speculation that recent offshore as well as onshore discoveries in the Caspian would provide "a new North Sea," modest oil exports from the Caspian region eventually will be brought to Western markets. However, this will take many years to accomplish. Complicating matters further, there is evidence to suggest that OPEC and non-OPEC members may be in collusion to maintain high oil prices.[5]

Dealing with OPEC will be a constant challenge to twenty first-century foreign policy practitioners, because OPEC's share of the world's oil supply will increase from today's 40 percent to approximately 50 percent. While it is true that the non-OPEC crude-oil supply will increase somewhat as well, the non-OPEC supplies will not challenge OPEC's supremacy in the near term. It appears likely that OPEC will remain very much at the center of the global energy debate because OPEC enjoys large reserves of crude oil and relatively low production costs.

Other experts suggest that not enough attention has been paid to future increases in energy demand from OPEC member countries themselves. For example, if Saudi Arabia were to "modernize" its economy to the level the United States enjoys today, its needs would move from 2.1 million BOE per day to over 12 million BOE per day by 2030. Though perhaps not of this magnitude in the near future, there will be significant local-demand growth in all OPEC countries and this will have a major impact on the export availability of oil from these countries.

The availability of spare productive capacity in the OPEC countries, particularly Saudi Arabia, Kuwait, and the United Arab Emirates, has contributed greatly to past abilities to avoid or significantly reduce the impact of oil-supply interruptions.[6] Spare capacity in non-Gulf OPEC countries has fallen significantly since 1997. The Gulf states witnessed their spare capacity fall by some 1.5 million barrels per day in 2000 due to internal consumption, although a spare capacity of some 2.5 million barrels per day remains. Gulf countries are currently debating the advisability of spending money to maintain spare capacity. It is likely that they will decide to permit spare capacity to decline in future years, to save money and to take advantage of high prices. Such a decision would raise severe security issues for the United States and Europe.

Environmental Trends

What had been a peripheral economic externality for the energy sector—compliance with environmental regulation—has become a major challenge to how the industry does business worldwide. Efforts to reduce greenhouse gas emissions are now focused on stationary sources of pollution, primarily oil and gas production, refining, petrochemicals, and the power industry as well as numerous other industrial processes. The priority of reducing carbon-dioxide emissions remains high despite the refusal of the United States, China, and several others to support the Kyoto Protocol. A commitment to reducing sulfur dioxide and nitrous oxides is also consistent with growing concerns about the burning of fossil fuels such as oil, gas, and coal.

This movement to reduce carbon-dioxide emissions will force changes in the energy industry. It will require increasingly systemic energy efficiency, renewable energy, and use of natural gas as a transition fuel for international environmental compliance. Emission trading systems are already being developed in the United States, the European Union, Australia, and Japan to lower overall greenhouse gas emissions, with the result being a greater role for environmentally benign technologies in the generation and utilization of energy.

These environmental constraints pose a major problem for oil producers who are sitting on substantial unrealized resources that may turn out to be worthless if not brought to market in the next few decades. All major oil companies have divested interests in coal holdings. Coal's share of the market today is slipping and its value will continue to decline.

A major question is whether the long-term impact of environmental concerns on oil and gas producers will mean that they will feel compelled to bring reserves to market as quickly as possible. If so, this is a strategy diametrically opposed to the supply-containment strategies that are more frequently talked about as forming the basic operating concept of the industry. It would also mean an artificial ceiling on the price of crude oil and energy, which may slow the investment in alternative energy solutions.

Global Implications

The key concerns for policymakers in the power centers of the world over the next 25 years go way beyond the question of simple access to fossil fuels. For them, it is not enough to predict the specific movements of supply and demand. They also need to grasp the importance of the oil market and its potentially disruptive implications for national and international interests, be they economic, political, or even security interests. These issues are global in nature and they have to do with understanding the trends outlined above.

These trends point to broader participation in the global energy economy by institutional investors in industrialized states looking for investments in developing states. The home bias of institutional investors has changed over the last 20 years and should continue to change as more institutional investors come from the new oil-producing states. What we have discussed above is the case of investors from developed nations possibly creating a much greater flow of financial capital into the capital markets of developing countries.

There are important forces at work in affecting both the supply and cost of fossil fuels over the next 30 years. Certainly the most important single trend is the rising Asian demand. Oil and gas are bought internationally. The medium of exchange is dollars. A major oil-price shock creates a tremendous sudden demand for dollars. That has very negative effects on the Asian economies. If, indeed, those economies collapse, the real price of oil to them skyrockets. With growing demand from developing countries in Asia, oil and gas are more important to their economies than they are to Europe and the United States. It is the resulting currency impact that creates the greatest damage to those economies. It is difficult to predict what oil-price shocks do to the relative value of those currencies. We are persuaded, however, that the transformations in the market trends discussed above will have price effects at least as significant and as enduring as the projected rise of oil demand relative to supply in the world.

While there is ample proof of supply being capable of meeting demand for the next few decades, there is a long-term depletion issue that has to be addressed. Three types of solutions are being discussed. One group advocates a reduction in demand for fossil fuels, another advocates technological solutions to the energy problem that do not rely on fossil fuels, and the last group is trying to develop incentives for carbon banking or the rapid natural reproduction of new fossil fuels. It is too early to pick a winner in this discussion. It is necessary to continue all of these dialogues, because current projections of economic growth of the seven most populous countries in the Third World highlight the problem the globe faces in less than 50 years.

The second issue identified in the trends is the heavy concentration of oil and gas reserves today. The Middle East—especially Saudi Arabia—for oil, and Russia for gas, will be the largest future sources. While there are other sources of both gas and oil, the difficulties of accessing these reserves will make the cost of extraction much more of a burden on consumers in the future. This will have grave implications for the poorer countries and for the poor in more developed countries.

Another major implication of our discussion is the trend of distribution or transportation being much more important than reserves for the next quarter century. The issue is clear in at last two different ways. First, it is necessary to understand the costs of energy as being inclusive of the costs of transportation and therefore dependent on efficient means of transit. Second, the potential for conflict over access to supplies means that nations are going to have to take a long-term look at how all can acquire access to sources in an economically feasible manner.

Notes

1. See figure 6.1. Many of the figures in this chapter come from an excellent set of tables provided annually by BP, available online at www.bp.com/centres/energy/index.asp.

2. See USGS, World Energy Resources, http://energy.cr.usgs.gov/oilgas/wep/wepindex.htm.

3. There is another factor for such slow exploration in the Caspian area. The Azeriis have been reluctant to allow new drilling rigs to be imported into the region for fear that the State Oil Company of the Azerbaijan Republic (SOCAR) would not profit from their use. This has been a problem that has hampered exploration since the beginning of this round in the "Great Game," a reference to the geopolitical "race" in central and South Asia by the Great Powers to Secure influence in the nineteenth century.

4. See source, note 1.

5. On May 1, 2001, *Kommersant Daily* reported that Russian President Vladimir Putin and Venezuelan President Hugo Chavez agreed to keep oil prices high and to create a bilateral commission to coordinate prices in the future. President Chavez also stated that he hoped the combined efforts of OPEC and Russia (a non-OPEC member) will prevent any decline in prices. More recently the discussions between OPEC and Russia over a cutback in production continue to show the weight of OPEC in setting world production levels.

6. For an in-depth review of regional resources and projections, see USGS World Energy Resources, http://energy.cr.usgs.gov/oilgas/wep/wepindex.htm.

7

Renewable-Energy Technologies

Gary Cook and Eldon Boes

The *Global 2000 Report,* and subsequent follow-up analyses (Barney 1999), have made it apparent that it would be highly desirable for the world to convert its patterns of energy consumption from carbon-dioxide emitting sources—that is, fossil fuels—to carbon-free sources, such as nuclear and renewable energy. The reasons for this desired transition run the gamut from the geopolitical to the environmental to the fact the fossil fuel resources are limited. Renewable-energy resources, for example, are ample, nondepletable, and available in all regions of the world. Hence, they are relatively free from geopolitical pressures. As these technologies become less and less expensive, renewable resources will help countries and localities sustain growing economies without having to depend on foreign resources. In addition, renewable-energy technologies are compatible with the environment, in terms of atmospheric emissions, and especially with regard to anthropogenic greenhouse gases. For example, one study suggests that, considered on a total fuel-cycle basis[1] and compared to electricity generated by a conventional pulverized coal plant, wind- and solar-generated electricity produce from 130 to 268 times less CO_2 per kilowatt-hour (San Martin 1989).

Renewable-energy resources are resources that are continually replenished or that are replaced after use by natural means. Such resources include wind energy, solar energy, running water, and biomass (plants and waste). Although strictly speaking, geothermal energy (heat from the earth) is not continually replenished, it is generally counted among the renewable resources.

This chapter provides an overview of the alternative sources of energy that can be relied on to fill the impending gap in fossil-fuel availability that may open in the next few decades. The chapter also surveys progress made in making these sources economically competitive. In addition, it suggests the contribution that renewable-energy resources might make to lessening the greenhouse warming problem discussed in chapters 8 and 9. Renewable-energy technologies are technologies developed to exploit renewable-energy resources. For most of human history, people have relied on sustainable energy sources such as wind, water, and especially the burning of wood and other biomass to provide heat and energy. With the advent of the industrial age, people began moving away from burning wood to fossil fuels—coal, then petroleum and natural gas—along with hydroelectricity and eventually nuclear energy, to provide the energy required to run the growing economies of the world. At the present time, the world relies on fossil fuels to supply more than 85 percent of its primary energy. (Energy Information Administration, 2002; International Energy Agency, 2000).[2] However, the World Resources Institute (WRI), which puts a greater emphasis on analyzing the use of more traditional fuels (wood, crop waste, animal dung), claims that the use of fossil fuels constitutes about 80 percent of the world's consumption. The WRI claims also that traditional fuels account for approximately 10.6 percent of world energy consumption, with those who live in rural sections of undeveloped countries still relying heavily on these traditional fuels (World Resources Institute, 2004). Either way, whether at 85 percent or 80 percent, the world's reliance on fossil fuels is extreme.

It is an irony of our age that to ensure sustained economic growth, to foster economic equity among nations, to help palliate geopolitical pressures, and to engender healthy environments, we are finding it most desirable to return to those more ancient but sustainable energy resources. But this is a return with a difference—today we can exploit renewable resources in ways never dreamed of in earlier centuries. These technologies not only promise to provide all forms of energy a modern economy demands, but could eventually meet all the world's energy needs cleanly, economically, and efficiently.

Consider the scale of these resources. The energy in solar radiation striking the earth's surface each year alone is more than 10,000 times that used annually by humans (*Solar Energy,* 2001); if we could efficiently harness only 0.01 percent of this energy, the world would have all the energy needed to run its economies in perpetuity.

Other renewables are similarly vast. In the United States researchers estimate that, under a moderate use of accessible land, there is enough wind-energy potential in just twelve Midwestern states to produce more than three times the electricity consumed by the nation today (Elliott and Schwartz 1993).[3] The good news is that advances in many renewable-energy technologies have not only been solid over the last two decades, but promise to continue for quite some time. As time goes on, this will enable us to exploit more renewables, more efficiently and economically.

What are these technologies? First, there are the mature technologies of hydroelectricity and the combustion of wood, waste, and other biomass for heat and electricity, currently constituting more than 88 percent of renewable-energy consumption in the United States (Energy Information Administration, 2003). Second, there are the so-called *emerging* renewable-energy technologies, including:

Bioenergy. Using wood and agricultural residues, grass, municipal waste, and other biomass to produce energy for heat and electricity as well as liquid and gaseous fuels

Geothermal. Primarily using the internal heat of the earth to generate electricity, but also to directly heat and cool living and working spaces

Photovoltaics. Utilizing solid-state semiconductor devices that directly convert sunlight into electricity

Solar thermal. Concentrating the heat of the sun to produce heat and electricity

Wind energy. Using the mechanical energy of wind to produce electricity

In the rest of this chapter we will discuss each of these emerging technologies in turn—what they are, their contribution status as of 1980, and their status today. We then present scenarios from several well-respected organizations concerning the possible contributions that renewable-energy technologies may make to enhanced ecological security in the next 20 to 50 years.

Bioenergy Technologies

The biomass resource—in the form of trees, grasses, crops, dung, agricultural residues, and forestry wastes such as sawdust, bark, branches, and wood chips—is enormous. These are the organic things we throw away in our dumps, and the methane generated as they decompose.

Biomass provides energy in many ways. We burn it to provide heat for our homes and buildings, and for industrial processes. We gasify it for use in turbines and fuel cells, and hydrolize, ferment, and distill it to turn it into fuel-grade ethanol, collectively known as *biofuel*. We also burn biomass to produce electricity, which is known as *biopower*. There are three general ways biomass generates electricity—cofiring with coal, direct-fired combustion, and gasification.

When cofired with coal, biomass supplements existing coal-fired boilers, constituting up to 15 percent of the total energy input. The advantage of cofiring is that it uses local resources, is low cost, does not decrease efficiency, and helps cut sulfur dioxide, carbon dioxide, and nitrogen-oxide emissions. Direct firing combusts biomass alone to produce steam, which is then used to produce electricity, or combined heat and power.

Gasification converts biomass to a biosynthesis gas (biogas)—a medium calorific gas made up primarily of hydrogen and carbon monoxide. Biogas is then used to drive turbines, with a high conversion efficiency—nearly 40 percent, about twice that of direct combustion. If used for combined heat and power, efficiency could reach 80 percent. The primary biofuel being researched and produced today is ethanol, which is mixed with gasoline and used in internal-combustion engines. Advantages of ethanol include high octane and high oxidation, which cuts certain smog-related emissions, and a decrease in carbon-dioxide emissions.

Wood has long been used for energy in the United States, primarily to heat homes, businesses, and for industrial processes. In 1980, out of the 2.4 quads[4] of wood energy consumed, less than 0.1 quad was used for electricity generation. Although ethanol was the original automotive fuel, by 1980 there was no measurable consumption of alcohol fuels. Over the last two decades, research and development (R&D) and tax and regulatory incentives have changed things substantially. Today, the United States has approximately 10,000 megawatts (MW) of bioelectric capacity generating nearly 70 billion kilowatt-hours (kWh) of electricity per year (Biomass Research and Development Board, 2001). Sixty ethanol plants produce about 2.3 billion gallons of ethanol per year, the great majority of which is used in a 10-90 ethanol-gasoline blend. Moreover, waste facilities supply more than 0.5 quad of energy per year. Together, they provide the United States with almost 3 quads of bioenergy each year (Energy Information Administration, 2003).

Today, almost all of the 2.3 billion gallons of ethanol used in the United States is produced from corn starch using acid hydrolysis. But using engineered enzymes to break down cellulosic and hemicellulosic biomass into sugars and then to ferment those sugars to ethanol (known as *enzymatic hydrolysis*) uses a far more extensive biomass resource and promises a far more efficient and cheaper conversion process. Using such technology, bioethanol consumption in the United States should reach nearly 12 billion gallons by 2020.

Most of the bioelectricity being generated today is done by independent (nonutility) producers, especially by the forestry industry, where paper mills and other processors use forest residues to produce heat and electricity to run the plants. Excess electricity is generally sold to utilities. Such plants rely primarily on direct-combustion technology; however, inroads to biolectric generation are being made by cofiring technology—principally applicable to utility-tied generation plants with coal boilers. This trend is expected to continue until at least 2020.

In the long run, gasification technology probably holds the most promise. First, it should soon be the most efficient biomass-generation technology. Second, it is scalable—it could be employed in both microturbines and large-scale plants, without loss of efficiency. Third, the gas produced could also be used in fuel cells. But most exciting is that gasification technology could lead to the emergence of the *biorefinery*[5]—the biological analogue of the petroleum refinery. Biorefineries would produce not only electricity, but a host of other products such as sulfur-free gasoline and diesel fuels, acids, alcohols, textiles, polyesters, plastics, and other chemicals. (The biorefinery could also arise from enzymatic hydrolysis of hemicellulose and cellulose to sugars, in which sugars become the platform chemical from which other chemicals and materials are derived.)

Geothermal Energy

The earth is an immense source of geothermal energy; the earth's core can reach temperatures up to 5000°C. This heat melts rocks to form magma, which sometimes flows to the surface as lava, but usually remains below, heating the surrounding rock. When water seeps into the earth and collects in fractured or porous rock heated by the magma, reservoirs of steam and hot water are formed, which can be tapped to provide heat and electricity. There are three primary uses of geothermal energy: for direct heat, with geothermal pumps for space heating, and for electricity generation.

Hot water from relatively low-thermal reservoirs can directly provide heat for industrial processes, crop drying, aquaculture, and heating buildings or municipal areas (district heating). Geothermal pumps use the ground as an energy-storage medium. During cool weather the pumps transfer heat from deep under the ground into a building. During warm weather, the process is reversed.

Geothermal energy can be used to produce electricity by drilling wells into reservoirs and piping the hot water or steam into a conventional power plant. There are three types of geothermal plants for producing electricity: dry-steam, flash steam, and binary-cycle. Dry-steam plants draw steam from underground reservoirs, where it is pumped to turbine generators. The spent steam is then condensed to water and pumped back into the reservoir. Flash-steam plants tap into very hot water reservoirs, which flow to the surface under pressure. As it nears the surface, the fluid pressure decreases and the water boils or "flashes" to steam. This steam is separated and used to drive turbines. The remaining water and condensed steam is returned to the reservoir. A binary-cycle plant uses lower-temperature underground reservoirs to vaporize fluids with lower boiling points than water. The vaporized fluid turns the turbines.

Geothermal resources have long been used, primarily as hot springs for spas. In the latter half of the nineteenth century, geothermal energy began to be used in America to heat buildings. Its first use for generating electricity was in the California Geysers area in 1921, when geothermal steam was used to generate 250 kW of electric capacity. But this plant soon fell into disuse because it was not competitive with other sources of electricity. The first large-scale geothermal electricity plant—based on dry-steam technology—was built in 1960 by Pacific Gas & Electric at the Geysers in California. The plant produced 11 MW of net power. By that time the first ground-source heat pump had been developed, and geothermal heat had begun to be used for several direct-heat applications.

In 1980, UNOCAL built the first geothermal flash plant, which generated 10 MW of electric power. By that year, there was approximately 900 MW of geothermal electrical generating capacity in the United States (Energy Information Administration, 2003). The great majority of this was located in California. These plants generated 5.1 billion kWh of electricity for a cost greater than 9¢ per kilowatt-hour.

Today, the United States has more than 2000 MW of geothermal electric plants that generate as much as 13 billion kWh of electricity at costs as low as 5¢ per kilowatt-hour. The nation also uses about 650 MW of direct heat from geothermal resources. With advances in drilling, exploration, and conversion technologies this nation could be tapping 10,000 MW of geothermal electric power by 2010, and as much as 40,000 MW of electrical capacity and 0.5 quad of geothermal heat energy by 2020 (National Renewable Energy Laboratory, 2001).

Practically all of our geothermal energy for the next two decades will be derived from *hydrothermal* resources—hot zones near the earth's surface that contain significant amounts of water. However, there are great geothermal reservoirs that are deeper and drier, such as *geothermal hot rock*—unfractured rock several miles below the surface, containing little water. Once technology to tap this deep resource is developed, the nation would be able to increase its use of geothermal energy by a factor of ten over that available through hydrothermal sources.

Photovoltaics

Photovoltaic (PV) cells use semiconductor materials similar to those used in computer chips to convert sunlight directly into electricity. When light is absorbed by these materials, the solar energy knocks electrons loose and produces electricity, a process called the *photovoltaic effect*. To produce usable power, individual cells are combined into modules, which are in turn mounted into larger units called arrays. Photovoltaic systems can thus be designed to almost any scale, from milliwatts to gigawatts.[6]

Some PV cells are built into collectors that use a lens to focus the sunlight onto the cells. This uses very little expensive semiconducting PV material while collecting as much sunlight as possible. But because the lenses must be pointed directly at the sun, concentrating collectors are limited to the sunniest parts of the country. PV systems can be connected to electrical utility grids, thus allowing the option to use the electricity on the spot or to transmit it elsewhere. Other PV systems are designed as stand-alone systems that provide electricity only to local applications. In such cases, PV systems need a storage technology such as batteries.

When the *Global 2000 Report* was published in 1980, photovoltaics had been used in space as a primary power source on satellites for slightly more than 20 years, but R&D for terrestrial applications had only been taking place for 5 or 6 years. Still, by 1980 this R&D had helped drop the cost of PV to nearly $50 per watt from about $200 per watt in 1959 (Chalmers 1976). The drop was made possible by advances in manufacturing and silicon-growth technology, increases in conversion efficiency, and further development of the PV market.

Compared with today, the PV technology of 1980 was limited and primitive. Manufacturing was slow and was labor- and energy-intensive. The principal semiconductor used was silicon, with less than 5 MW of total installed capacity; even this was confined to single-crystal silicon modules in stand-alone applications, remote applications, and demonstration projects.

Today, things have changed dramatically. Photovoltaics have grown into an industry that shipped 740 MW of capacity to markets around the world in 2003 (Maycock 2004). This is an annual worldwide module market that is worth more than $3 billion and is growing rapidly. The reasons for this growth are myriad. Manufacturing technology has become automated, using less labor, energy, and materials. Modules have become more efficient and reliable, with the typical silicon module having an expected lifetime of about 30 years, converting sunlight to electricity with an efficiency of around 15 percent. Module costs have dropped to $3–$5 per watt, generating electricity that costs as little as 20¢ per kilowatt-hour, as opposed to about 4¢ per kilowatt-hour for electricity generated by a state-of-the-art coal plant. Moreover, applications have increased considerably and today include residential and commercial power, telecommunications, villages in the developing world, and remote hospitals, ranches, and farms. PV technologies are integrated into roofing, structures, or building facades, or broadly distributed across power grids.

The future of photovoltaic technology is even more promising, with dramatic advances expected during the next three decades. These are projected to include cells with conversion efficiencies greater than 50 percent; quantum-dot cells that could convert the entire solar spectrum to electricity, with efficiencies tending toward the thermodynamic maximum of 66 percent; and polymer-based cells that are both cheap and flexible. Such advances would result not only in modules that could cost 50¢ per watt or less, but will also enable PV systems to be easily integrated into other technologies.

With continued cost reductions and growth in applications, the industry expects the international PV market to grow at an annual rate of 25 percent or more for the next two decades, reaching a cumulative 70,000 MW of installed capacity by 2020. In the United States, it could reach 15,000 MW (U.S. Photovoltaic Industry, 2001). At that rate, by 2030 the United States would have about 140,000 MW of cumulatively installed PV systems (National Renewable Energy Laboratory, 2001).

Solar Thermal Energy

Solar thermal is energy from the heat of sunshine. It can be used to provide light, to heat and cool spaces in buildings, to heat water, or to generate electricity. *Concentrated solar power* (CSP) plants produce electricity by using mirrors to concentrate solar energy to produce heat, which then runs a conventional generator. These systems can be modular and sized for small applications requiring as little as 1 kW of electric power or for grid-connected applications requiring more than 100 MW of power. Some systems use thermal storage to allow them to operate during cloudy periods or at night.

CSP is best applied in areas where there is plenty of direct sunlight available, such as in the Southwestern United States. *Trough systems* use curved mirrors to focus sunlight on a receiver tube that runs along the length of the mirror. The fluid within the tube then produces steam, to power electrical turbines. A *dish-engine system* is a stand-alone unit that uses mirrors on a dish-shaped surface to focus solar energy onto a receiver, which transfers it to an engine, converting the heat to mechanical and electrical power. *Power-tower systems* use hundreds or thousands of heliostats (large mirrors that track the sun) to focus sunlight onto a receiver tower. The focused energy heats molten salt flowing through the receiver, which is used to generate electricity in a conventional steam generator.

In 1980 there were no products or systems using concentrated solar power to generate electricity. The first power tower—Solar One, a 10 MW system—was not built until 1982, and then only as a demonstration technology. In 1992 the Solar One facility was redesigned as Solar

Two to test and demonstrate new technologies, especially that of molten salt used for energy storage and electricity production.

Today, the United States has 354 MW of CSP generating capacity, all of which comes in the form of trough technology. There are no commercial dish-engine systems or power towers in use. All 354 MW of troughs are part of nine large plants located in the Mojave Desert in California. These are hybrid systems that use natural gas as backup, and that generate electricity for between 12¢ and 14¢ per kilowatt-hour. This is a decrease from 35 cents per kWh when the first plant was installed in the mid-1980s. Since that time these systems have generated more than 7.0 billion kWh of electricity. But after installation of the last plant in 1992, dropping energy prices and the elimination of tax credits have made further investments not commercially viable. To reverse this trend, costs would have to be halved, which may be possible with the development of a new combined-cycle hybrid system, advanced storage options, lower-cost, longer-lasting mirrors, and eventual economies of scale.

The power-tower technology has not yet become commercially competitive, although a consortium is exploring the possibility of building a commercial plant in Spain. To become competitive the technology would have to deliver between 100 and 400 MW of electric power and integrate with a fossil-fuel system. Advocates project this may happen as early as 2005 or 2010.

Dish-engine systems have yet to be commercialized, partly because no engine has been demonstrated that can efficiently and reliably capture and convert the high solar flux to electricity. However, this problem may be on the verge of solution, and the dish-engine concept is currently being demonstrated in several states, including a 1 MW system in Nevada.

Although the commercialization of this technology has been stalled, its outlook is not bad. The dish-engine system should become commercial in niche markets soon. Other engine-converter concepts are also being explored, including the use of high-efficiency PV systems at the focal point of the dish, and a heat-pipe engine/receiver concept in which liquid sodium metal is vaporized on the absorber surface of the receiver and condensed on the heater tubes. Either approach would result in greater efficiency and reliability. With these kinds of advances, we may see tens of thousands of modules being produce per year by 2030.

For parabolic troughs we should see the emergence of advanced heat-collection systems and advanced collectors that incorporate lighter, more durable, less costly reflectors. These advances, along with integration of better hybrid technologies, will help reduce the cost of electricity to as little as 5¢ or 6¢ per kilowatt-hour in the next decade, making parabolic trough systems competitive with conventional electricity generation. As a result, we could see as much as 20,000 MW of installed capacity worldwide by 2020 (Electric Power Research Institute, 1997).

Wind Energy

Wind-energy systems capture the kinetic energy of the wind and convert it into electrical energy. The usual system consists of a rotor, nacelle, and tower. A *rotor* typically consists of two or three propeller-like blades mounted on a low-speed horizontal shaft. The blades capture the wind and rotate the low-speed shaft at a rate determined by the wind speed and the shape of the blades (typically at 20 to 60 revolutions per minute, or rpm). Only two or three blades are used to provide enough spacing between blades to minimize turbulence, required for effective rotor operation. The *nacelle* is a housing that holds the drive train, the yaw system, and electronic controller. The *drive train* consists of the aforementioned low-speed shaft, a gearbox, a high-speed shaft, and a generator. The *gearbox* accepts the low-rotational speed from the *low-speed shaft* and, via mechanical advantage, transmits a high-rotational speed (typically from 1200 to 1500 rpm) to the *high-speed shaft,* which turns the *generator,* which produces ac electricity. The *yaw system* keeps the rotor and blades properly oriented into the wind as the wind direction changes. The *electronic controller* monitors the condition of the wind turbine, starting it up and shutting it down at appropriate wind speeds, stopping it in case of malfunction, and communicating the status of the wind turbine to computers on the ground. The *tower,* generally made from tubular steel or steel lattice, provides mechanical support for the rotor and nacelle, which are mounted on top of the tower at a height that enables the blades to turn freely, maximizes wind capture, and minimizes turbulence. Today, utility-scale turbines are mounted on towers that are 50 meters and taller.

The U.S. government began an R&D program in wind energy shortly after the 1973 oil embargo. A wide variety of turbines were researched, from smaller 50–150 kW systems to those with outputs rated as high as

4.5 MW and with blade diameters as large as 300 feet. In 1980, the cost of wind-generated electricity was about 40¢ per kilowatt-hour. When the U.S. government began tracking wind energy in 1984, grid-connected wind-generated electricity was far less than 1 billion kWh. However, in the early to mid-1980s, the market began to strengthen as a result of new development policies and federal and state tax incentives. *Wind farms* with hundreds of turbines were established in good wind-resource areas and began selling electricity to the utilities. By the late 1980s, grid-connected wind electricity in the United States had grown to more than 25 billion kWh. The U.S. market began to stagnate in the late 1980s, as tax and other incentives were removed. But decreasing costs, increasing durability and power-production capabilities, as well as subsidies, helped the international wind market to flourish, especially in Germany and Denmark.

Today, extensive testing and modeling have allowed us to better understand how wind interacts with wind blades and other turbine structures and materials. Blades are now designed specifically for wind turbines, and are made from lighter composites that last much longer and produce significantly more energy, more efficiently. Other improvements have been made in tower materials and electronic monitors and controls to orient blades properly in the wind. Turbines have also become much larger, reaching generating capacities of 750–1,000 kW and greater. The result has been to lower the cost of wind-generated electricity to between 4¢ and 7¢ per kilowatt-how, and sometimes even lower, depending on the wind-resource and financing options. Along with government subsidies, these changes have helped the wind industry grow at a sustained rate well above 20 percent per year for more than a decade. Today, there is more than 40,000 MW of wind-energy systems installed worldwide, and annual turbine sales have topped $8 billion per year. With continued growth and with the right incentives and policies, some contend that worldwide installed wind energy capacity could surpass 1200 GW by 2020. (European Wind Energy Association, 2004).

The United States has recently experienced a rebirth in the wind-energy market. In 2000, wind turbines generated more than 51 billion kWh of grid-connected electricity; by the end of 2003, wind capacity had reached 6374 MW. If the U.S. market maintains its current growth rate, the U.S. Department of Energy expects as much as 80,000 MW of installed wind capacity by 2020 and 200,000 MW by 2030 (National Renewable Energy Laboratory, 2001).

Dramatic growth could be spurred by advances in energy technology, which could drop the cost of wind-generated electricity to 3¢ per kilowatt-hour and lower. These advances include turbines that operate efficiently at low wind speeds, dual-output turbines that generate electricity for direct use, or produce hydrogen via electrolysis of water, and turbines that could operate on the oceans to take advantage of the immense offshore wind resource.

Scenarios and Projections for Renewable Energy

According to the U.S. Energy Information Administration, while renewable energy continues to show remarkable technological progress and increased competitiveness, renewable sources contributed only about 8.0 percent to the world's energy consumption in 2001—32.2 quads out of a total of 404.9 quads (Energy Information Administration, 2004). This is not much more than the 7.6 percent contributed in 1990.

However, for its international data the Energy Information Administration compiles only the electric energy produced by renewable energy resources. Thus it does not take into account the renewable energy consumed in other forms, such as the traditional uses of burning wood or waste for cooking, heating, and other applications. With this in mind, between 1980 and 2001 worldwide production of renewable electricity climbed nearly 11.35 quads, with about 8.5 quads of this increase due to the growth in hydroelectric production of electricity (7.6 quads of which came from growth in developing countries), and 2.8 quads due to electricity from emerging renewable energy technologies. The increase in electricity from emerging renewable energy technologies represents a 600 percent growth from 1980, an indication that these technologies are starting to make an impact in world energy usage. In fact, some of these technologies, such as wind and photovoltaics, have grown by an average annual rate of more than 25 percent per year for more than a decade and show the promise of continuing this rapid pace for the next decade or more. These technologies are quickly becoming important industries, both in terms of energy production and economic impact (U.S. Photovoltaic Industry, 2001; American Wind Energy Association, 2001).

The Shell Scenarios

Many organizations have tried to analyze and forecast future energy use; expectations for renewables range all over the map, from optimistic to conservative. The most optimistic, often cited by environmentalists, is a scenario proposed by the Royal Dutch–Shell Group in 1995, which asked "What if renewable energy were able to expand its supply as fast and sustainably as oil did in the early 20th century?" (Shell International, 1995). Based on this assumption, Shell expected several trends to emerge: renewable energy would become a significant contributor by 2020; fossil fuel would continue to spur growth until about 2030, when it would begin to decline against advances in renewable technologies; and renewable energy would gain a 50 percent share of the world energy market by 2050.

This scenario is based on the highest potentials expected of renewable energy. Yet they are not completely out of step with projections or scenarios offered by others—in particular those of the Union of Concerned Scientists, suggesting that renewable energy could supply 20 percent of U.S. electricity needs by 2020 and 37 percent by 2030. A more recent long-term plan by Shell projects that renewable sources will account for 33 percent of worldwide energy consumption by 2050 (Shell International, 2001). This assumes a world in which innovation will provide superior consumer options in transportation, space heating, and electricity generation. Fuel cells, along with developments in nanotechnology, communications, and materials technologies, will spur sustained growth of renewable energy. This presents one possible path toward an affordable, sustainable energy system.

A decade ago, the World Energy Council and the International Institute for Applied Systems Analysis (WEC/IIASA) (1995) developed six scenarios on global energy use in the twenty-first century. Half of the scenarios were based on assumptions of sustained high economic growth; one was based on moderate economic growth. The remaining two assumed the international community would cooperate aggressively on policies and technologies to protect the environment and promote international equity. Under the latter two scenarios, renewable energy is expected to provide more than 20 percent of the world's energy by 2020, 38 percent by 2050, and 80 percent by 2100. These are optimistic numbers, and rival those suggested in the Shell *sustained-growth* scenario for 2020 and

2050. In fact, under all of the scenarios described by WEC/IIASA, renewable energy does rather well, providing from 16.2 to 21 percent in 2020 and from 22.2 to 38 percent in 2050.

The strength of renewable energy under these environmental scenarios is due both to an absolute increase in dependence on renewables and a large increase in conservation and energy efficiency; growth in total energy consumption rises only by about 43 percent in 50 years. However, other scenarios project global energy use to grow by as much as 150 percent, with fossil-fuel consumption growing by more than 115 percent. Such an increase in fossil-fuel use would lead to large increases in carbon-dioxide emissions.

At the opposite end of the spectrum from these estimates are the relatively conservative projections made by the U.S. Energy Information Administration (EIA). Every year, the EIA makes energy-consumption projections for both the United States and the world, accounting for current trends, expected economic growth by nation and region, and assumptions about future economic energy intensities (energy use divided by GDP). These are used to produce 20-year projections of energy consumption for the world and by region, as well as of the consumption of major resources (oil, natural gas, renewable energy, and so on).

The latest EIA reference-case projections forecast that worldwide use of renewable energy will grow from 32.2 quads in 2001 to 50.4 quads in 2025 (Energy Information Administration, 2004). Most of this increase will come from growing use of hydroelectricity in Asia and other developing areas, as well as wind energy in many industrial countries. The reference-case scenario also projects that the relative contribution of renewable energy will stay steady at about 8 percent through 2020. Most of the increase in consumption over the next two decades is expected to come from fossil fuels, which the EIA expects to increase by about 200 quads. This would clearly not support attempts to reduce carbon-dioxide emissions and the threat of global warming.

Renewable-energy technologies are the world's most promising avenues for displacing, and eventually replacing, fossil fuels. None of the renewable-energy technologies produces greenhouse gases, with the possible exception of biomass technologies. Yet, while conversion of biomass to electricity or fuels does produce greenhouse gases, this could be considered part of the carbon cycle—growing biomass absorbs about as much carbon dioxide as is emitted during the harvesting, transporting, and energy conversion of the biomass. Hence, biomass has essentially net zero production of carbon dioxide, especially if forest and agricultural residues are used as raw material.

The bottom line is that all renewable-energy technologies are exceptionally adept at offsetting greenhouse gas emissions. The amount of offset depends on the kind of energy production they displace. If we assume that renewable technologies displace electricity otherwise produced by today's average utility mix for the United States, then each kilowatt-hour generated by renewable-electricity technologies will offset about 175 grams of carbon equivalent, or 644 grams of carbon dioxide (Energy Information Administration, 2001; U.S. Department of Energy and U.S. Environmental Protection Agency, 2003).[7] A typical crystalline silicon module could provide as many as 28 years of "free" energy and carbon-dioxide offset; a PV system rated at 1 kilowatt, with a typical capacity factor[8] of 20.5 percent, would annually generate approximately 1,796 kWh of electricity and offset 308 metric tons of carbon (1,130 metric tons of carbon dioxide).[9] During its lifetime, such a system would offset more than 32,000 metric tons of carbon dioxide. The situation may be even better for wind-energy systems. Over a 30-year lifetime (a goal of the U.S. R&D program), 1 kW of installed wind-energy capacity would offset nearly 45,000 metric tons of carbon dioxide.

An unpublished paper prepared by the National Renewable Energy Laboratory (NREL) for the Department of Energy estimates that by 2010, renewable-energy technologies may be able to offset as much 65 million metric tons of carbon equivalent (MMTC$_e$) (National Renewable Energy Laboratory, 2001). This is rather optimistic, assuming that markets for renewable-energy technologies would continue to have high growth rates, and that federal R&D funding would double. With the expected growth of GDP and energy consumption, the offset due to renewable energy would not decrease the amount of carbon the United States produces—rather, it would mitigate a greater increase than might otherwise occur.

The same report suggests that renewable-energy technologies may be able to offset as much as 200 MMTC$_e$ in the United States by 2020 and 450 MMTC$_e$ by 2030. But even this apparently large amount of offset will not begin to reduce the nation's emission of carbon, if the projections made by the U.S. Energy Information Administration are near their targets. These projections suggest that emissions of carbon dioxide in the United States will rise by 384–588 $MMTC_e$ by 2020 (Energy Information Administration, 2004).

Conclusion

There are at least three compelling reasons why the United States and the world must soon move away from over-reliance on fossil fuels. First, we are taxing the ability of the earth's natural systems to absorb the impact of fossil-fuel consumption; this may have dire consequences, especially with respect to global warming. Second, our growing reliance on fossil fuels will continue to accrue deleterious socioeconomic and geopolitical costs. Third, fossil-fuel resources are limited, and within the next two or three decades the world may witness a decline in the production of oil and gas, with possible grave negative consequences for the world's economies and socioeconomic order.

Renewable-energy sources are the best bet to replace fossil energy because such resources are immense and available everywhere. As emerging renewable energy technologies become more and more competitive, they will provide a growing portion of all the forms of energy a modern economy needs to heat, light, and cool its homes and buildings, power its businesses and industry, and fuel its transportation systems. But can we expect these technologies to supply a substantial share of the world's energy anytime soon? Not if we believe the projections of the U.S. Energy Information Administration and the International Energy Agency, which forecast that in the next 20 or 30 years much of the world (including the United States) will increase its use of fossil fuels. Yet if we can believe the optimistic scenarios presented by Shell and by WEC/IIASA, we may begin to see an absolute decline in fossil-fuel dependence and carbon dioxide emissions toward the middle of the century. Much of this shift will be due to the increasing presence of renewable energy. These technologies—and others not yet imagined—may mean an energy future far different from what we are capable of imagining today.

Notes

1. Analysis of emissions on the basis of a total fuel cycle takes into account emissions associated with extraction and transportation of a fuel, plant or system construction, and plant operation, in addition to emissions due the generation of the energy, in this case electricity.

2. Primary energy is all of the energy consumed by end users excluding electricity, but including the energy consumed to generate electricity.

3. The wind potential was calculated relative to the electricity generated in the United States for 1990; we have restated it in terms of the electricity generated for 2000.

4. A quad is 1 quadrillion Btu = 10^{15} Btu.

5. The biorefinery could also arise from enzymatic hydrolysis of hemicellulose and cellulose to sugars, in which sugars become the platform chemical from which other chemicals and materials are derived.

6. A milliwatt is one-thousandth of a watt. A gigawatt is 1 billion watts.

7. The amount of offset will vary in accordance with the type of renewable technology employed.

8. The capacity factor for an electric generating unit is the ratio of the amount of energy produced during a given time period (usually expressed in kWh) to the energy that could have been produced had that unit operated at its rated capacity for that time period. For example, there are 8,760 hours in a year. So, a 1-kW PV system would produce 8,760 kWh of electricity, if the system operated at its rated capacity for the entire period. But because the availability and intensity of sunshine is intermittent, a typical PV system will operate at only 20.5 percent of its rated capacity (1 kW × 8,760 hrs. × 0.205 = 1,796 kWh).

9. 1,796 kWh × 175gC/kWh = 308 metric tons of C × 3.667 (the ratio of the molecular weight of CO_2 to C) = 1,130 metric tons of CO_2.

8

Future Socioeconomic and Political Challenges of Global Climate Change

Matthias Ruth

Since the dawn of human history, technological and social innovation has sought to stabilize environmental conditions and decouple economic growth and sociocultural development from the vagaries of environmental change. Pottery facilitated storage of food away from moisture and rodents, increasing supplies for humans. Terraces reduced erosion rates and helped to maintain agricultural productivity. Aqueducts controlled distribution of water and equalized supply across regions. Use of firewood and fossil fuels helped to maintain indoor temperatures throughout the seasons; fiber garments provided year-round protection from the elements. Other improvements include the development of institutions to coordinate human activities and ensure that they harmonize with environmental conditions (Ausubel 1999).

Many of these technologies and institutions have helped to reduce human vulnerability to adverse environmental conditions and to broaden the scope of economic activity—to a significant extent, these define how we live and who we are. They have also fostered increased materials and energy throughput, requiring more energy of higher quality to produce and distribute ever larger quantities of goods and services (Daly 1991). Early energy sources included muscle power, wood, and peat, each of which had only limited ability to provide heat or power (Ayres 1978; Smil 1997). These were ultimately replaced significantly by fossil fuels—most notably coal, oil, and natural gas (Grübler and Nakicenovic 1999). Fossil-fuel combustion began to proliferate across all sectors of industrializing economies by the mid-1800s, a process that continues in the developing world today.

For decades, economic growth closely followed increased fossil-fuel use (Schipper and Meyers 1992), but confidence that perpetual growth and development could occur irrespective of biophysical constraints was punctured by the temporary oil shortages of the 1970s and 1980s. Rapid population increases, growing wealth disparities, loss of pristine ecosystems and biodiversity, and accelerated urbanization also generated concern among an increasing number of analysts (Meadows et al. 1972; Barney 1980). Some have argued that economic growth has not reduced environmental damage, but has instead fueled additional consumptive expansion (Daly 1991). In contrast, others dismissed these trends as temporary challenges, to be overcome by continued technological progress. This worldview believes conversion of natural resources and environmental services into capital goods enhances future generations' abilities to meet their needs (Simon 1980, 1996).

While the debate about the adequacy of finite natural resources and the ability of technology to overcome limits continues to be waged, a set of new, global issues has shifted the debate from an emphasis on the sources of material wealth to the sinks for waste by-products. Losses of stratospheric ozone have been tied to the release of chlorofluorocarbons (CFCs) from industrial processes and consumer products; elevated UVB radiation associated with ozone loss has been identified as a contributor to human disease and declines in ecosystem health. Elevated carbon levels in the atmosphere—triggered by the combustion of fossil fuels—have been linked to changes in global atmospheric temperatures. Subsequently, the list of gases that potentially contribute to global climate change has been extended to include, among others: methane from rice paddies, livestock, and termites; CFCs used in air-conditioning, refrigeration, and plastics; and sulfur dioxide from coal-fired power plants (Wigley 1999). Today, a confluence of changes in population, increased energy and materials consumption, loss of habitat and species diversity, the spread of disease, and the decline of waste-assimilation capacities are all seen as potentially related to climate change. These revelations have occurred at a time in human history when decoupling economic growth and development from the vagaries of the environment seemed within our grasp.

Societies around the globe have slowly begun to respond to new scientific knowledge about global environmental change (Lemons and Brown 1995). Strategies to reduce emissions of ozone-depleting CFCs have been readily identified and implemented, in part because the number of sources was limited and substitutes for many CFCs were available. Reduction of emissions of gases contributing to climate change has proven much more challenging, because these emissions are intimately related to all aspects of life—the food we eat, the houses we occupy, the clothes we wear, the entertainment we enjoy, and the way we move goods, services, people, and messages.

Recognition of the multitude of cultural, social, and economic interactions with the natural environment, and heightened sensitivity to previously unknown uncertainties and risks, also occurred at a time of increased disillusionment of the public with official scientific expertise (Ravetz 1999) and at the turn of the century and dawn of a new millennium—a time when deeper perennial questions of human existence tend to emerge (Hicks 2000). Calls came for humans to be not mere custodians of the planet, but also to rekindle spiritual values (Barney 1999) and shape a viable future, with a meaningful legacy for posterity (Valemoor and Heydon 2000). Others critiqued what they called the "threat industry" for a tendency to seek out problems and capitalize on the subsequent attention, while belittling people's ability to adapt and meet new challenges (Ausubel 1999).

It is in this context that I discuss the challenges of climate change for human decision making. As humanity grapples with the underlying complexities and tries to make investment and policy decisions in the face of profound uncertainty, special attention needs to be paid to the diverse and changing environmental contexts, the vulnerability of social and economic systems, as well as their adaptive capacities, and to the full range of potential strategies. The following sections address each of these issues in turn. The chapter closes by analyzing the implications for human decision making and institution building, in the presence of global climate change.

Past and Future Climate Change

The earth's climate is partly regulated by the presence of gases and particles in the atmosphere that are penetrated by short-wave solar radiation and trap the longer-wave radiation reflected back from earth. Collectively, these are referred to as greenhouse gases (GHGs). Water, the main GHG, affects the overall energy budget of the globe—the hydrological cycle works like a steam-heating system to transfer energy across regions. Other notable GHGs are carbon dioxide (CO_2), methane (CH_4), nitrous oxide (N_2O), and chlorofluorocarbons (CFCs). Each has different chemical and physical properties, including concentration and persistence in the atmosphere. As a consequence, each has a different capacity to upset the radiation balance, a dynamic known as *climate forcing*. Geographic patterns of radiative forcing are relatively uniform for CO_2, CH_4, N_2O, and CFCs, because these gases are relatively long-lived, and therefore more evenly distributed. In contrast, the effects of short-lived substances such as aerosols and ozone are closely tied to their emission sources (Wigley 1999).

The steep increases in atmospheric GHG and aerosol concentrations since the industrial revolution began are unprecedented in the earth's history. As a result, the global average surface temperature has increased by about $0.6°C$ over the twentieth century, with the 1990s as the warmest decade (and 1998 the warmest year) on record since 1861 (Intergovernmental Panel on Climate Change, 2001a).

While average temperature changes may serve as a useful indicator, they are only one of many ramifications of higher GHG concentrations. Since disruption of the earth's energy balance is neither seasonally nor geographically uniform, effects of climate disruption vary across space as well—higher latitudes have warmed more than the equatorial regions (Office of Science and Technology Policy, 1997). There has been a widespread retreat of mountain glaciers during the twentieth century, as well as a decrease in Arctic sea-ice thickness (Intergovernmental Panel on Climate Change, 2001).

The net loss of snow and ice cover, combined with an increase in water temperatures and thermal expansion in the oceans, has resulted in a rise of global average sea levels between 0.1 and 0.2 meters during the twentieth century, which is considerably higher than the average rate during the last several millennia (Barnett 1984; Nicholls and Hoozemans 1996; Intergovernmental Panel on Climate Change, 2001b; Douglas 2001a). Yet the extent of sea-level rise varies across the globe; some areas such as England and Western France have already lost ground, while others such as Scandinavia and Scotland have been emerging from the sea (Doornkamp 1998). In some cases, land subsidence from mining, natural gas, or groundwater extraction has significantly speeded the potential effects of climate-change-induced sea-level rise (Gambolati and Teatini 1999).

Many of these changes are likely to be discontinuous—many environmental systems have been shown to abruptly "flip" to alternate states (Kay and Schneider 1994). A gradual temperature increase could trigger localized changes in species composition, which may in turn affect ecosystem elements such as soil properties or pollination, with the potential to impact crop production, food supplies, livelihoods, water cycles, and the spread of disease. Such impacts would then likely trigger further changes in local societies and economies.

Heat fluctuations throughout the atmosphere and oceans, combined with changes in the reflectivity of the earth's surface and an altered composition of GHGs and particulates in the atmosphere, may also affect the frequency and severity of climate events around the globe (Easterling and Mehl 2000; Mehl and Karl 2000). For example, there was a 2–4 percent increase in the frequency of heavy precipitation events in the mid- and high latitudes of the Northern Hemisphere in the last half of the twentieth century, while regions such as Asia and Africa have experienced more frequent and intense droughts in recent decades (Intergovernmental Panel on Climate Change, 2001a). The timing and magnitude of snowfall and snow melt may also be significantly affected, influencing erosion, water quality, and agricultural productivity (Frederick and Gleick 1999).

Efforts are underway to explore the complex causal relationships between human activities and climate change via computer modeling, which enables scientists to explore a range of likely climate futures, based on alternative assumptions about biogeochemical mechanisms and human activities (Intergovernmental Panel on Climate Change, 2001b). Most projections indicate that global averaged surface temperature is likely to increase by 1.4°C–5.8°C between 1990 and 2100, a rate much larger than the observed changes of the twentieth century, and very likely larger than the changes of the last 10,000 years (Wigley 1999; Intergovernmental Panel on Climate Change, 2001a). The frequency of daily, seasonal, and annual warm temperature extremes are also expected to increase, while the frequency of daily, seasonal, and annual cold-weather extremes will likely decrease. Such temperature changes could be accompanied by larger year-to-year variations in precipitation, regionally distinct rates of snow- and ice-cover changes, and changes in sea level (Klein and Nicholls 1999; Intergovernmental Panel on Climate Change, 2001b).

Climate-change models increasingly show climate responses that are consistent across very differently specified models and recent observations, thus giving researchers confidence that humanity has indeed embarked on a real-world climate-change experiment of monumental proportions. However, despite their growing sophistication, climate models continue to suffer from uncertainties about the underlying biogeochemical processes and a fundamental inability to anticipate human responses to change. Moreover, it is difficult to model potential discontinuities within climate processes, which are instead often portrayed as incremental changes (Schelling 1992).

Variations in Vulnerability

Many climate-change discussions are concerned with identifying the main culprits causing climate change, the winners and losers, and whether and how winners should compensate losers. Any analysis of human vulnerability to climate change must be sensitive to the potential for both negative and positive impacts. Such an analysis should also take into account that these impacts will likely vary by economic and social sectors, as well as across regions and time—specific vulnerabilities will be intricately tied to these variations. For example, tropospheric methane, carbon monoxide, and ozone levels over the region with the world's greatest population density—extending from Nepal, Bangladesh, Burma, and Sri Lanka to Pakistan—are higher than elsewhere. Rainfall patterns in the belt's highest mountains have changed significantly, though adjacent coastal areas show no such trend (Hingane 1996), resulting in differential impacts on human welfare within the region.

Geographic variations will likely be exacerbated by differing capacities to cope with vulnerabilities. The financial and technological resources in less developed countries are unlikely to be sufficient to significantly mitigate and adapt to climate change, leaving many societies, environments, and economies in peril. The fact that conflicts between economic and environmental goals often remain unresolved adds to the plight of many social, economic, and environmental systems (Ipsen and Rösch 2001).

Although it is difficult to generalize the geographic distribution of climate-change impacts, differences will be most pronounced between industrialized and developing nations, as well as within regions of the developing world. There is growing recognition that industrialized economies, which were not required to address global environmental challenges during their development phase, significantly benefited from an ability to expand fossil-fuel use and land conversion, and that imposing constraints on developing countries today may reduce their economic potentials. While industrialized nations now have the financial and technological means available to reduce their GHG emissions, industrialization in the developing world often entails the expansion of heavy industries that are notorious for high energy intensity and GHG emissions (Han and Chatterjee 1997).

The rapid cycling of materials and energy through socioeconomic and environmental systems is often not matched by sufficiently rapid increases in the effectiveness of technology and institutions to avoid increased social, environmental, and economic stresses. Changes in climate can add to that stress, as is becoming increasingly apparent in Bangladesh, where the interaction of population growth, land conversion, and sea-level rise has resulted in an increasingly precarious situation for the local population (Al-Farouq 1996). Economic pressures associated with globalization have also been shown to modify or exacerbate existing vulnerabilities (O'Brien and Leichenko 2000).

Environmental impact is related to population, affluence, and technological potential as well. In many developing countries, both population size and living standards are rising, resulting in increased demand for food, raw materials, and energy, and also resulting in growing pollution of land, water, and air, even as technological change reduces impacts per person or unit of economic activity. Higher living standards often mean more cars, refrigerators, and air-conditioners, thus lowering ambient air quality. Emission from power plants and end-use devices such as cars also means increased heat-island effects and changes in local temperature and precipitation patterns.

Cities deserve special attention, because urbanization rates are increasing around the globe. The changes in climate regimes of cities observed in Turkey (Tayanc and Toros 1997), Austria (Böhm 1998), South Africa (Hughes and Balling 1996), and elsewhere may be a harbinger of a new round of induced energy demand for cooling and air-conditioning, further disrupting local and global climates.

Vulnerable Populations

In 1994, approximately 37 percent of the world's population lived within 100 kilometers of a coast—seventeen of the world's twenty-five largest megalopolises are located along coastlines (Cohen and Small 1997). In the United States, more than half the population lives in coastal counties; estimates suggest that by 2010, that population will have increased 60 percent over its 1960 levels (Culliton and Warren 1990). As coastal development accelerates, more infrastructure becomes located in these zones (Nicholls 1995; Timmerman and White 1997). However, the advantages that have historically led to the location of cities on the coast (e.g., geographic control, access to food sources, transportation, and trade) are eroding at the same time that transportation, flood-control, and sewage-treatment infrastructures are impacted by climatic change. Areas most prone to sea-level rise include small island states with a limited ability to prevent encroachment by rising seawater, or to protect local freshwater resources from saltwater intrusion.

Individuals and institutions may be harmed by some manifestations of climate change while benefiting from others. Climate change has far-reaching implications for the distribution of wealth and welfare, across regions and time; the costs and benefits of climate change will be distributed unevenly across generations (Portney and Weyant 1999). Understanding the temporal variability of climate-change vulnerabilities requires that we simultaneously consider changes in both biogeochemical processes and in socioeconomic institutions and infrastructure. Where the potential for rapid human adaptation to changing environmental conditions exists, vulnerabilities can be reduced significantly.

Connections between climate change and human health have also begun to receive heightened attention (Balbus and Wilson 2000). Changing environmental conditions may favor airborne, waterborne, or vector-borne diseases, thus posing heightened or new threats to plants, animals, and people. Vulnerability to disease outbreaks is highest in countries and regions lacking early-warning systems and access to disease control, such as medical systems or drugs. Changes in climate conditions may also directly threaten human health through severe climate events such as flooding and drought, or from periods of temperature extremes, with long-lasting and far-reaching impacts on housing, food production, water systems, and the spread of infectious disease. Elevated temperatures result not only in heat stress—most notably among the elderly and urban poor—but also exacerbate local air pollution, leading to respiratory problems.

Sectoral Vulnerabilities

To date, most of the work on climate-change impacts has been on individual economic sectors, agriculture in particular (Schmandt and Clarkson 1992; Rosenberg 1993; Rosenberg and Crosson 1993; Crosson and Rosenberg 1993; Cohen 1996, 1997a; Huang and Cohen 1998). However, the number of studies conducted on regional and integrated impacts of climate change is increasing. These studies suggest that the sum of sea-level, energy, water, and recreational impacts far exceeds those to agriculture (Ruth and Kirshen 2001). If air-pollution and health impacts are included, the toll is even greater. Even if the lowest estimated economic impacts of sea-level rise hold true, the combined infrastructure damages for energy, water, and recreation would still significantly exceed agriculture (Yohe and Neuman 1996). While this should not divert attention from the danger posed to agriculture and the food supply, it highlights that other disruptions are likely to be similar and potentially more concentrated, because most infrastructure is typically located in urban areas. While these immediate effects may be principally urban, they will undoubtedly ripple through the social and economic fabric to affect the larger regions with which cities interact. Cities are often the drivers of economic growth, development, innovation, and finance; climate-induced infrastructure losses and reduced quality of life are likely to have much broader impacts, nationally and globally.

Historically, the implications of climate change for food production have been of particular concern. The combination of higher temperatures, especially during the growing season, and reduced water availability may prove lethal to plants, animals, and humans. Beyond any direct impacts on health and well-being, reduced agricultural productivity and water scarcity may also exacerbate tensions among social classes, ethnic groups, or geographic regions. Though these trends are perhaps most pronounced in the developing world, industrialized countries will not be immune to them. Dramatically expanded irrigation in upstream agricultural areas is not likely to improve relations with countries or regions downstream. Large-scale displacement or migration related to climate impacts may lead to considerable challenges when trying to integrate or assimilate migrants in receiving regions, in addition to the challenges to the economies and societies from which people flee. The loss of human capital may be felt for decades in the form of reduced agricultural productivity, economic instability, and deteriorating social networks. On the other hand, migration has been an integral driver for technological and socioeconomic development throughout human history (Pieterse 2000). Cultural diversity is partly facilitated by constant population redistribution of people around the globe, and may be essential to increase humanity's resilience in the face of new challenges (Pirages 2000).

Primary-sector activities (e.g., agriculture, fishing, and forestry) are not the only economic activities that are highly vulnerable to climate change, as has commonly been assumed or implied (Ausubel 1991; Schelling 1992). Even highly advanced industrialized economies could suffer noticeably—just-in-time procurement systems and information technologies both benefit from stable environmental conditions. If climate change spurs more intense and more frequent climate events, transportation by ship, rail, or road may be impaired; power lines may be cut; communication networks may be disrupted; and power plants may be shut down to protect ambient air quality during the hot summer months. As a result, both manufacturing- and service-industry operating efficiencies could be jeopardized, resulting in operating losses or reduced investment in the susceptible sectors.

Capacity to Adapt

The industrialized world's ability to achieve significant reductions in environmental impacts per unit of economic activity is relatively low when compared to the potential in the developing world. Developed economies have already picked most of the "low-hanging fruit" of increased efficiency, so additional improvements will be more costly. In contrast, the efficiency of many processes in the developing world could be raised by adopting technologies already widespread in the industrialized world. This is not unlikely, because many developing countries have begun replacing obsolete technology and infrastructure at relatively rapid rates.

Unprecedented opportunities exist to raise material and energy efficiencies, and to cut production costs and reduce GHG emissions, in these countries (Price and Michaelis 1998). However, most major technology and infrastructure investment in the last several decades has occurred in the industrialized world. Many of these investments have expected lifetimes spanning several decades (Marland and Weinberg 1988; Ausubel 1991), making a large-scale overhaul rather unlikely.

Throughout the world, rapid economic growth frequently overwhelms efficiency improvements. While per capita energy and water consumption and emissions per production unit may decline, population and economic output often increase at higher rates, resulting in increased environmental impacts. How such effects are distributed depends in part on the capacity of technologies, infrastructure, and institutions to respond flexibly to observed and anticipated changes. It also depends on the extent of inter-generational wealth transfers—compensation for the damage from climate change—as well as on the development of new technologies, infrastructure, institutions, and knowledge capable of addressing tomorrow's problems.

While human adaptation to climate is not new, the scale and rate at which climate is changing pose new challenges. Even if GHG emissions could be reduced to preindustrial levels, many gases would remain in the atmosphere for decades and even centuries. As a consequence, climate change will continue for the foreseeable future. Even if the cumulative impacts of climate change are less than the impacts of nonclimate factors, the marginal effect may noticeably compound existing stresses on resources, infrastructures, and institutions.

To date, the climate-change debate has concentrated mainly on direct, negative impacts on current generations. Global response strategies have been identified to address what has been perceived, in essence, as a global problem. More and more attention is being given to adaptation strategies, especially those that are beneficial in the absence of climate change but that would also lead to development that is robust in light of climate change. This section briefly reviews some of these strategies, concentrating on two broad categories—efforts to mitigate the greenhouse effect, and measures to adapt to climate change. Both acknowledge that humans are not passive victims of climate change, and that simply preventing adverse effects avoids the moral dimensions of climate change, while jeopardizing the solvency of the insurance industry. The timing and extent of either mitigation or adaptation is influenced by tensions between the perceived need to resolve remaining uncertainties, and the need to act with precaution (Pearce 1991; Lemons and Brown 1995).

The UN Framework Convention on Climate Change, which took effect in 1994, established the goal of stabilizing GHG concentrations in the atmosphere "at a level that would prevent dangerous anthropogenic interference with the climate system" (UN Framework Convention on Climate Change, 1992). Toward that end, parties to the convention are obliged to develop national inventories of GHG sources and sinks; promote and cooperate in the development and diffusion of technologies that can prevent GHG emissions; promote conservation and enhancement of GHG sinks and reservoirs; cooperate in preparing for adaptation; share information; and promote education, training, and public awareness. In addition, industrialized countries are asked to provide developing countries with financial resources to meet their commitments under the Framework Convention. At the 1997 Kyoto Conference of the Parties, a protocol was signed that laid out mechanisms to achieve the Framework Convention's goals (UN Framework Convention on Climate Change, 1997).

Each of the various mechanisms laid out in the Framework Convention includes the intent to provide incentives to countries to reduce emissions beyond their own targets and to collaborate internationally to achieve cost-effective emissions reductions. Special focus was given to economic incentives, such as marketable emissions permits, and to new institutions, such as the Global Environment Facility to foster environmentally friendly development.

The promotion of technological change is critical in the climate-change and development context (Edmonds and Roop 2000). While some innovations may boost output and reduce fossil-fuel costs, these also tend to increase GHG emissions. On the other hand, efficiency and knowledge improvements tend to decrease GHG emissions and mitigation costs. The issue is made more complex by the fact that knowledge and efficiency improvements are often related to higher production rates, which generate revenue to invest in new technologies. Moreover, knowledge often improves as cumulative production increases (Yelle 1979; Ruth 1993). As relative prices change and development spreads throughout an economy, consumer preferences are likely to change. Substitution among production inputs, consumer goods, and leisure activities is a key determinant of GHG emissions (Jorgenson and Goettle 2000). Yet current international agreements pay scant attention to the indeterminate net effects of substitution and technological change, or to changes in preferences, for GHG emissions.

A multitude of other policy instruments are presently available in many countries to achieve emissions goals, or to leverage the effectiveness of market-based climate-change policies. These include environmental-labeling requirements for electricity sources, demand-side management, tax credits and accelerated depreciation schedules, planning and siting preferences for renewable-energy facilities, renewable-energy portfolio standards, land reclamation and reforestation policies, and trace-gas collection requirements for landfills. Many were originally implemented to improve energy security, raise ambient air quality, maintain ecosystem health and species diversity, or increase energy efficiency. Coordination of these instruments may help to further leverage GHG emission reductions (Dernbach 2000).

The Framework Convention's call for climate-change mitigation has spurred governments, industries, and academia to identify specific means of meeting the targets, as well as the costs and benefits of alternative mitigation strategies (Gwilliam 1993; Bernstein and Bromley 1999; Ruth and Davidsdottir 2000). The debate has centered on "no-regrets" strategies (which make economic sense even without climate change), the coordination of multiple policy instruments (Ruth and Davidsdottir 2000), and an emphasis on the broader social and environmental costs of energy use, beyond those of energy conversion, emissions, or mitigation (Berry and Jaccard 2001). Solutions are being sought that transcend narrowly defined technological fixes and place technology policy in the broader context of developing adequate local capacity and essential support systems (Ruth and Davidsdottir 2000). Scientists have also begun to emphasize that non-CO_2 GHGs have caused most of the observed warming, and that it may be more practical and cost-effective to reduce these emissions first (Hansen and Sato 2000).

Adaptation has often been perceived as the antidote to mitigation. Mitigation emphasizes our ability to reverse human-induced environmental trends. In contrast, adaptation means adjusting to climate change, in order to reduce social and ecosystem vulnerabilities; this is frequently perceived as an admission of humanity's inability to noticeably reverse climate change in a timely manner.

While successful mitigation depends on international cooperation (with global benefits), successful adaptation depends on local financial, technological, and human resources (with localized benefits). As a consequence, mitigation has frequently been promoted as *the* proper response to the global issue of climate change. However, pursuit of adaptation strategies is neither an admission that climate change is unstoppable, nor need it be a mere treatment of symptoms instead of an eradication of the causes. As I discuss in more detail below, mitigation and adaptation can go hand in hand, and spending scarce resources on appropriate policy and investment strategies may successfully advance both mitigation and adaptation.

Adaptation strategies can range from sharing or bearing losses, to actively reducing or preventing vulnerabilities. Some adaptations may occur as reactions to specific climate events—such as the installation of pumps in basements and tunnels in response to increased rainfall, or increased chlorination of drinking water to prevent the spread of diseases at higher temperatures. Others may be anticipatory, such as creating early-warning systems for extreme weather events, adjusting agriculture and forest-management practices, genetically engineering crops, redesigning bridges to reduce scour at high-flow events, moving power lines underground to minimize susceptibility to wind and ice, or establishing corridors for migrating species (Frankhauser 1996). Like some mitigation strategies, many climate adaptations generate benefits to society even if the climate does not change, through reduced susceptibility to extreme weather events (Burton 1996) and corrected economic inefficiencies (Toman and Bierbaum 1996).

Given a finite natural resource base and clear biophysical limits on material and energy conversions (Ruth 1993), increased emphasis needs to be placed on lifestyle changes that significantly reduce materials and carbon from economic cycles—not just per unit of GDP or per person, but in total. Since such changes are slow in coming, missed opportunities today will almost inevitably translate into economic and social costs tomorrow.

Lessons for Decision Making and Institution Building

This chapter opened by stressing humanity's ability to respond to environmental challenges. While history may give us considerable hope for our ability to further improve living standards, it must be pointed out that such improvements are neither inevitable, nor guaranteed to arrive soon enough, or on a scale capable of avoiding significant short-term costs. Therefore, I will close with six lessons for human decision making and institution building that rest on the discussion above. Whether we consider these lessons when crafting responses to climate change will significantly affect our success or failure in reducing or alleviating human vulnerabilities to climate change.

1. Avoid the Dangers of Ambulance Chasing

For years, climate change has been a hot topic in science and policy discussions. Major efforts are being made worldwide to reduce remaining uncertainties about biogeochemical processes, with billions of dollars spent on research programs that support the activities of tens of thousands of scientists. The lion's share of those funds go to the natural sciences for monitoring and modeling projects, attracting ever larger numbers of investigators to compete for available funds. This growth in climate-change research has helped to reduce some uncertainties and led to the discovery of others. The fundamental complexities of the climate system and its interactions with human activities suggest that some significant level of uncertainty about the future climate will always remain (Ausubel 2001). An open-ended expansion of research to eliminate remaining uncertainties is disingenuous and may damage the credibility of those involved in the long run.

The practice of tying ever more topics to the climate-change issue—from migration and local wars (Foley 1999) to the spread of diseases (Martens 1996, 1998)—may sometimes be justifiable, but may also divert attention from more important factors. Improper emphasis may also sometimes be placed on addressing climate change, at the expense of other more immediate challenges. The implications drawn from thinking about climate change highlight current shortcomings of infrastructures and institutions (broadly defined), as well as the social costs associated with existing systems. Revisiting these flaws and identifying alternatives that make good economic and political sense in their own right seems the honest and prudent thing to do.

2. Foster a Diversity of Problem-Solving Approaches

The desire to find the factors driving complex environmental, social, and economic processes may be topped by the urge to identify quick fixes to perceived problems. Climate-related susceptibilities in agriculture may be addressed with genetically engineered crops (GMOs), new diseases may be combated by raising the chlorine content of water or spraying insecticides, or nuclear power may be promoted as apparently GHG-free energy. Focusing on easy solutions to these challenges may mean missed opportunities for more fundamental structural change. Widespread use of GMOs may seriously erode the genetic diversity of noncultivated plants, more aggressive chemical treatment of water or disease vectors may have unanticipated environmental and human health consequences, and an expanded nuclear energy industry will certainly exacerbate existing challenges of dealing with nuclear waste.

But even if individual strategies can be clearly identified as improving human welfare in light of climate change, there is a danger of investing in a small set of strategies while neglecting to explore others. A broad range of cost-equivalent technological and institutional strategies should be capable of reducing human, social, and economic vulnerabilities in the long run (Gritsevskyi and Nakicenovic 2000). The evolution of such strategies is strongly path dependent; it is not possible to identify an optimal development strategy a priori. Consequently, there is a need for a diversity of strategies, so that the potential for positive spillover is increased and sufficient flexibility will exist to shift the path of development in the future.

3.   Leverage Interdependencies among Infrastructures and Institutions

The potential connections between infrastructure systems, between infrastructure and environmental change, and between infrastructure and socioeconomic systems are countless, yet these systems are typically managed and analyzed in isolation. If we instead strove to understand how various system components are interrelated, we might begin to develop management strategies that permit adjustment within a given system, as new information becomes available about others. For example, water systems can be overwhelmed by increased demand during droughts, or by excess water during storm events—both of which may directly affect water quality. Water quality may also be directly or indirectly affected by ambient temperatures—through changes in biological oxygen demand, bacterial growth, or the concentration of particulates following evaporation. Severe storms may impair transportation and lead to delays, accidents, and economic loss. For energy technologies that require significant quantities of water, drought may be a constraint, in turn disrupting transportation and communication systems. As private transportation technologies become increasingly electricity-based, new demands are placed on energy infrastructures, which rely on information technologies for power generation and distribution. Moreover, fuel distribution is susceptible to changes in surface transportation and storage conditions. Thus, water quantity and quality, electricity generation, and transportation are deeply interrelated issues, though each is typically managed by separate institutions and analyzed by specialized experts.

This example highlights only some of the many potential interrelationships between environmental and infrastructure systems. Research that is able to explore ways that change in one component transfers through space and time to affect entire systems will be able to inform management systems and strategies that can anticipate such dynamics. Modern computer models and scenario-building approaches may provide tools for such systems-based analysis, as well as sensitizing decision makers accustomed to focusing on individual system components (Ruth and Hannon 1997; Deaton and Winebrake 2000; Hannon and Ruth 2000; Robinson 2001).

Modeling environment-infrastructure-society interactions is a means to comprehensively represent system dynamics, to explore mitigation and adaptation strategies, and to identify investment needs. The key to achieving such goals is the choice of appropriate indicators capable of exploring the environmental and socioeconomic parameters under which systems reach critical states, estimating crisis response times and quantifying costs to avoid system breakdown.

By definition, indicators are abstractions derived from models; the search for better indicators is also a search for better models. Unfortunately, efforts to model biogeochemical processes associated with climate change have not been matched—in extent or sophistication—by the social sciences. Instead, disproportional emphasis has been placed on detecting climate signals. As long as the social sciences lack the methodological and computational tools to explore response strategies, the climate debate will continue to be dominated by discussions about uncertainties, rather than the identification and implementation of optimal strategies to address vulnerabilities of socioeconomic systems.

4.   Establish and Implement Forward-looking Design Standards
Traditionally, design criteria and standards have been developed and established on the basis of historical observations. In many cases, modern infrastructure is built on the assumption that in the future, the climate will look like it has in the past. Management of these systems is also based on past experience; managers are trained to react to real events, with physical rather than economic or institutional tools. The deep uncertainties about future climate—which are unlikely to ever be fully resolved—are significant barriers to action (Schilling and Stakhiv 1998). Identifying new standards and technologies to resolve them is only part of the challenge. Another potentially more daunting challenge is to change the institutions that coevolved with the respective technologies (Unruh 2000; Geels and Smit 2000). For example, in many countries large-scale, centralized fossil-fuel-based or nuclear power plants spawned government agencies for oversight of those plants, agencies to control energy distribution and prices to consumers, and consumer groups contributing to decision-making processes. Public and private R&D laboratories emerged to address the refinement of those technologies; financial markets evolved to broker energy. This coevolution of institutions and technologies often "locks in" systems that make it difficult to promote alternatives. As a consequence, development of new technologies is often relatively simple, when compared to their social and institutional implementation (Elliott 2000). Significant effort should therefore be directed toward understanding and promoting the institutional adaptation necessary to accompany technological and environmental change.

5.   Get Multiple Bangs for the Buck
Earlier, I contrasted mitigation and adaptation strategies to address climate change. Yet some policy and investment choices can be cost-effective, while simultaneously reducing GHG emissions and vulnerabilities to climate change. For example, installing distributed solar-power systems could translate not only into energy and cost savings to households and industries, but also reduce interruptions when power lines are downed, air-quality standards are surpassed, or cooling water for power plants is scarce. If centrally installed, solar-power systems could help to avoid costly expansion of generation and transmission capacity, and reduce fuel and other operational and maintenance costs. In either case,

they would reduce GHG emissions per unit of electricity used. Similarly, expansion of natural gas-fired combined-cycle generation or combined heat and power plants in nonattainment areas could improve air quality, reduce transmission congestion, and stimulate economic development (Center for Clean Air Policy, 2001).

In each of these examples, GHG emissions would be reduced, costs cut, and system reliabilities increased. A nontechnological strategy would be to increase home-ownership rates in metropolitan areas, economically and socially revitalizing those communities. Investments in insulation and energy-efficient appliances are more likely to be made by home owners, who bear both construction and ongoing energy costs; increased home ownership may also strengthen community development. Regardless of whether strategies are technological or social in nature, they must be selected based on their ability to generate simultaneous economic, environmental, and societal benefits.

6. Promote International Collaboration without Stooping to Lowest Common Denominators

While each of the previous lessons mainly addressed actions on the local or sectoral scale, where policy and investment decisions are ultimately implemented, there is little doubt that successfully addressing climate change will require some level of global collaboration. This insight has often been understood to imply common emission goals with which individual nations must comply, and institutional mechanisms implemented on a multination scale to reduce emissions and encourage those responsible. The Kyoto Protocol is a prime example of this logic (UN Framework on Climate Change, 1997). But attaining an international agreement acceptable by most (if not all) signatories, required that emission targets be set at levels too low to have any noticeable effect on climate change, with complex institutional mechanisms to guide decision making, monitoring, and enforcement by government and businesses around the globe.

Could alternative approaches be envisioned to lead to larger GHG emission reductions with lower administrative burdens? There is a good chance that such alternatives will someday be more thoroughly explored. While such improvements might occur through climate policy, they may begin in efforts to address other economic and societal goals. Where sufficient resources exist, improvements may be funded by industry and governments to foster their own institutional and infrastructure development. But since the bulk of future GHG emissions are expected to come from the developing world, technological, infrastructure and institutional improvements may also be part of bilateral or multilateral agreements or foreign-assistance programs. In either case, the goal should be to foster a diversity of problem-solving approaches, tuned to existing cultural, social, economic, institutional, and technological constraints. Rather than striving globally for minimal emission reductions, a more productive strategy may be to maximize social benefits through correcting existing or anticipated inefficiencies (including those induced by climate change), as well as the misallocations of resources and the associated environmental, social, and economic costs.

9

Global Climate Change: Policy Challenges, Policy Responses

Jacob Park

During the turbulent times of the French Revolution and Napoléon's reign in the early nineteenth century, the philosopher and mathematician Jean Baptiste Joseph Fourier began to ponder the question of how the earth stays warm enough to support life. In a paper titled "General Remarks on the Temperature of the Terrestrial Globe and Planetary Spaces" published in 1824, Fourier hypothesized that some of the sun's energy is trapped by water vapor and other gases when it is reflected back into the atmosphere from the oceans and land masses. When over 150 delegates from nearly 100 governments met in Shanghai to deliver the results of Working Group One's *Third Assessment Report* of the Intergovernmental Panel on Climate Change (IPCC) in January 2001, one might say that the backdrop to this meeting was Fourier's observation that the earth's atmosphere acts like an immense garden greenhouse and traps the sun's heat to warm the planet (Christianson 2000a).

This is a story of how an obscure scientific theory from the nineteenth century turned into one of—if not the greatest—global policy dilemmas in the twenty-first century. Climate change[1] will remain an important global priority for the foreseeable future, though emphasis is likely to change from scientific questions toward normative and stakeholder concerns. This is already evident in the Conference of the Parties (COP) climate negotiations and is likely to become more pronounced over the next three decades. This chapter begins by examining the emergence of climate change as a scientific concern using the *Global 2000 Report* (Barney 1980) and the *Third Assessment Report* of the Intergovernmental Panel on Climate Change (2001b) as key reference points. The second part describes how climate change evolved into a global policy dilemma. The third part discusses the critical issues and questions that will guide the development of global warming policy over the ensuing decades. The fourth and final part of the chapter examines some of the scenarios and pathways by which climate change may develop as a global policy dilemma later in the twenty-first century.

Climate Change as an Evolving Scientific Concern

In the early 1890s—some 70 years after Fourier published his paper on "un effet de verre" or an effect of glass—this largely forgotten research drew the attention of the Swedish chemist Svante August Arrhenius, who was then exploring the potential effects of the carbon-dioxide buildup in the atmosphere. Arrhenius calculated that a doubling of carbon-dioxide in the atmosphere would lead to an average temperature increase of 5°C–6°C (9°F–11°F). However, Arrhenius, who eventually received a Nobel Prize for his work on electrolytic dissociation, believed global warming or what he called the "hothouse" effect to be a positive thing because it would likely lead to an expansion of agriculture and a reduction in the harshness of winter in places like Sweden. Moreover, he thought that the process of doubling the atmospheric concentration of carbon dioxide would take at least three millennia (Christianson 2000a).

One of the earliest American scientific proponents of the global warming thesis was the geophysicist Roger Revelle, who argued for and eventually won support in the 1950s for the establishment of permanent stations to monitor carbon-dioxide levels in the atmosphere. The first high-level government mention of global warming was noted—with as much significance as a footnote—in a 1965 White House report on the nation's environmental problems. In 1977, the National Academy of Sciences issued a study titled Energy and Climate, which concluded that, given the possibility of global warming, further research should be devoted to addressing the remaining scientific uncertainties (Sarewitz and Pielke 2000).

Global warming, or what scientists at that time referred to as "inadvertent modification of the atmosphere," remained the intriguing hypothesis of a few scientists but generated little concern among the public or environmentalists throughout the 1960s and 1970s (Sarewitz and Pielke 2000).

The *Global 2000 Report to the President*

By the time former President Jimmy Carter issued a call in 1977 to the Council on Environmental Quality and the U.S. Department of State, in cooperation with other federal agencies, to study the "probable changes in the world's population, natural resources, and environment through the end of the century," the issue of global warming was starting to get more attention from policy makers in the U.S. and abroad. In addition to the 1977 National Academy of Sciences study, *Energy and Climate*, the World Meteorological Organization (WMO) issued a statement citing environmental implications of climate change in 1976. The WMO followed up in 1979 with the First World Climate Conference (Obasi 1999).

The *Global 2000 Report to the President* itself highlighted what it called six notable "environmental consequences" at the end of the twentieth century: impacts on agriculture, water resources, forest losses, nuclear energy, species extinction, and the world's atmosphere and climate. Though published a quarter of a century ago, the *Global 2000 Report* reads as if it had been written much more recently with its references to terms like ecological instability, human vulnerabilities, and resource scarcity.

Moreover, the report was hardly ambiguous when it concluded that greenhouse gases and ozone-depleting substances are expected to increase at rates that might significantly alter the world's climate by 2050. The report noted that if the projected rates of increase in fossil fuel consumption were to continue, a doubling of carbon dioxide in the atmosphere could be expected after the middle of the twenty-first century, along with significant changes of precipitation patterns around the world.

Global 2000 and the IPCC 2001: A Comparison

The Intergovernmental Panel on Climate Change (IPCC) was established in 1988 by the UN Environment Programme and the World Meteorological Association with a goal of assessing the scientific, environmental, and socioeconomic impacts of climate change. While the *Global 2000 Report* did not focus exclusively on global warming, its conclusions are noteworthy, especially when read side by side with the conclusions of the latest IPCC *Assessment Report.*[2] A comparison of these two reports shows to what degree scientific knowledge of global climate change has increased over the past 25 years. There is now much more compelling evidence that most of the global warming observed over the past 50 years is attributable to human activities. Going beyond the 1995 IPCC climate-science assessment report, which had concluded for the first time that the "balance of evidence suggests a discernible human influence on global climate," the 2001 IPCC climate-science assessment report provided even more concrete evidence that so-called natural climate-change agents alone could not explain the warming in the second half of the twentieth century. While many of the uncertainties identified in the 1995 IPCC report remain, climate models have improved significantly. Based on the current scenarios and taking into account the estimated uncertainties in the models, the projected global average temperature increase by the year 2100 ranges from 1.3°C to 5.6°C. Such an increase would be much larger than the observed twentieth-century changes and without precedent in the last 10,000 years (Evans 2001).

Although the *Global 2000 Report* made several references to the environmental threat posed by the buildup of greenhouse gases in the atmosphere, this report did not have access to the climate-change models that were used to supply data and analysis to the IPCC reports. While the *Global 2000 Report* did warn of the potential dangers posed by changes in precipitation patterns and the relationship between rising temperature, melting of the polar ice cap, and rising sea levels, it had little of the scientific certainty and precision of the IPCC 2001 report. For example, based on "proxy" data from tree rings, corals, ice cores, and historical records, the IPCC 2001 report suggested that the average temperature increase in the Northern Hemisphere over the twentieth century is likely to have been the largest of any century during the past 1,000 years.[3]

In addition to greater scientific certainty and precision, the IPCC 2001 report provided a comprehensive sketch of a wide range of climate-change-linked impacts and vulnerabilities. Whereas the *Global 2000 Report* offered preliminary analysis of the environmental threats posed by changing precipitation patterns, the IPCC 2001 report provided an integrated assessment of the socioeconomic and public health impacts of global warming–linked changes in weather patterns, water resources, and ecosystem disturbances. As a *Washington Post* article on the IPCC 2001 report observed;

In the most comprehensive look yet at the existing and long-term effects of global warming, the report by a United Nations panel warned of the potential for large-scale and irreversible climate changes—including large reductions in the Greenland

and West Antarctic ice sheets and a substantial slowing of the circulation of warm water in the North Atlantic. Rising global temperatures already responsible for shrinking glaciers and vanishing permafrost eventually could touch off climate changes that would literally alter ocean currents, wipe away huge portions of Alpine snowcaps and aid in the spread of cholera and malaria. (Pianin 2001)

The IPCC 2001 report also presented much better scientific evidence of global warming as a key agent in the rapid increase in the number and severity of so-called "natural" disasters like floods, tornadoes, and earthquakes (Abramovitz 2001; International Federation of Red Cross and Red Crescent Societies, 2001). Although the 1990s were named by the United Nations as the International Decade for Natural Disaster Reduction, it was a decade marked by more than $608 billion in disaster-related economic losses worldwide, more than the previous four decades combined. Moreover, over 2 billion people were affected by disasters worldwide, which is more than those now estimated to be displaced by conflict.[4] What is particularly disturbing is the growing scientific evidence that global warming coupled with deforestation, wetlands destruction, and ecologically destructive human-settlement practices is permanently altering—if not unraveling—what Janet Abramovitz of the Worldwatch Institute describes as our planet's ecological safety net (Abramovitz 2001).

For many years, climate change was a technical issue that only concerned a small number of scientists and policymakers. As recently as the early 1980s, climate change was regarded as an obscure scientific issue that was the exclusive domain of physicists, forest ecologists, and chemical engineers. The release of the *Global 2000 Report* did not change the prevailing wisdom that climatic change was no more than an interesting scientific hypothesis. Today, while many outstanding climate-science issues and questions remain, science is no longer the driving force in climate-change policymaking. The transition from an obscure scientific issue to a globally prominent policy concern represents a key shift in the transformation of ecological concerns—at least in perception—into key global policy priorities.

Climate Change's Policy Salience: A Capsule History

How did climate change become a prominent global issue and what was the institutional and historical context from which this transformation took place? The increase and eventual decline of climate change's policy salience can be grouped into three distinct stages: 1980–1992, 1992–1998, and 1999–2004.

1980–1992   The remarkable record of bipartisan environmental legislation in the United States in the 1970s, including the Clean Air and Water
acts, Endangered Species Act, and the Toxic Substances Control Act,
abruptly ended with the election of Ronald Reagan in 1980. President
Reagan viewed environmental conservation as fundamentally at odds
with economic growth and prosperity and sought to reverse or weaken
many of the environmental policies enacted in the previous decade (Vig
and Kraft 1997). But by the mid-1980s, even the Reagan administration
could not ignore the critical change that was taking place in terms of the
way scientists and policymakers viewed the climatic impact of the consumption of fossil fuels. When the Second World Climate Conference was
held in Villach, Austria, in 1985, it became clear that climate change had
become established on the policy agenda and there was a growing scientific consensus on the potential seriousness of global warming.

Despite President Reagan's efforts to abolish the Council on Environmental Quality and curtail the regulatory mandate of the EPA and
other environment-related agencies, Congress successfully initiated a
national program to combat global warming. Led by Representative
Albert Gore (D-Tennessee) and Senator Timothy Wirth (D-Colorado),
Congress pushed through a number of bills supporting increased funding
for climate research and a wide assortment of energy-conservation and
renewable-energy programs in the 1980s. The most important climate-
change-related bill during this period was the 1987 Global Climate
Protection Act, which called for the development of a coordinated
national policy on climate change (Fisher-Vaden 1997).

The unusually hot and dry summer of 1988 proved to be the perfect
backdrop for a series of international conferences and congressional hear-
ings that were held on global warming. In what could be considered the
first major international conference that brought scientists and policymakers together to discuss the possible policy ramifications of global warming,
the Toronto Conference on the Changing Atmosphere formulated a pledge
for industrialized countries to voluntarily cut CO_2 emissions by 20 percent
by 2005. Also, the congressional testimony of James Hansen of NASA's
Goddard Institute of Space Studies in the summer of 1988 is particularly
noteworthy because it represented the first time that a climate expert testi-
fied that there was a "conclusive" link between human-made greenhouse
gases and the changing weather.[5] Although the actual scientific confirma-

tion of the human influence on global climate would not come until the 1995 Intergovernmental Panel on Climate Change's *Second Assessment Report*, the testimony of Hansen and other scientists enabled global warming to have political credibility, which was something that this issue had not had despite many years of environmental activism (Rosenbaum 1998).

Even though the position of the first Bush administration (1988–1992) could be described as less ideologically opposed to the international climate-change negotiation process, it did not deviate far from the stance adopted by the Reagan administration. Despite the almost-universal plea from OECD environment ministers for recognition of the "precautionary principle" (i.e., preventive actions should be taken even if scientific certainty has not yet been achieved), during the ministerial-level climate-change forums held in 1989 and 1990 the United States refused to endorse any binding emission commitment because of fears that such a commitment would have a severe negative impact on American industrial competitiveness.

Toward the end of the first Bush administration, two subtle but important changes in the U.S. climate-policy agenda could be detected. The first was a shift in perceptions of climate-change from a scientific to an economic and political concern, with important ramifications (mostly negative) for American manufacturing and energy industries. The second change was a growing emphasis on domestic politics (at the expense of international diplomacy) in the climate-change debate. All major climate-change-related policy decisions began to be discussed within domestic policy forums like the Bush administration's Domestic Policy Council, often without the participation of U.S. State Department diplomats and climate scientists.

Fueled by new scientific evidence of the environmental threat posed by global warming, the prominence of climate change as a U.S. foreign-policy issue did increase, particularly toward the latter half of the Bush administration. At the same time, this increase in prominence also increased political complexity by attracting the involvement of environmental NGOs, business and commercial enterprises, and Congress. While the participation of nongovernmental stakeholders like NGOs and labor unions in the climate-change debate can be interpreted as a triumph of civil society, this also vastly complicated the task of scientists and diplomats, who had been the traditional power brokers in the climate-change debate.

1992–1998   The election of Bill Clinton and Al Gore in 1992 raised enormous expectations that the United States would dramatically alter its go-slow diplomatic stance on climate change and other global environmental issues. Many American environmental activists considered Vice President Gore to be one of the most committed green political leaders in the United States, and hopes ran high for an activist global environmental policy agenda. Climate change continued to develop as a prominent foreign-policy issue during the Clinton administration; four events marked this growing prominence.

The first was the Clinton administration's 1996 environmental diplomacy initiative. While environmental issues had been a part of U.S. foreign policy for a number of years, the 1996 initiative was arguably the first real attempt to "institutionalize" global warming and other global environmental problems as part of U.S. foreign-policy architecture. Former Secretary of State Warren Christopher gave a speech in 1996 in which he outlined the premise of the Clinton administration's new environmental diplomatic strategy. He argued in his speech that our ability to advance global and national interests was linked to how well we manage our planet's natural resources, and the Clinton administration was determined to place environmental concerns in the mainstream of American foreign policy (Christopher 1996).

The second major event was the decision of the Clinton administration to agree to binding (as opposed to voluntary) emission targets in 1996. At the Second Conference of the Parties to the Climate Change Agreement (COP-2) in 1996, the United States dramatically increased the visibility of global warming as a national political issue by acknowledging that nonbinding efforts of individual countries would not be enough to achieve the goals of stabilizing emission at 1990 levels by the year 2000. Tim Wirth, the head of the U.S. delegation, proposed that future negotiations should focus on an agreement that sets realistic, verifiable, and binding medium-term emission targets. Although the U.S. proposal did not include any specific references to emission targets and timetables, Wirth's support of binding emission targets caused a seismic shift in the politics of climate change.

This shift in U.S. climate policy angered many Republican members of Congress, who were privately assured by Clinton administration officials that the United States would not be supporting any binding emission protocols at COP-2. This also raised fears in the business community that the binding emission targets would be accompanied by increases in energy taxes and more stringent fuel-efficiency standards for automobiles. The Clinton administration knew that this decision would be controversial, but they did not want to be diplomatically isolated, nor to be perceived as contesting the IPCC *Second Assessment Report's* conclusion that there is strong evidence of human impact on the global climate.

The third event was the adoption of the Byrd-Hagel Senate Resolution in 1997. The Clinton administration's climate diplomacy suffered a huge setback when the U.S. Senate endorsed the Byrd-Hagel resolution (named for its two chief sponsors, Senators Robert Byrd (D-West Virginia) and Chuck Hagel (R-Nebraska)) in 1997. It stipulated that the United States refrain from signing any climate-change agreement that does not impose equal commitments on industrialized as well as developing countries and that may potentially have a serious impact on the U.S. economy (*Global Change,* 1997). Although the resolution was non-binding and highly questionable in terms of international environmental law, the unanimous passing of the resolution signaled that Congress was not going to let the White House have the policy discretion to set the U.S. climate-change agenda. By the middle of 1997, global warming had become too important a foreign-policy concern for it to be ignored by Congress.

The final event was the adoption of the global climate protocol at the 1997 Global Climate Change Conference (COP-3) held in Kyoto. The adoption of the Kyoto Protocol (with the United States agreeing to reduce its greenhouse gas emissions by 7 percent below its 1990 levels over the 2008–2012 period, and the European Union agreeing to an 8 percent and Japan a 6 percent reduction) may have been the best outcome anybody could have imagined at that time. However, the political divisiveness and the lack of consensus in international climate negotiations were mirrored in the contradictory conclusions drawn after the end of the conference. Anti-climate-change treaty forces were upset at the prospect of a binding global climate-change agreement, while pro-climate-change treaty groups were frustrated that the Kyoto Protocol did not go far enough in addressing the long-term threat posed by global warming.

1999–2004   The fourth and fifth climate-change conferences held in 1998 and 1999 represented attempts—albeit failed—to gain consensus on the many important unresolved details of the Kyoto climate-change protocol. These included definitional and operational issues concerning the treatment of carbon sinks, compliance with the protocol obligations, developing-country participation, and rules and modalities for the Kyoto "flexible mechanisms" (emission trading, the clean-development mechanism, and joint implementation). These unresolved details formed the core issues addressed at the sixth Climate Change Conference (COP-6) in the Hague in November 2000.

The prominence of climate change as a national and international policy dilemma can be best noted by comparing the relatively small number of participants at the 1988 Toronto conference with the huge gathering at the 1998 Buenos Aires climate-change conference (COP-4). In 10 years, climate change was transformed from a relatively unknown scientific issue to, according to Melinda Kimble, former Acting Assistant Secretary of State for Oceans, Environmental, and Scientific Affairs, arguably the greatest diplomatic dilemma confronting the U.S. government (Kimble 1988). Whereas only a few hundred scientists, governmental officials, and representatives of environmental groups from 48 countries attended the 1988 Toronto conference, more than 5,000 government officials, representatives of nongovernmental organizations, and business executives from 166 countries participated in COP-4. While a handful of midlevel government officials made up the U.S. delegation in Toronto, a battalion of more than 50 government delegates, drawn from the White House (the Council on Environmental Quality, the Council on Sustainable Development, the National Security Council, and the Climate Change Taskforce), the U.S. Departments of State, Energy, Justice, and Defense, and the Environmental Protection Agency, formed the U.S. delegation at the Buenos Aires climate-change conference.

At the 1999 climate-change conference in Bonn, the U.S. delegates to the UN-sponsored negotiations circulated a motion to postpone the sixth climate-change conference (COP-6) to the spring of 2001 because of fears that the high-stakes, high-profile international negotiation sessions would take place just days before the U.S. presidential elections. The proposal was turned down, ensuring that climate change would remain a campaign issue in the 2000 presidential elections. With American voters putting the environment as one of their most important policy concerns (ahead of such issues as gun control and school vouchers)[6] and the intense media scrutiny of the Kyoto Treaty, global warming became a legitimate national political issue. A 1997 *New York Times* article offered this cogent analysis of the climate-change issue in the 2000 presidential elections:

As the debate begins over the agreement to reduce global gas emissions, many Republicans sense that they have a political opportunity reminiscent of the health care fight of 1994. The country then supported the basic idea of health insurance for all, just as it now supports strong environmental action. But Republicans skewered the health plan on the details, and painted President Clinton as a big government liberal in the process. Some now think they can repeat their success and this time tar Vice President Al Gore. (Mitchell 1997)

November 2000 proved to be a critical point for climate-change politics both in the United States and abroad. COP-6, held in the Hague, ended in failure after a bitter dispute between the European Union (EU) and the United States over how to curb greenhouse gas emissions, and George W. Bush was elected the forty-third president. Despite initial promises made during the 2000 presidential elections that carbon dioxide would be regulated in some form as part of a comprehensive national environmental policy strategy, President Bush decided to abandon the 1997 Kyoto Protocol in March 2001, arguing that the environmental treaty was against American economic interests. The European Union reacted with anger and shock, and the Council of Europe's parliamentary assembly passed a resolution in April 2001 that cast doubt on the United States' reliability as a global partner. Despite some initial policy waffling, Japan also criticized the U.S. decision to abandon the Kyoto climate treaty and laid the groundwork to ratify the protocol whether or not the United States decided to seek treaty ratification.

COP-6 Part II, held in July 2001 in Bonn, brought a breakthrough when 178 nations reached a last-minute compromise to salvage the Kyoto climate accord. Even without the formal participation of the United States, the Kyoto treaty continued to survive, albeit in a much weakened state. Ironically, many of the agreed on points at COP-6 Part II were things that had been long favored by the United States. These included no limits on emission trading as a means of meeting the Kyoto commitments and no limits on all three forms of greenhouse gas credits allowed under the protocol's so-called flexible mechanisms (i.e., carbon credits achieved via emission trading, clean-development mechanism, and joint implementation) (Kopp 2001). COP-7, held in Marrakesh in November 2001, finalized the terms for implementing the Kyoto climate accord, but was overshadowed by the political fallout from the terrorist attacks in the United States months before.

With the preparation underway for the COP-10 in Bueno Aires in December 2004, Russia stills seems reluctant to agree to a specific timetable to implement the Kyoto Protocol. In May 2004, during WTO accession negotiations with the European Union, Russian President Vladimir Putin said that Russia would move toward approving the Protocol, but gave no timetable. In the short term, Russia's decision to ratify the Kyoto Protocol may depend on which entity Putin feels he can afford to antagonize—the European Union, which strongly supports the Kyoto Protocol, or the United States, with which Putin has established close ties in the fight against international terrorism.

In the long run, Russia's decision to support the Kyoto Protocol may mean little if the greenhouse gas emissions in the highly industrialized countries continue on their rapid growth patterns. According to a 2003 report by the UN climate-change secretariat, the European Union, Japan, the United States, and other highly industrialized regions could grow by 8 percent from 2000 to 2010 (to about 17 percent over the 1990 level) despite domestic measures to limit emission levels. While Europe's total emissions decreased by 3.5 percent from 1990 to 2000, emissions increased in most other highly industrialized areas, including Japan (11 percent), the United States (14 percent), Australia (18 percent), and Canada (20 percent).

Responding to Complex Environmental Phenomena

The development of global warming policy over the next two decades will not resemble that of the previous two. Though the future trajectory is difficult to predict, three factors are likely to guide how and in what manner climate change will continue to develop as a global policy concern. First, what strategies will the international community choose as responses to various complex, climate-driven environmental phenomena? Second, how will ethical or social-justice issues influence future climate-change policymaking? Third, what roles will nonstate actors play in global climate governance?

One of the most important underlying components of sustainability thinking is the notion that humanity and nature are inextricably linked in a dynamic socioecological system. Consequently, offering any kind of greenhouse warming solutions remains difficult because of the high level of complexity and uncertainty endemic in such a dynamic system. The science of global climate change is extremely complex, due to the dynamic and often-surprising interrelationships that arise when components of the global ecosystem—the biological, physical, chemical, and human dimensions—interact.[7] Climate science offers one of the best case studies of policymaking in a world where things are interconnected, where unintended consequences of our actions are unavoidable, and where the total effect of behavior is not equal to the sum of individual actions (Jervis 1997; Roe 1998).

Compared to many other types of environmental dilemmas, global warming is extremely abstract—it is not experienced in the same way as a toxic-waste spill or a clear-cut forest. As Daniel Sarewicz of the Columbia Center for Science, Policy and Outcomes and Roger Pielke of the National Center for Atmospheric Research argue, global warming is abstract in such a manner that even scientists often disagree over whether they have observed it or not. It is also unlikely that scientists would ever be able to pinpoint with any degree of accuracy whether global warming was the cause of a specific hurricane or a heat wave (Sarewitz and Pielke 2000).

Another methodological challenge posed by climate science is how to predict changes that are at best episodic, discontinuous, and surprising. This is particularly important in the case of climate-change research because there is growing scientific evidence the resilience of many ecosystems has become undermined to the point that even the slightest disturbances could make them collapse. After decades of continuous change imposed by human activity, many of the world's ecosystems remain dangerously susceptible to sudden catastrophic change. According to a report titled *Abrupt Climate Change: Inevitable Surprises* that was released by the National Academy of Sciences (2001a), most climate-change research has focused on gradual changes. However, new evidence shows that periods of gradual change in the earth's past were punctuated by episodes of abrupt change, including temperature changes of 10°C.

Whereas in the early 1980s a major preoccupation of climate science was to develop better and technologically advanced computer models, climate science in the twenty-first century is likely to be concerned with how to make sense of socioecological issues that are highly abstract, complex, and uncertain. Putting even more resources into global climate-change research is not likely to reduce this level of complexity and uncertainty. For example, over one decade, the U.S. Global Change Research Program spent nearly $18 billion. Doubling or even tripling the research budget is not likely to appreciably remove many of the key question marks surrounding climate science.[8]

Moving toward Equity in Climate-Change Policy

Equity considerations remain central to the climate-change debate. Which country bears the greatest responsibility for greenhouse warming? Which are at greatest risk from the impacts of warming? According to Article 3 of the 1992 UN Framework Convention on Climate Change, the forerunner of the Kyoto Protocol, the concept of equity is acknowledged as one of the guiding principles of the climate convention with its reference to "common but differentiated responsibilities." As Eileen Claussen and Lisa McNeilly of the Pew Center on Global Climate Change once observed,

Of the many pending issues within the climate change debate, the question of what constitutes equitable international commitments may be the most difficult to address. Long unresolved divisions about the distribution of resources and equitable access to them must be considered by climate change negotiators in order to agree on a fair and effective global response. (Claussen and McNeilly 1998, 1).

Equity has been or will continue to be one of the pivotal issues that define whether and to what degree the objectives of the Kyoto Protocol are successfully addressed.

Equity and justice concerns surface in climate-change policymaking in two important ways. First, there is the question of an equitable allocation of emission levels. Global carbon emissions average around 1 metric ton per year (tC/year) per person. Japan and Western European nations emit between 2 and 5 tC/year per person, while the U.S. per capita emissions exceed 5 tC/year per person. In comparison, per capita emissions of the developing world currently stand at 0.6 tC/year per person, and more than fifty developing countries have emissions under 0.2 tC/year per person. This presents a formidable policy challenge because the average worldwide emissions must be stabilized at levels below 0.3 tC/year per person for a future world population of 10 billion, if we are to prevent greenhouse gases from exceeding twice the preindustrial levels (Baer et al., 2000). Thus, the key question is who bears the most responsibility and should pay for mitigating the effects of climate change?

The second equity issue concerns the uneven impacts of global climate change. According to the IPCC report released in 2001, the impacts of climate change are expected to fall disproportionately on poor countries in Africa, Asia, and Latin America. Long-term climate change will have a greater impact on the world's poor because a larger portion of less developed economies depend on climate-sensitive sectors such as agriculture.[9] In addition to greater mortality from heat stress and higher exposures to disease, the IPCC report predicts that there will be decreased crop yields in tropical and subtropical regions and decreased water availability in many areas. Most coral reefs could disappear within 30 to 50 years due to warming oceans, while three-quarters of the world's mangrove forest in the Sundarban regions of India and Bangladesh could be flooded by a sea-level rise of 18 inches.[10] The most perverse consequence of climate change from the standpoint of equity and burden sharing is that countries that produce the smallest amounts of greenhouse gas emissions are likely to suffer the worst effects of global warming. According to the latest impact studies from the Tyndall Centre for Climate Change Research at the English University of East Anglia, Afghanistan, Ethiopia, Sierra Leone, and Tanzania are the most vulnerable countries to the impacts of climate change, while Luxembourg, Ireland, Britain, and New Zealand are likely to suffer the least. With the projected increases in sea levels and greater incidence of tropical storms, small island states in the Pacific Ocean remain the most vulnerable. They already suffered more than $1 billion in damages in the 1990s from various weather disturbances (World Bank, 2000a).

To many climate experts from the developing world, global warming is an issue of fairness. As Jyoti Parikh (2000, 2) of the Indira Gandhi Institute of Development Research in India notes,

The problem is rooted in inequity. It is important to realize that greenhouse gas accumulation is only one of the many manifestations of a larger malady of a highly inequitable world where 25 percent of the population is consuming 75 percent of the world's resources. Many constraints are imposed indirectly on the way developing countries take decisions today on policy options regarding issues such as what energy sources to use, how to generate power, how to use land, and what crops to grow. . . . The risks to poor countries should be the primary focus of the climate change analysis rather than costs to the developed countries.

Finally, though hardly a concern in the early 1980s, it is now nearly impossible to discuss the management of any global issue without first factoring in the possible role to be played by nonstate actors, particularly private business interests and nongovernmental groups.

Multinational corporations (MNCs) have been the subject of scholarly attention since the 1960s, but the research on the impact of MNCs on world affairs has been unable to keep pace with the huge surge in the growth of MNCs driven by advances in information technology, market liberalization, and global deregulation. Whereas the earlier research on MNCs tended to focus on the extent to which the MNC acts in terms of its own needs, without regard to national sovereignty or control, some of the most pressing and relevant questions about MNCs now center on their social and environmental responsibilities. The annual revenue of some MNCs is larger than the gross domestic product of many countries—the annual revenue of American retailer Wal-Mart is equal to the gross domestic product of Greece, the computer giant IBM is close in size to Egypt, and the electronic company Sony is similar in size to the Czech Republic (Stopford 1999). Yet until very recently, theories of multinational corporate behavior were largely devoid of environmental and social variables as if cross border business activities are neutral to environmental and social impacts (Choucri 1993).

From the early 1970s to the mid-1980s, MNCs and the business community complied with environmental regulations only when absolutely necessary and often fought the enactment of early antipollution measures such as the Clean Air Act. By the mid-1980s, however, corporations began to recognize the importance of integrating environmental issues into their overall business strategies. With regulations moving away from mandating compliance—toward emphasizing results—companies began adopting corporate environmental-management programs. Often these yielded large cost savings and significant reductions in waste emissions.

One important shift in the attitude of the business sector toward global warming occurred when John Browne, chief executive officer of the petroleum giant BP, called for a "precautionary approach" in dealing with the climate-change problem in a speech delivered at Stanford

University in 1997.[11] His remarks were significant because he was the first CEO of a large MNC to adopt a proactive approach to the climate-change issue, signaling the first real division in the business community between those who support and those who oppose the objectives of the Kyoto Protocol.[12]

Another important development has been the rapid growth in the number of pro-climate-treaty business groups (e.g., Pew Center on Global Climate Change, World Business Council for Sustainable Development, and others) and industries that are energy intensive enough to gain from increased energy and resource efficiency. While there are still many anti-climate-treaty companies and business groups, the international business community is no longer a monolithic force working to defeat the Kyoto Protocol. The growing influence of proactive businesses means that there is for the first time credible support for a vigorous climate-change policy from the global business community. According to Robert Watson, former IPCC chair, "The fact that we've got negotiations going on here (COP-6 in the Hague, The Netherlands) sends a signal to business. And the fact is, business may lead" ("Climate Talks May Be Moot Amid Green Power Advances," 2000).

The emergence of global environmental problems such as climate change coincided with another important development in international affairs—the rise in the number and influence of nongovernmental organizations (NGOs). Whether one subscribes to the view that the rise of the NGOs reflects the breakdown of the absolutes of the Westphalian system—territorially fixed states where everything of value lies within some state's border (Matthews 1997)—or that NGOs are transcending their role as transnational pressure groups and becoming political actors in their own right (Wapner 1995), it would difficult to dispute that NGOs are distinctive entities with important skills and resources to deploy in the process of international environmental cooperation (Raustiala 1997). In the 1990s, there was a remarkable rise in the number and prominence of NGOs and in their ability to precipitate change. According to the *Yearbook of International Organizations,* the number of transnational NGOs grew from 176 in 1909 to more than 20,000 in 1996. Up to 70 percent of the NGOs operating in the United States have been created in the last three decades, while the number of NGOs operating internationally—those with a presence in three or more countries—has quadrupled to 20,000 over that same period ("The Non-governmental Order," 1999; Runyan 1999).

In the case of NGOs that work on global warming–related issues, more than fifty groups make up the U.S. Climate Change Network, an umbrella organization for climate-policy activities in the United States. Environmental NGOs in this network can be classified into three broad categories: those affiliated with international NGOs (e.g., the Worldwide Fund for Nature and Greenpeace International), environmental organizations whose primary interest is advocacy work in the United States (e.g., Sierra Club, U.S. Public Interest Research Group, and so on), and research-oriented environmental research groups and think tanks (e.g., World Resources Institute, Pew Center on Global Climate Change, and so forth). Several groups—such as the Environmental Defense Fund and the Natural Resources Defense Council—are organizational hybrids, in that they do substantial advocacy work with offices spread across the country, but also do extensive policy research.

The effectiveness of the U.S. Climate Change Network has been hampered in recent years by conflicting policy objectives and a clash of organizational styles between more advocacy-oriented groups like the U.S. Public Interest Research Group and more research-oriented groups like the Environmental Defense Fund. There are hopeful signs, however, that environmental NGOs are working hard to coordinate their advocacy and public information campaigns. In the fall of 1999, a number of environmental organizations, including the National Environmental Trust, the Union of Concerned Scientists, and Physicians for Social Responsibility, formed a coalition to launch an $11 million information campaign to educate the American public about global warming. The campaign included one of the largest television advertising strategies launched by NGOs as well as a website that allows individual citizens to contact members of Congress with their concerns about this issue.[13]

Climate Change in the Age of Globalization

What are the specific scenarios and pathways by which climate change is likely to develop over the next three decades? One way to envision the development of climate change as a policy concern over the next 30 years is to use the four scenarios outlined in the UN Environment Programme's

(2002) *Global Environment Outlook–3* (GEO-3) report, which highlights four possible scenarios, spanning developments in overlapping factors such as population, economics, technology, and governance, over the next 30 years.

In the "Markets First" scenario, most of the world adopts the values and expectations prevailing in today's industrialized countries. Trust is placed in further globalization and liberalization to enhance corporate wealth, while ethical investors, together with citizen and consumer groups, try to exercise corrective influence on corporate-led globalization but are undermined by economic imperatives. The "Security First" scenario assumes a world of striking disparities of wealth and resources where inequality and conflict prevail. Socioeconomic and environmental stresses lead to waves of social protests and counteraction, and powerful and wealthy groups opt for self-protection in the form of gated communities. This is already happening in a number of places around the world, most notably in Brazil's cities, but also in certain parts of the United States.

A more hopeful future can be seen under the "Policy First" scenario, in which decisive initiatives are taken by governments in an attempt to reach specific social and environmental goals. Costs and gains are factored into policy measures and regulatory frameworks and are further reinforced by fiscal incentives such as carbon taxes. Under the "Sustainability First" scenario, a new environment and development paradigm emerges in which there is a radical shift from confrontation to collaboration between stakeholder groups in the decision-making process.

Under these four scenarios, differences in the likely policies on climate change are quite stark. The "Market First" and "Security First" scenarios are "business-as-usual" situations, in which the fossil-fuel-driven global economy would continue to emit greenhouse gasses at an unsustainable rate, causing great harm to small island states and other climate-vulnerable countries. What is absent in these two scenarios is the development of sophisticated policy mechanisms needed to respond to global-equity concerns and complex environmental problems as well as the critical stakeholder collaboration between governments, nongovernmental organizations, and private enterprises. While some measures to effectively deal with global warming are present in the "Policy First" and the "Sustainability First" scenarios, what is questionable is the likelihood of these two more hopeful scenarios prevailing over the next 30 years.

However unlikely the "Sustainability First" scenario might now appear, one should not assume the "Security First" scenario as a fait accompli. When the UN Conference on the Human Environment was held in Stockholm in 1972, only one environment minister attended the conference because most countries did not have independent environmental agencies or ministries at that time. Thirty years later, 6,500 official delegates—including more than 100 heads of state—attended the 2002 World Summit on Sustainable Development in Johannesburg. While the *Global 2000 Report* raised concerns about climate change as a potential global ecological threat, it was not until over a quarter of a century later (in the form of the IPCC report) that the scientific connection between human activities and climatic change was firmly established.

Scientific certainty and political consensus frequently move at a pace inconsistent with the threat posed by global climate change. While the "Sustainability First" scenario may not realistically prevail over the next 30 years, one should not assume the dark and gloomy prophecy of the "Security First" scenario as inevitable. In the United States and elsewhere, there has been a gradual but noticeable erosion of the "Market First" ethos as well as a growing emphasis on the importance of public policies to guide corporate accountability and responsibility.

California and other U.S. states appear more committed to reducing greenhouse gas emissions, having declared their intention to challenge the federal government's role in setting national environmental policy. Shortly after President Bush rejected the Kyoto Protocol in 2001, New England's governors joined their eastern Canadian counterparts to announce their own climate-change action plan that calls for each state and province to reduce greenhouse gas emissions to 1990 levels by 2010 and 10 percent below that by 2020.

A "Sustainability First" Future in a "Security First" World

Climate science in the early twenty-first century has progressed to the point where certain conclusions can be clearly drawn. There is now almost undeniable evidence that human activities have caused climatic change. Nine of the ten warmest years since 1860 have occurred since

1990, and observed temperatures are rising three times as fast as in the early 1990s, according to findings of the World Meteorological Organization ("This Year Was the 2nd Hottest, Confirming a Trend, UN Says," 2001). Yet while climate-change research has helped build awareness and establish global warming as a public-policy concern, a credible and effective policy remedy to address climate change has not been established. Climate change has been and will continue to be an important domestic and foreign-policy concern for the United States. However, the question remains whether this issue will continue to be overshadowed by other more politically and economically salient priorities.

In the next 5 to 10 years, there is little chance of a major policy breakthrough on the climate-change front. Even if the U.S. government eventually signs the Kyoto Protocol (or a successor treaty), it would not "solve" the problem of climate change. At best, the Kyoto Protocol fills a short-term policy gap until longer-term solutions that can deal effectively with thorny issues such as equity and greater stakeholder involvement are devised and implemented.

What often gets overlooked in the ever-pressing search for a solution to the climate-change problem is that there is no simple solution. Even more important than the eventual fate of the Kyoto Protocol are the small but important steps through which the international community can—if it chooses—establish the groundwork for a less carbon-dependent global economy. The crucial question for the international community over the long term is whether it has the vision and foresight to establish a critical policy link between the present and the future in the form of sustainable energy and mobility programs.

Even before the September 11 attacks, deep divisions existed over the purpose of American power and how to maintain a delicate balance between unilateral actions and multilateral cooperation. No matter who is occupying the White House and which political party is controlling the U.S. Congress, global warming will remain an important global problem. Achieving global consensus on any issue as complex, science-driven, and full of uncertainties as climate change is truly a Herculean challenge for the international community. This is certainly the case now and it is likely to represent an even greater global challenge in the coming decades.

Notes

1. Although *climate change* is the term preferred by scientists and environmental policymakers, *global warming* and *climate change* will be used interchangeably in this chapter.

2. All IPCC working group reports from 1990, 1995, and 2001 are available online at www.ipcc.ch.

3. Many of the data, scenarios, and conclusions from the IPCC 2001 report were supported by the analysis of the National Academy of Sciences' June 2001 report, *Climate Change Science: Analysis of Some Key Questions* (National Academy of Sciences, 2001b).

4. The military conflicts in Afghanistan and Iraq will obviously change some of these assumptions.

5. For more, see Anderson, 2001.

6. Based on the "What Worries Americans" poll conducted by ICR for the *Washington Post*. For a summary of the results, see "A skeptical Electorate Searches for Leadership," 1999: A1.

7. See the description of the Biocomplexity in the Environment program of the National Science Foundation online at www.nsf.gov/home/crssprgm/be.

8. The budgetary figures for the U.S. Global Change Research Program are drawn from *Our Changing Planet,* FY2002, available online at http://globalchange.gov/pubs/ocp2002.html.

9. See the Summary for Policymakers, *Climate Change 2001: Impacts, Adaptation, and Vulnerability,* available online at www.unep.ch/ipcc.

10. For more information, see the Summary for Policymakers, *Climate Change 2001: Impacts, Adaptation, and Vulnerability,* accessible online at www.unep.ch/ ipcc.

11. John Browne's 1997 speech can be found online at www.bp.com/speeches/sp_970519.htm.

12. It should be stressed that virtually all of the *prominent* anti-climate-treaty business groups (e.g., Climate Action Coalition, Business Roundtable, U.S. Chamber of Commerce, and so on) are either based in the United States or run by Americans.

13. Information on the Global Warming Campaign, including press releases and background information, can be found online at www.hotearth.net.

14. Further information is available online at www.hotearth.net.

10

Forest Degradation, the Timber Trade, and Tropical Region Plantations

Patricia Marchak

Degradation of tropical forests has occurred since the beginning of human history, but like many environmental conditions, has become a serious ecological security problem within the past 50 years. Hunting bands and shifting cultivators lived in these forests for thousands of years without causing extensive damage, so long as their numbers remained small and their tenure in any one location was limited to 2 or 3 years. Selective timber extraction always caused disruption to surrounding vegetation and soils, but until roads and large-scale industrial equipment existed, the damage was limited. While assaults on the forest attributable to urban expansion, settlement, and agriculture are still the major causes of deforestation, forestry has steadily increased its proportional impact since the 1960s.

Although not widely acknowledged at the time of the *Global 2000 Report to the President* (Barney 1980), tropical deforestation was identified as a problem during the 1980s, spurring several initiatives by international bodies such as the UN Food and Agriculture Organization (FAO) and the International Tropical Timber Organization (ITTO), including the International Tropical Timber Agreement (ITTA) and the Tropical Forestry Action Program (TFAP). These issues gained wider recognition through publication of the World Commission on Environment and Development's report (Brundtland report) in 1987, and through ongoing media interest in some of the more extreme examples of devastation.

The tropics currently supply a small proportion of total world forest products, but the trade in chips, plywood, and pulp from these regions has grown rapidly since 1970. The FAO has predicted that world demand for forest products will increase at about 3 percent per year over the next three decades (Dore, Johnston, and Stevens 1997; Apps and Price 1996), and the Northern countries can no longer meet that increased demand.

Basic Definitions

There are diverse tropical-forest types, but this chapter concerns only *closed tropical rainforests* and *seasonal tropical forests,* often grouped together as *tropical moist forests.* These generally exist between the Tropics of Cancer and Capricorn, but a few are found in New South Wales, Australia; in the Himalayan foothills of upper Myanmar, India, and southern China; and near Rio de Janeiro, Brazil (Whitmore 1990).

Deforestation is a problematic term, because forests can be severely degraded, even destroyed, yet still contain standing trees. The FAO defines deforestation as the "permanent conversion of the forest to other uses," but often tropical forests are destroyed without converting the land to other uses. Instead, the more flexible term *degradation* is preferred, because it refers to the destruction of ecosystem integrity.

Tropical-forest plantations are not forests but agricultural crops, established to produce wood for construction or fiber suitable for pulp and paper production. They play an important role in tropical forestry, because they are often planted on previously forested land, and, paradoxically, are also touted as the best way to save tropical forests.

Limitations of Regeneration and Management

The earth's temperate forests are remarkably resilient, having regenerated from overharvesting and natural disasters again and again (though sometimes this process takes centuries). We often assume that tropical forests have the same capacity, but most of the nutrients in these ecosystems are found in the foliage rather than in the soil or shallow root systems. Recovery from selective logging may occur, if trees are chosen with extreme care and extracted without damaging those remaining. If small patches are removed (as in shifting agriculture), regeneration may occur within 30 to 40 years. Similarly, carefully logged, narrow strips can regenerate successfully, though this technique can also cause severe harm to animals who become isolated by the strips. Each of these operations requires great sensitivity to forest conditions, to multiple types of vegetation and the interdependence of vegetation and fauna—an awareness rarely manifested in tropical-forest logging.

Timber plantations are often established by first removing natural forests, then replacing them with commercial timber species, which are often exotic to the region. Other species and vegetation are discouraged by poison or other means. Usually fertilizers are needed to counteract nutrient depletion in soils (Jordan 1991, 165–166), which often leads to chemical runoff into local water tables.

Degradation and Ecological Security

The degradation of tropical forests is a threat to global ecological security for many reasons. The three most significant are the impacts of degradation on carbon and hydrological cycles, the loss of quality habitat and biodiversity, and the negative effects to indigenous and landless farmers.

Growing forests of all types are *carbon sinks*—by storing carbon in their tissues, they help keep the earth's climate in balance. Deforestation and other forms of degradation release nonfossil carbon dioxide into the atmosphere. Since about 1950, the release of carbon from tropical-forest degradation has exceeded carbon emissions from all other nonfossil sources combined (Houghton 1996; Dore, Johnston, and Stevens 1997). Removal of the tree canopy also interrupts local and regional hydrological cycles, causing springs and shallow wells to dry up and precipitation to decline.

Tropical forests are home to an estimated two-thirds of the major plants so far identified by scientists (Whitmore 1990), and to a similar proportion of animals; Collins (1990) notes that these regions provide habitat for 30 million species of insects. Biodiversity in tropical forests is greater than in any other region on earth. Many of these species are endemic to particular regions; they may be destroyed before we even become aware of their existence. Because tropical forests exhibit a high degree of interdependence between plants and fauna, destruction of one species necessarily means destruction of others.

This loss of biodiversity is also a loss to humanity, as potential medicines and other tropical products are destroyed. Nontimber forest products and services include gums, resins, latex, nuts, fruits, spices, and a vast range of medicinal and pharmaceutically useful biochemicals (Panayotou and Ashton 1992). Some are vital food supplies for forest dwellers, or otherwise essential to their well-being. Exports of these products can also provide important income. The potential benefits of many tropical species are still unknown, though they may be destroyed before we understand their properties.

Indigenous forest dwellers and landless farmers are also directly victimized by tropical deforestation. An estimated 50 million people (half in Southeast Asia) currently inhabit tropical forests; some are hunter-gatherers, more are shifting cultivators. Small bands of cultivators typically burn small clearings in the forest, then plant yams or similar vegetables for 2 to 3 years, before moving to more fertile ground. When forests are invaded for resource extraction and settlement expansion, both kinds of forest dwellers are pushed further toward the margins (if not killed outright). The same fate befalls the poor who grow vegetables in forests because they have no other land or means of subsistence. Labeled "encroachers" when they try to evade forest guards, their impact was minimal when their numbers were few and their cultural capacity to limit population was intact. However, this is now beginning to change. Deforestation begets deforestation, as growing numbers of impoverished forest dwellers continue to cut down the forest unless an alternative means of subsistence is available.

The Extent and Causes of Degradation

The FAO estimates that an average of 15.4 million hectares of tropical forests disappeared per year during the last two decades, a 50 percent increase over the 1970s (World Resources Institute, 1992). Statistics also reveal an annual loss of 4.6 million hectares of rainforest and 6.1 million hectares of moist deciduous forest during the 1980s. Figures were highest in Asia (2.2 million), followed by Latin America and the Caribbean (1.9 million); Brazil and Indonesia each lost 1 million hectares of rainforest per year in that decade. None of these official figures account for the vast acreage of illegal logging that occurs each year (Rodenberg 1992).

Over the past decades, many economists have attempted to analyze the importance of alleged deforestation causes (Dore, Johnston, and Stevens 1997). Such analyses fail to support many of the claims about causal factors, revealing that simple cause-and-effect explanations are rare, and that clear definitions of key terms are still elusive. However, standardized measures of deforestation are also rare, further complicating research efforts (Palo, Merey, and Salmi 1987; Phantumvanit and Panayotou 1990; Allen and Barnes 1986; Capistrano and Kiker 1995).

The general causes of deforestation would seem simple—forests are destroyed for settlements, roads and railways, and agriculture and ranching, as well as through many industrial forestry practices. However, conclusive results are hard to find. In 1993, Burgess determined that roundwood production per capita is correlated with deforestation, but was unable to show whether logging was a by-product of conversion to agriculture or industrialized forestry.

Others have attributed deforestation to social and economic factors such as political turmoil and insecure property rights. Deacon (1994) proposed that such contexts would discourage investment, thus decreasing logging pressures. While he found the hypothesis was not supported, he argued that variables like transportation infrastructure and forest access needed to be coinvestigated. Dore, Johnston, and Stevens (1996) claim that this blurs endogenous and exogenous variables. Arguing that property rights "may be neither necessary nor sufficient to curb deforestation," they point to the privately owned forests of Chile, where deforestation is rapidly accelerating.

Others have focused on the role of economics (including debt), but this evidence is also weak (Kahn and Mcdonald 1995). Dore, Johnston, and Stevens (1997) suggest this may be due to dynamic and recursive causal patterns. In 1994, Dore and Nogueria argued that the initial cause in Brazil was inflation. Interest payments on foreign debt inhibited attempts to improve living conditions for displaced forest dwellers, who then cleared more forests. In a country with extreme disparities in land ownership as well as with chronic inflation and foreign debt, this cycle became permanent.

Ecologists have instead argued that Amazon degradation is caused by agricultural and ranching practices inappropriate for tropical soils. Others have proposed the "hamburger thesis," that tropical cattle ranching expanded to provide beef for the U.S. fast-food industry (Hecht and Cockburn 1989; Myers 1984). The theory does not bear out—the U.S. does not allow the import of fresh Brazilian beef, on grounds that it fails to meet health standards. Instead, the domestic beef market is used to sustain a presence in areas where the Brazilian government is keen to demonstrate sovereignty.

Industrial Forestry and Global Markets

A different explanation is that developing countries will generally use their natural resources to create wealth or reduce debt, in response to global market and investment opportunities. It is well known that industrialized countries have recklessly exploited the resources within their own borders, and have historically appropriated such wealth from poorer countries. However, the importance of tropical forests for biodiversity and climate modulation, tropical-soil fragility, and the difficulty of renewal after industrial logging, lead to different opportunities for tropical nations today, beyond the obvious economic and social factors.

In the past, industrial forestry has not been a major agent of degradation for several reasons. Tropical timber is rarely of the quality needed for construction, though some species are used for high-value decorative purposes. Temperate forests produce much higher quality construction lumber, and Northern producers dominate world markets. Finally, Southern countries have lacked the technology and infrastructure to develop a full-scale industry. However, beginning in the 1960s, changes in pulping technologies, biotechnology, declining stocks in the Northern Hemisphere, and world market conditions changed the potential for industrial forestry in tropical regions.

The first development was the demand for plywood in Japan, whose companies began logging Southeast Asian forests. Forestry in the Philippines, Indonesia, and Papua New Guinea (PNG), as well as on the island of Borneo expanded to supply Japan with plywood. In 1975, Indonesia stopped log exports and created a domestic plywood industry, which eventually became the major world supplier. Log exports continued into the 1990s in PNG and Malaysia.

At the same time, accessible timber in the Northern Hemisphere was in decline, and second-growth forests had not yet matured, or were inadequate. Pulping technologies were being developed that would make hardwoods more valuable. Researchers also developed subspecies of eucalyptus, acacia, albizzia, and other fast-growing trees that could produce high-quality pulp. These developments all led to the creation of tropical plantations, where trees grew to maturity in 7 to 10 years, yielding substantially more pulp, at much lower cost, than northern conifers. These plantations were first established in the 1970s; the countries of the global South began to develop markets by the late 1980s. Several also began to supplant imports with domestic paper products of their own.

Japan emerged from the postwar period as a major paper manufacturer, with an apparently insatiable domestic market demand. Already a major buyer of tropical timber for plywood and decorative purposes, Japan soon became a primary force in these new developments, as a major investor in tropical plantations and mills and as a major market for pulp.

By the mid-1970s, timber plantations began providing pulpwood in several Southern countries. Biotechnology and conventional forestry became major research activities throughout Brazil and in other new centers of production, as these countries attempted to limit the problems associated with plantations. Brazil began by establishing large timber plantations on land earlier sown to other plantation crops; today, these plantations provide increasing quantities of pulp and paper for domestic markets, plus a small but steadily growing quantity for export.

However, in the last decade expansion efforts began converting forested lands to plantation species. Pulp mills are now established throughout Southeast Asia and the Amazon region to supply pulp and paper markets in Japan, Southeast Asia, South America, the United States, and Europe. Both Malaysia and Indonesia explicitly seek to displace tropical forests with species suitable for pulp. Sumatra is home to the world's largest pulp mills, which are gradually transforming their huge natural forest concessions into acacia plantations. Pulp exports from these mills go to paper mills in China, Taiwan, Korea, and India.

The process of logging natural forestlands for new plantations is beginning now in Malaysia, whose forests are being cut mainly by Japanese companies and exported to Japan to be manufactured into plywood. A few timber barons own most concessions, and corruption within the police and government bureaucracies is endemic. The business thrives on cheap wood, lack of inspection or regulation, and export incentives. Malaysia's great dipterocarp forests are almost at an end—deforested for conversion to plantations of fast-growing pulp species.

Plantation development strategies are consistent with growing literacy rates, increased local demand for paper products, and import substitution policies, but the particular means by which timber production and extraction are pursued often directly contradict other social goals. For example,

Indonesia's 1999 Forest Act has been strongly criticized by environmentalists, academics, indigenous peoples, and community leaders for depriving indigenous peoples of customary rights and limiting their forest access. Although the act employs fashionable terms such as *accountability, sustainability,* and *equity,* critics point out that it is wide open to corruption, and that it continues to serve the interests of established logging concessions (Lebel 1999c).

Despite legal restrictions, large-scale logging continues in Cambodia and Myanmar—the military regimes of both countries are implicated (Lebel 1999a, 1999b). Logging (both legal and prohibited) occurs at a rapid pace in the Philippines, much of Central America, and the African tropical regions. Much of Africa is being deforested by pressures associated with civil war, lack of alternative cooking fuels, and urban expansion. The forests of the Amazon have been assaulted by many groups, but industrial forestry companies have made inroads in the past decade. These companies have goals similar to those in Southeast Asia: replacing natural forests with fast-growing species suitable for pulp.

Recent growth of the Chinese pulp and paper industry has been phenomenal, supplied by illegal logging in Myanmar. Thai companies also log in Myanmar, despite a ban in their own nation. Korea and Taiwan have become paper manufacturers as well, though they have no domestic fiber supplies at all. The same may be said for Germany, France, and Italy, who are producing increasing quantities of paper with hardly any fiber supplies of their own. As table 10.1 demonstrates, paper is now being produced in countries with very little or no pulp production capacities, and pulp is being produced in countries that until recently had no pulp-production forests or facilities. While Northern countries are producing more pulp and paper than in the 1970s, their production as a proportion of the total has declined. Though their role as dominant pulp and paper suppliers is losing momentum, these countries are now supplying the engineering services, machinery, chemicals, and construction agents for the new mills being established elsewhere.

The strength of environmental movements in Northern countries has many governments rethinking their approaches to resource exploitation. Apart from the boreal forests in Canada, Northern countries have slowed logging in their remaining forests. The Scandinavian countries supply the paper mills they established in Western Europe from world markets;

Table 10.1
Pulp and paper production (millions tons)

	Pulp		Paper	
	1975	1998	1975	1998
Brazil	*	6.7	*	6.5
Canada	14.8	23.5	9.8	18.7
Chile	*	2	*	*
China	2.9	16.5	3.6	28
Finland	5.2	11.4	4	12.7
France	2.8	2.7	4.1	9.2
Germany	1.5	1.9	5.3	16.3
Indonesia	*	3.4	*	*
Italy	1	*	3.6	8.2
Japan	8.6	10.9	13.6	29.9
Korea	*	*	*	7.7
New Zealand	*	1.4	*	*
Portugal	*	1.7	*	1.1
Spain	*	1.6	1.8	4.2
Sweden	8.3	10.5	4.4	9.9
Taiwan	*	*	*	4.2
United States	36.8	57.9	46.2	85.9

*Volume under 1 million tons.
Source: Pulp and Paper International Fact and Price Book, 1996 and 2000.

U.S. companies have shifted away from the Northwestern states toward the Southeastern pine plantations, but also seek more of their wood supplies from world markets.

Investment, exchange, and consumption patterns also vary by country. Japanese paper companies in search of international fiber sources have purchased shares (usually half or less) in both pulp mills and plantations. Koreans and Taiwanese have followed suit, though on a smaller scale. North American companies are not major international investors in forestry plantations at this point. More common are domestic investor groups (often aided by state banks), who join with Northern partners, or benefit from international development assistance. While Northern multinationals may not dominate anymore, it would be naive to ignore international market pressures, debt, and increasing consumer demands in developing countries. Forestry has become a global industry; countries with forest resources have become economically, politically, and socially integrated into the global marketplace.

International Efforts to Reduce Forest Degradation

In March 2001, President George W. Bush informed the Summit of the Americas in Quebec City that the United States would provide funding for the preservation of tropical forests. Yet this gesture is not likely to reduce tropical forest degradation—there have been many international efforts to limit deforestation over the years, yet only a few have been effective.

The Convention on International Trade in Endangered Species of Wild Fauna and Flora (CITES), initially negotiated in 1973, has since been adopted by 167 countries. Though not designed to save forests, it has supported conservation of some endangered tree species. Unfortunately, the effect has sometimes been to shift pressures onto other marketable species.

International Forest Reserves were first proposed by the UNESCO *Man in the Biosphere* program and other organizations in the 1980s. These have provided some protection for biodiversity, but have done little to save larger ecological systems, because these reserves have met neither the ecological nor the social needs of poor countries. An alternative would be for wealthy countries to fund the establishment of reserves (Rubinoff 1982).

The International Tropical Timber Agreement (ITTA), signed in 1983, was a binding agreement between the consumers and producers of tropical timber, under the umbrella of the International Tropical Timber Organization (ITTO). The agreement established international guidelines for sustainable management of tropical forests and plantations. However, the viability of tropical-forest management has not been proven, given the fragility of the soils and the nonregenerative capacities of nature in equatorial climates (Johnson and Cabarle 1993; Goodland et al. 1990; Colchester 1990). Due for renegotiation in 1994, the agreement broke down when consuming nations were unwilling to accept trade restrictions and refused to donate new funds. While eventually an agreement was reached, the ITTA remained limited in its scope.

The Tropical Forestry Action Program (TFAP), devised in the mid-1980s by the UN Development Program (UNDP), the World Bank, and the World Resources Institute, was to rehabilitate, manage, replant, and preserve forests around the world. The United States and other donors contributed funding, though never as much as originally anticipated (Sizer 1996). The program was designed to help countries establish timber plantations, in order to reduce pressures to log natural forests. The organizers argued that their efforts would reduce encroachment, enrich degraded soils, save forests, and provide foreign-exchange earnings to impoverished tropical countries. Because they did not expect these nations to log natural forests before establishing plantations, they failed to guard against such an outcome. Nor did they anticipate the sovereignty and development concerns at odds with international interest in environmental management. By the 1990s, the program was in disarray, and funding had dwindled (Oksanen et al. 1993; Colchester and Lohman 1990).

Several other initiatives were proposed at the 1992 UNCED Conference in Rio. A nonbinding set of principles was negotiated, including Chapter 11 on Forestry (in Agenda 21). The Framework Convention on Climate Change promotes reforestation and advises against deforestation; the Convention to Combat Desertification was signed in 1994. Funding mechanisms were put in place to implement Agenda 21 and the conventions on a Global Environment Facility (GEF) and Capacity 21 of the UNDP, including forestry programs in developing countries. While many have expressed concern for deforestation, a binding convention has not been possible, because governments fear the loss of control over their own resources or trade policies. Also, large-scale funding has yet to emerge.

Elsewhere, the so-called Montreal Process established protocols for assessing sustainability in temperate and boreal forests. Uruguay and Argentina subsequently joined Australia, Canada, Chile, China, Japan, the Republic of Korea, Mexico, New Zealand, Russia, and the United States as signatories to a comprehensive set of seven criteria of sustainable forest management, with sixty-seven indicators to assess progress. While quantitative measures were deemed possible for some topics, there remain many for which quantitative measures are inappropriate or otherwise elusive (e.g., social sustainability and some aspects of biodiversity). Nevertheless, this is a beginning to the process of creating systematic assessment criteria for forests, deforestation, degradation, and community participation.

The Forest Stewardship Council (FSC), consisting of representatives from indigenous peoples, business, NGOs, and the scientific community, was established in the mid-1990s to influence forestry management in North America and Europe. Many tropical countries have since become interested in certification. However, caution is advised, because alternative stewardship programs have been developed that are less stringent and universal agreement on the definition of sustainable forestry remains elusive.

Such international initiatives have put tropical forestry on the agenda, increasing problem awareness and pressuring both consuming and exporting countries to devise solutions. But growing demand for wood and paper products (domestic and international) and developmental challenges have exerted enormous pressures on tropical countries to use their forests to generate income.

Other Suggested Alternatives

While these international efforts have been unable to deliver solutions, several alternative strategies have been suggested (summarized in Marchak 1995): log export bans, increased prices for tropical wood, increased logging costs, and import bans.

The experiences of both Indonesia and Thailand have shown that log export bans lead either to increased domestic production (an improvement for local investors and workers) or increased illegal logging—they do not halt logging. Bans are unrealistic unless accompanied by strategies to increase wealth through other activities.

Market forces will eventually cause the price of tropical wood to rise, but there is no guarantee that this would occur before tropical forests are biologically decimated. However, it is unclear whether an artificial price increase would reduce deforestation, since each extracted tree would simply add to overall profits. Such a price increase may reduce pressures to replace forests with plantations, inasmuch as natural woods take on more value.

If governments asserted their rights to public lands, they could, at least theoretically, increase the stumpage rate for logging. If the cost increased substantially, the cost might inhibit industrial activity. But since governments also seek short-term rents and have colluded with extractive industries in the past, they are unlikely to increase costs beyond the profit-seeking elasticity range for logging companies. The same is true in temperate regions today.

Environmental organizations have won a reprieve for what remains of the temperate forests in my own region of the world (British Columbia, Canada), by campaigning in Europe against the purchase of logs from unsustainable logging operations. Market controls began to work once campaigners convinced importers to buy wood only if it met certified standards. Importers were so affected that some forestry companies changed their logging methods, phasing out clear-cutting and agreeing not to log particularly fragile or ecologically unique areas. However, British Columbia (like much of the Northern conifer-production regions) is no longer price-competitive with Southern plantations—land, resource, and labor costs are far higher, yields are smaller, and regrowth cycles are much, much longer. In any event, other industries have supplanted forestry as a major source of regional income, creating a very different context from the developing forest regions of the global South.

Import bans may work for certain high-value, decorative species, provided potential buyers could be persuaded to do without teak, mahogany, or ebony wood. Yet many of these trees are logged illegally, and few countries are likely to halt illegal operations, given that international demand would be unlikely to disappear. Moreover, countries that have developed carefully managed plantations of such species should not be punished for their efforts. Import bans may make the consumer-country populations feel virtuous, but they often harm exporting countries, without stopping the decimation.

Economic Development and Management

Bans, plans, promises, good intentions, and international pressures have not broken the cycle of degradation in tropical forests. The final alternative is to accept the fact that these lands are important economic resources to developing nations (as they have been throughout the developed world). Preservation of small areas may be feasible, but conservation will best be achieved through resource management that allows for plantations and limited agriculture to sustain growing populations. This can only work if land-tenure systems are substantially changed in most tropical countries. For example, Brazil has encouraged the poor to settle the Amazon because no land is available for them elsewhere. The movement of poor populations into areas unsuited to agriculture is a function of the inequality of land-holding practices and policies, not of overpopulation.

Though plantations have had many ecological problems attributed to them, they are a good alternative when established on already-marginalized lands with semistable soil conditions. However, portraying plantations as universal solutions is unrealistic. Apart from growing domestic and international demand for pulp, plantations do not provide fuelwood or subsistence for the poor; alternative supplies would have to found or these social problems will persist. Experiments are underway in both Southeast Asia and Brazil to grow subsistence crops beneath plantation tree species and plant small woodlots for fuel.

Integrated Forest Management

As is clear from the inadequacies of the efforts described here, no simple scheme to limit tropical-forest degradation is likely to be successful. The alternative is to develop integrated ecosystem-based management approaches to all forest uses (and abuses): agriculture, forestry, mining, recreation, and nontimber industries. International and national government programs to reduce poverty and improve conditions for aboriginal and landless people are essential. Grainger (1993, 179) makes a case for making forestry and agriculture more productive and sustainable, and to stop the eviction of shifting cultivators (indigenous people who plant crops for short period) from their forest homes. With respect to managed plantations, he recommends the establishment of agroforestry systems where subsistence crops are grown along with plantation species (known throughout Asia as the *taungya* system).

Many tropical researchers oppose the practice of cattle ranching in Amazonia. Others have argued against oligarchic (including military) control of land and of potential plantation areas in Africa and Asia. Virtually all writers have argued strongly against land-tenure systems that privilege wealthy minorities, displacing poor and indigenous peoples and leaving them without land or other means of subsistence (Westoby 1989). Such systemic injustices not only punish the marginalized, but reduce a country's potential, because these peoples are prevented from legally participating in the process of development.

Conclusion

In summary, none of the international projects so far devised and none of the suggested solutions—short of land-tenure reform and the redistribution of benefits—are likely to succeed in stopping tropical degradation. Many causes lie beyond market forces, but even where market-based approaches are possible, developing countries cannot be expected to put forest conservation ahead of their own economic interests, especially when the Northern countries have only recently (and marginally) begun to do so.

If the international community were genuinely concerned about the ecological security of tropical forests (which is, after all, a global issue), their optimum contribution would come in the form of technical as well as material aid for integrated forest management, guided by domestic policies to enable the displaced poor to obtain land or other means of survival. Plantations are inevitable. Skilled management of these plantations to preserve soils, reduce atmospheric and hydrological impacts, and offset the dangers of monocultures would be in the best interest of companies hoping to benefit from long-term development.

11

Biodiversity and Ecological Security

David W. Inouye

Biodiversity is a term coined so recently (1985) that it was not in use when the *Global 2000 Report* (Barney 1980) was prepared. Although people had begun to consider the environmental pressures and associated problems created by human overpopulation, such as the loss of wildlife habitats and possible extinctions, there was far less emphasis on these topics or their ramifications than one would see if the report were being written today. But though *biodiversity* was not part of the scientific or popular vocabularies in the late 1970s, its importance was clearly suggested in the opening paragraph of the *Global 2000 Report*: "Serious stresses involving population, resources, and environment are clearly visible ahead" (p. 1).

Biodiversity: The Richness of Life

Biodiversity may be a relatively new concept, but it has already worked its way into public discourse. Biologists define the term more broadly than most laypersons, because the concept encompasses diversity at many levels, from genetic variation, through arrays of species, to arrays of genera, families, and higher orders of organization, and even to the diversity of ecosystems (Wilson 1992). Thus, biodiversity refers to the variety of life in all forms, from viruses and bacteria to plants and animals, and at all levels of organization. Sometimes the ecological and evolutionary processes that generate, maintain, and benefit from this diversity are also included in definitions of biodiversity; accordingly, it is useful to differentiate structural biodiversity (species and populations) from functional biodiversity (the variety of interactions among those species) (Hunter 1996).

A sobering indication of the state of our biodiversity knowledge is suggested by the fact that we do not know how many species there are on the planet. Estimates have ranged from 5 to 50 million (with a consensus of maybe 12.5), but only about 1.5 million species have been named by taxonomists. These estimates are much higher than those of the *Global 2000 Report*, reflecting two additional decades of research. The primary reason for the rapid growth of the field of conservation biology is concern for potentially large-scale biodiversity losses, from genetic variation within species, to the species level and higher, including possibly even the ecosystem services (Daily 1997) provided by the current biodiversity.

The Importance of Biodiversity

Biodiversity has both utilitarian and nonutilitarian value. The former includes economic value (Hanemann 1986), which can be difficult to quantify (Norton 1986). How is it possible to place a monetary value on a particular species or habitat? The emergence of ecotourism—including tours to see mountain gorillas in Rwanda, coral reefs and rainforests in the tropics, or penguins in Antarctica—attests to this economic value. The widespread harvest of wildlife resources, for example through recreational fisheries or big-game hunting, points to the economic value of such resources, which bring millions of dollars each year to local communities. Utilitarian benefits also include the value to the economy of medicines derived from various species, and the benefits to agriculture of the genetic diversity of wild relatives of our crops.

The nonutilitarian values of biodiversity can include the aesthetic value associated with plant or animal species we consider beautiful, which is underscored by the effort we put into collecting them in places such as zoos, aquariums, and arboretums. The increasing attempts of some religious groups to addres the significance of biodiversity loss reflect a recognition of the existence value of species. Independently of how one thinks those species came to be (e.g., evolution, creation, or another mechanism), the efforts to preserve them are testimony to the importance we have begun to assign to preventing their extinction.

Perhaps less widely recognized, but just as important economically, is the value of genetic biodiversity as a source of variation for plant and animal breeding. This form of diversity helped to create the productivity of modern farming, and is a continuing source of new genes for improvements in growth rates, disease resistance, and fecundity. If we someday manage to create a perennial corn variety, or disease-free crops, it will likely be due in large part to use of the genetic diversity found in the wild relatives of those crops. An interesting story about the collection of a wild tomato from Peru and its subsequent use in plant breeding is told by Iltis (1986); he estimated the cost of the collection at $42 and the potential value of the traits found in that plant at $8 million per year. A similar example involves the discovery of a wild relative of corn in Mexico that has disease-resistance and perennial-growth traits that could be tremendously valuable if they can be transferred to domesticated corn (Wilson 1992).

A more globally significant aspect of biodiversity is ecosystem services, which emerge from the interaction of plant and animal species and the physical environment. Again, such functions were presaged in the *Global 2000 Report:* "The environment will have lost important life-supporting capabilities" (Barney 1980, 39). Scientists have since developed long lists of life-support services that intact ecosystems provide (Daily 1997), and have even tried to put a dollar figure on their value. Such services include the purification of water and air, regeneration of soil fertility, flood control, and the detoxification and decomposition of wastes.

In 1996, the New York City water department chose to enhance ecosystem services by spending $1.5 billion to preserve the Catskill and Delaware watersheds, rather than the $6 billion needed to construct a new water-treatment system (Daily and Ellison 2002). The ecosystem services provided by these enhanced watersheds include the cleansing, collection, and storage of water. Freshwater ecosystems also provide nonextractive benefits such as recreation, transportation, flood control, and habitat for birds and other wildlife, and can help to dilute or remove pollutants (e.g., wetlands can transform, detoxify, or sequester wastes) (Postel and Carpenter 1997).

Another ecosystem service that has only recently begun receiving attention is pollination. Although scientists have not completely cataloged all of the species that function as pollinators, over 100,000 invertebrate species (e.g., bees, moths, butterflies, flies, beetles) and 1,000 vertebrate species (e.g., birds, mammals, even reptiles) known to pollinate flowering plants have been identified (Nabhan and Buchmann 1997). Around 90 percent of the estimated 250,000 species of flowering plants (Heywood 1993) require the services of pollinators for sexual reproduction. Pollinators are essential to the production of over 150 food crops in the United States; their economic value has been estimated at more than $8 billion for managed honeybees (in the absence of native pollinators), and $4 to $6 billion for other pollinators (Nabhan and Buchmann 1997). Unfortunately, many of these species are in decline (Allen-Wardell et al. 1998). North American honeybee populations have been declining over the past decade (following the appearance of parasitic mites), forcing the agricultural industry and others to recognize the economic importance of native pollinators (honeybees were introduced from Europe). Other pollinator losses follow from pesticide poisoning and the invasion of Africanized honeybees, but even more common factors are habitat loss and fragmentation, which jeopardize both nesting areas and the floral resources needed by pollinators.

Pollinators and the services they provide are a good example of how interlinked biodiversity issues can be. Pollination has played an important role in the evolution of much of the diversity of flowering plants and could be considered a keystone service in both human-managed and natural ecosystems.[1] Without pollinators, flowers may not be able to produce the fruits and seeds that support many animal species, or to maintain the mutualistic relationships between plants and their seed dispersers. This is only one of many ecosystem services that depend on the maintenance of existing biodiversity and that are threatened by its loss.

Yet another benefit of biodiversity may be its link to ecosystem stability (resistance to disturbance). The ecological consequences of biodiversity changes are not well known, but the potential for biodiversity losses to affect ecosystem processes has spurred recent research in this area. For example, several studies have focused on the effect of plant-community diversity on productivity (Tilman 1999; McCann 2000). There is also some evidence that more diverse plant communities have increased resistance to invasion by weedy species (Naeem et al. 2000).

Threats to Biodiversity

Many biologists believe we are in the midst of a mass extinction, rivaling any in the planet's geological history. As human populations grow, we are losing not only individual species, but also genetic diversity within populations, and even entire ecosystems. Noss, LaRoe, and Scott (1995) reported that in the United States alone, more than 30 ecosystem types were critically endangered (i.e., suffered more than 98 percent loss of the original size). Another 58 ecosystems types were considered endangered and 38 threatened. The World Conservation Union's Red List of Threatened Species now encompasses at least one of every eight plant species in the world, and almost a third of those in the United States (IUCN, 2000). Of the 16,000 plant species native to the United States, 13 are known to have gone extinct in past 200 years; 125 more have not been seen for many years, and some 700 are threatened or endangered. Similar stories can be told for animal species, both globally and within the United States.

The principal causes of such biodiversity loss are diverse, but all can be traced ultimately to the growth and resource use of a single species—our own. The range of threats include habitat loss (including whole eco-systems), fragmentation (splitting once-large habitats into small, separated pieces), overharvesting of natural resources (plant and animal), the effects of invasive species, and most recently (and perhaps most universal), global climate change.

Most species of plants and animals have somewhat specific habitat requirements, and many have relatively narrow geographic ranges. If those habitats are significantly altered (or disappear), the biodiversity they harbor can be placed at risk. Habitats can be very small areas, such as a single spring, or as large as a whole biome, the largest habitat category, which can be continental in scope. At all scales, we can find examples where human activities have placed biodiversity at risk.

Even when pieces of habitat remain intact, they may be reduced to a size too small to maintain viable populations of some of their original inhabitants. The fragmentation of previously larger habitats is likely the primary reason for the demise of much biodiversity today, as humans have expanded into previously undisturbed areas in quest of natural resources and arable land. Fragmentation can disrupt foraging patterns as well as the dispersal of plant and animal species, reduce populations to the point where inbreeding becomes an issue, and increase the likelihood of local or even global species extinctions.

Overharvesting is another threat that affects both individual species and whole ecosystems. In the past, we have seen the collapse of fisheries (e.g., California sardines, Northern Atlantic cod); species extinction from overhunting (e.g., passenger pigeons and heath hens); desertification due to overgrazing; and the loss of commercially viable populations of some animal and plant species (e.g., Ecuador's sea cucumber fishery, or the localized loss of wild ginseng). Only rarely has a fishery ever been sustainable; fishing methods may cause significant ecosystem-level habitat disturbance (Pauly et al. 2002). Much of this harm is attributable to what has been called the "tragedy of the commons," by which communally owned natural resources are highly vulnerable to degradation or loss through overuse (Hardin 1968; Hardin and Baden 1977).

We have only recently become aware of the threats posed to biodiversity by both the intended and unintended introduction of plant and animal species to areas where they are not native. Introduced species have contributed to the decline of 42 percent of endangered and threatened species in the United States; we have transplanted some 50,000 species around the world, many introduced for landscaping, erosion control, range forage, and other uses.[2] Invasive species also threaten commercial food and fiber production; associated economic costs run into the billions of dollars each year.[3] Some 900 such plant species have been identified in the United States alone, covering 10 million acres. These nonnatives disrupt ecosystems throughout the United States, competing with indigenous insects, birds, and other wildlife for sources of food and shelter, and replacing and eliminating native species and their habitats. Invasives are also known to disrupt plant-animal associations such as pollination, seed dispersal, and host-plant relationships, to alter ecological processes such as plant succession, to change the frequency and intensity of natural fires, and to have hydrological and other significant impacts (Mack et al. 2000). Weed control is another problem associated with invasive exotic plants. Consider, for example, the problems associated with kudzu in the Southeastern United States, or the invasion of tamarisk (salt cedar) in the Southwest.

The most recently recognized threat to biodiversity that has human origins is global warming. Climate change may put whole ecosystems at risk, as temperatures rise and precipitation patterns change. Species in these ecosystems may be unable to migrate to higher latitudes or altitudes, in order to maintain themselves within the climate zones to which they are adapted; intricate evolved relationships between plants and animals (e.g., pollination and seed dispersal) may break down. Significant extinctions may result from this kind of disruption.

Another significant aspect of global warming is the consequent rise in sea levels. It has been reported that the Chesapeake and Delaware bays (the two largest estuaries in the Eastern United States) have already lost significant areas of marshland due to sea-level rise, and that all coastal marshes in these bays could disappear before 2100 (Kearney et al. 2002). Such loss significantly affects food chains and the productivity of fisheries in those estuaries, but also impacts water quality and increases the quantity of carbon being released to the atmosphere.

Perhaps the most serious long-term threat to biodiversity is the effect of human activities on the evolutionary potential of existing and new species. Many forces that have contributed to natural selection in the past (leading to the current biodiversity) have been irrevocably altered. Removal of predators, reduced population sizes (and associated genetic variation), and habitat destruction, fragmentation, and isolation all affect natural selection in ways that may be detrimental to the long-term survival of a species (Soulé 1980). The behavioral and physiological traits most suited for life in nature preserves, arboretums, aquariums, or zoos may not be conducive to survival in the wild, or to adaptation to a changing environment.

The Future: Biodiversity and Environmental Security

There are many signs that biological resources are in short supply and may become the source of future conflicts. Both domestic and international conflicts have already occurred over fisheries. In Japan, competition among fishermen—in a great many instances motivated more by economics than pride—is intense and the disregarding of official regulations and lawbreaking more frequent and flagrant (Ruddle 1987). In Canada, conflicts over fisheries are well documented (Dobell and Longo 1996); the collapse of the Atlantic cod fishery (Harris 1998) and the turbot war between Canada and Spain (Matthew 2002) are examples where disputes over the access to fish populations has threatened to end in violence. Beginning in the 1960s, technological innovations allowed the exploitation of deepwater ocean fisheries, some of which were spectacularly successful; 40 percent of the world's trawling fisheries now operate in waters beyond the continental shelves (Roberts 2002). However, the economic viability of most of these fisheries has been short-lived, because these slow-growing fish populations are easily overexploited. In less than a decade, the stock of orange roughy near New Zealand and Australia collapsed to less than 20 percent of its preexploitation density. The Patagonian toothfish (often marketed as "Chilean sea bass") is another example of a recently discovered but already threatened deepwater fishery.[4] These slow-growing fish can live up to 50 years, not reproducing until they are 10. They now face commercial extinction within 5 years because of (mainly illegal) overfishing.

A similar tale could be told about timber resources. A driving force for the deforestation that threatens much of the tropics is the growing demand for timber, although much forest destruction can also be blamed on slash-and-burn agriculture. We have already cut about 50 percent of the world's closed-canopy tropical rainforests, and by some estimates the current rates of removal will leave only scattered remnants by 2025, except for parts of the Amazon Basin and Central Africa. The loss of this habitat, which houses an estimated 3–7 million species of plants and animals, would be devastating for the planet's biodiversity.

When countries exhaust domestic supplies, they may turn to other places for resources. For example, Asiatic ginseng (*Panax ginseng*) was extirpated by overharvesting in its natural habitats centuries ago. Deprived of a plant so important to their traditional medicine, the Chinese began looking for alternatives. American ginseng (*Panax quinquefolius*) is a small herbaceous plant that grows in the understory of the Eastern deciduous forests of North America. Prior to 1900, American ginseng was harvested from the wild and exported primarily to China, Hong Kong, and Korea. Though the United States began to export cultivated ginseng by the early twentieth century (Carlson 1985), the price of wild roots is substantially higher. Consequently, a large volume of wild ginseng is still traded internationally, and the health of wild populations of American ginseng is uncertain. This led the Convention on International Trade in Endangered Species of Wild Fauna and Flora (CITES) to list American ginseng in 1975. Ginseng is only one small example of how economic forces may threaten biodiversity.

Protecting Biodiversity

How much biodiversity ought to be conserved, and where should it be conserved? This issue has ecological, economic, and political dimensions. Should we attempt to preserve all biodiversity? Most of it? Only the "most" valuable? How would we define such value? We clearly lack the financial resources (and the political will) to protect all biodiversity. From an ecological perspective, progress has been made in identifying the means to preserve the most biodiversity with limited funds, by identifying regions and locales of greatest diversity.

One approach that has been suggested is to attempt to preserve representatives of all ecosystem and habitat types. Toward this end, the World Wildlife Fund has tried to identify the world's most outstanding examples of each major habitat type (Olson and Dinerstein 1998). Preservation of these habitats would maintain species diversity, while preserving distinct ecosystems and their ecological processes. Rather than identifying areas based on political boundaries, ecoregions were used as a unit of analysis; worldwide, 233 have been identified with outstanding biodiversity and representation values. These included terrestrial, freshwater, and marine habitats. Forty-seven percent of the terrestrial ecoregions are considered critical or endangered, 29 percent vulnerable, and 24 percent relatively stable or intact. Although data for temperate freshwater habitats were harder to find, most of these habitats face some threat, from pollution, dams, or invasive exotics. The same is true of many marine areas, which are threatened by habitat destruction and overfishing.

Another approach (championed by Conservation International) has been to identify "hotspots" of biological diversity, to be targeted for preservation. Hotspots are defined as areas rich in biodiversity and under imminent threat of destruction. Twenty-five hotspots have been identified, comprising only 1.4 percent of the earth's land surface, but containing 44 percent of vascular plant species and 35 percent of all vertebrate groups (birds, mammals, reptiles, and amphibians). Myers et al. (2000) have estimated that an average of $20 million per hotspot per year, or $500 million annually, could preserve much of this biodiversity; this is contrasted with an estimated $300 billion required annually to protect biodiversity worldwide. The fact that most of these hotspots are found in the world's less affluent regions, some of which are areas of political tension, focuses attention on political aspects of biodiversity conservation.

Biodiversity and Ecological Security

The interaction of human population growth and commercial exploitation of endangered and threatened species may have unanticipated consequences for human health. One hypothesis for the origin of the HIV/AIDS epidemic is that it resulted from the infection of hunters who had killed chimpanzees. A subspecies of chimpanzee in west-central Africa carries a simian immunodeficiency virus (SIV); it has been suspected that HIV may have emerged when hunters came into contact with chimpanzee blood. Similar SIVs occur in other primates in Africa, raising the possibility of these diseases moving to humans as a consequence of the large and growing trade in bushmeat.[5] Similarly, it is thought that some outbreaks of the Ebola virus may be a consequence of contact with infected chimpanzees and gorillas through the bushmeat trade.

The human population reached 6.3 billion in 2003—more than 1 billion of these have been added since 1988. For comparison, consider that it took about 4 million years to reach the first billion mark, and that the United Nations predicts that by 2050 we will have added another 3 billion. There is uncertainty about how much longer the population will continue to expand, but one model suggests an 85 percent chance that growth will stop by 2100, and a 60 percent probability that we will not exceed 10 billion people before that time (Lutz, Sanderson, and Scherbov 2001). Although it is reassuring that there may be a foreseeable end to the recent rapid growth of the human population, it seems likely that in the coming decades we will see severe conflicts over resources ranging from space, to food, and even to water—with dire ramifications for much of our biodiversity.

Reasons for Optimism

Perhaps the foremost cause for optimism has been the response of biologists to the threat of biodiversity loss, highlighted by the emergence and growth of the discipline of conservation biology. The first international conference in this new field was held in 1978, and the first book on the topic appeared the same year as the *Global 2000 Report* (Soulé and Wilcox 1980). There are now scores of textbooks, journals, websites, and organizations devoted to conservation biology. In the past decade, more than thirty new graduate-level programs have appeared, and courses in the field have been added to the curricula at most colleges and universities (Jacobsen 1990).

This new research is beginning to bear fruit, as we begin to identify what factors put biodiversity at risk, and how to manage resource use in order to minimize biodiversity loss. For example, recent research on fisheries has shown how the establishment of reserves benefits fishing in adjacent areas (Roberts et al. 2001). Work on the impact of coffee plantations has suggested ways coffee can be grown while promoting bird diversity (Greenberg et al. 1997). The consequences of fragmentation are being recognized (Saunders, Hobbs, and Margules 1991) and the use of habitat corridors to minimize negative effects is being investigated (Beier and Noss 1998). The impacts of roads and road building have also been studied (Trombulak and Frissell 2000), and efforts to preserve wilderness areas are underway.

Biologists are also becoming more politically aware and active, as is evidenced by the Washington offices opened by the Ecological Society of America and the Society for Conservation Biology. Prominent biologists are devoting significant effort to educating the press, the public, and politicians about the value of biodiversity and threats to it. Collaborative efforts between academics, nongovernmental organizations, government agencies, and industry are evident in projects such as the North American Pollinator Protection Campaign,[6] a group of more than forty affiliated organizations that seek to encourage and help coordinate efforts at pollinator conservation.

There is also a growing public and political awareness of threats to biodiversity and its real value. The belief that biodiversity (at all levels) is a heritage that should be preserved, for both utilitarian and nonutilitarian reasons, has become more common. While it may be easy to support the biodiversity of charismatic species such as blue whales, giant pandas, whooping cranes, and tigers, realization that even the loss and fragmentation of habitat leads to a loss of biodiversity is gradually spreading beyond the circle of professional conservation biologists.

The 1992 Earth Summit in Rio de Janeiro lifted the idea of sustainable development (which has many implications for biodiversity) onto the world political agenda. At that conference, 158 countries signed the Convention on Biodiversity; it has since been ratified by 166 countries (the United States is not among them). The convention requires signatories to take action to protect biodiversity and to use it sustainably; many have subsequently generated action plans to protect habitats and species. Although funding for implementation of such programs has been insufficient, the convention is likely to remain a significant driving force for protection of biodiversity.

The field of economics is also beginning to consider the problem of biodiversity loss. One indicator of this is the development of the field of ecological economics, which now has its own society, journal, and graduate programs. As we find better ways to value biodiversity and ecosystem services, it may become easier to convince people that these warrant conservation. The rise of green consumerism, which encourages consumers to purchase products that are grown or harvested in ecologically sustainable ways even when they cost more, is another sign of increased recognition of a link between biodiversity and economics (Hardner and Rice 2002). These efforts have been particularly directed toward timber, but one can also buy coffee, cocoa, and beef that are certified as having been produced in ways that promote biodiversity protection. Conservationists have also begun to recognize the possibility of using "conservation concessions" to protect biodiversity, outbidding logging companies for timber concessions that are auctioned off by governments needing to generate income (Hardner and Rice 2002). Daily has collected several examples of how economic incentives can be used to further conservation efforts (Daily and Ellison 2002).

Recognition of the importance of the ecosystem services provided by biodiversity is also indicated by the 2001 launching of a four-year Millennium Ecosystem Assessment. The goal of this project is to research ecosystem conditions and the effects of the changes they are undergoing, as well as to identify response options. It is hoped this effort will improve understanding of the linkages between ecosystems and the goods and services they offer, and provide a scientific underpinning for national and international programs that address environment and development changes. Economic analysis is an important part of this program.

There may also be a growing recognition that we need to address the causes of problems associated with biodiversity loss rather than just the symptoms. Ultimately, human overpopulation and excessive consumption (with the United States leading the list of consumers) are fundamental threats to biodiversity. Political, philosophical, anthropological, social, and economic factors are as important as biology in the conservation of biodiversity.

Conclusions

Discussions of national or global security have been in flux since the end of the Cold War, as ideas about threats apart from warfare have been introduced as part of the reframing of conventional categories of security (Dalby 2002). One such shift has been to include ecological considerations, including reductions in biological diversity, as human security concerns, as formalized in a 1994 report from the UN Development Program (1994). In that same year, the Environmental Change and Security Project of the Woodrow Wilson International Center for Scholars opened in Washington, DC. The project is an example of how scholars are exploring the links between factors such as population growth, biodiversity, resource depletion, and degradation of ecosystems, and their implications for conflict, security issues, and foreign policy. Given the rapid pace of contemporary globalization, it may not be surprising that biodiversity was still an invisible issue to policymakers in the 1980s. Today, as part of international policy discussions and programs, biodiversity is a global security issue that must be considered by both states and individuals in the future.

How should we decide where to conserve biodiversity and what parts of it to protect? How should economic assistance for biodiversity conservation be obtained and disbursed? What is the economic value of biodiversity, and who should benefit from it? In the near future it will become increasingly important to answer these questions; they will need to be resolved if we are to minimize or prevent future conflicts related to biodiversity. There are promising signs that the value of biodiversity is being increasingly recognized, that greater effort is being devoted to its identification and protection, and that these efforts will have benefits for the ecological security of all states and their citizens.

Notes

1. See http://esa.sdsc.edu/ecoservices.
2. See www.nps.gov/plants/alien/apwgaction.htm.
3. See www.esa.sdsc.edu/invas3.htm.
4. See http://news.nationalgeographic.com/news/2002/05/0522_020522_seabass.html.
5. See www.bushmeat.org.
6. See www.nappc.org.

12

Twenty-Nine Days: Responding to a Finite World

Ken Cousins

Understanding the natural world and humanity's role in it is a difficult task, one that has changed dramatically as we have increased our capacity to alter the world to our own ends. We have learned of the world's ecological limitations, even as our impacts on ecosystems and species continue to grow. All of the authors in this book have noted the difficulties inherent in attempting to create sustainable societies, and have revealed some of the complexities of our interactions with nature. While each has acknowledged the ecological factors that directly affect our survival, each has also emphasized the importance of social values and institutions.

Environmental policies are the principal means by which societies attempt to adapt to ecological constraints, and to mediate between competing demands and values. Yet translating ecological knowledge into anticipatory policy has proven difficult, for several reasons. Perhaps most important, scarcity and the irreversibility of many investments will always constrain the range of policies possible in a given context. Our ability to overcome such inertia is challenged even more by the complexity of most ecological and social systems, which make forecasting difficult under the best of conditions. Moreover, though policies may be developed at regional, national, or global levels, local implementation requires commitment across a multitude of ecologically and socially heterogeneous settings. Since effective policies must be grounded in an awareness of local conditions, expanded participation will be critical to achieving sustainable solutions to ecological challenges.

Then and Now

Although the "IPAT" framework, first introduced by Paul Ehrlich and John Holdren in 1971, explicitly addressed both affluence and technology (but not distribution), most analysts (including Ehrlich and Holdren) have tended to focus on the environmental impacts of population. In *The Limits to Growth*, these effects focused on understanding what might happen if demand increased against a stable resource base (Meadows et al. 1972). Accordingly, the analysis focused on population and capital dynamics, both aggregated at the global level. Though functional ecosystems were considered important for food production and waste absorption, that project emphasized limiting both population and economic growth. In the years following its publication, the project was criticized as ignoring the potential of market forces and innovation (Day and Koenig 1975; Poquet 1978). However, while careers have been made attacking the various projections of *The Limits to Growth* (e.g., Simon 1980, 1981, 1996; Simon and Kahn 1984), most of the original projections remain on track (Meadows, Randers, and Meadows 2004). Only in the next few decades will we be able to know whether the concerns of Meadows et al. were fully justified.

As Pirages says in chapter 1 of this book, the *Global 2000 Report to the President* also tended toward the scarcity-focused reasoning of *The Limits to Growth*. Demands on agriculture, forests, and water supplies were projected to approach critical levels by the turn of the century, again principally driven by the demands of a growing global population (Barney 1980). Although many of the substantive issues addressed by both *The Limits to Growth* and the *Global 2000 Report* did overlap, the latter focused more directly on policy issues, addressing sectoral issues (e.g., tropical forests) that the first effort had subsumed under the broad heading of renewable resources.

Perhaps the most prescient observation in the *Global 2000 Report* concerned the future importance of carbon dioxide buildup. While the current consensus is that anthropogenic sources of greenhouse gases are a real threat to future climate stability, reaching such a conclusion in the late 1970s exhibited great foresight, as Park points out. Even though *The Limits to Growth* had included a generalized model of environmental waste absorption, few could have anticipated then that a truly global-level sink would be significantly affected by human activities.

New Challenges and New Solutions

Even as advances in science and technology have enabled us to perceive and understand the world with greater subtlety, they have also introduced new, less tangible threats. While most of these may be exacerbated by a rising human population and increasing consumption, many are difficult to understand as a function of scarcity. Perhaps most surprising are the unexpected problems associated with successful control of population growth. Here, both chapters on population offer persuasive evidence that reduced growth rates have created serious challenges to public policy. For aging societies, the combination of fewer births and deaths presents an unexpected variation on the classic model of demographic transition (Kirk 1996). But as several authors also note, other societies have achieved lower growth rates only through the crushing burden of HIV/AIDS. Again, although dramatic shifts in population structures can be expected to have significant (though indeterminate) ecological impacts, such dynamics are difficult to interpret simply in terms of resource scarcity.

In 1980, the economist Julian Simon convinced Paul Ehrlich (an entomologist) to place a wager on the future price of five metals. Many of the neo-Malthusian predictions of the preceding decades had focused on such nonrenewable resources; a steady rise in the prices of these metals in the immediate postwar years led Ehrlich and Holdren (as well as physicist John Harte) to accept the bet, despite their belief that limits were more likely to be seen in the growing demand on renewable resources and ecological services (Holdren, Ehrlich, and Ehrlich 1980). Simon's confidence was based on his absolute faith in two economic and technological processes: dematerialization and substitution (although some suggested that the early 1980s recession also served to drive prices down). After losing on four of the metals (copper prices had actually risen 10 percent over that period), Ehrlich and biologist Stephen Schneider offered another wager, this time emphasizing global ecological indicators and the availability of renewable resources (Ehrlich and Schneider 1995). Simon refused, claiming he was only interested in direct measures of human welfare. While their differences may have been more than intellectual, the shifting focus of their decades-long debate reveals important lessons for both sides. First, it is often possible to reduce our demand for a given resource through dematerialization and substitution. Second, while alternatives may exist for many resources, these are not always economically or socially feasible. Third, the distribution of a resource is often more critical than its scarcity in absolute terms. And finally, human welfare is sustained by a multitude of ecological services, few of which can be priced or sold.

Regeneration and Functional Ecosystems

Renewable resources may potentially be consumed in perpetuity, but they can also be made extinct if their ability to regenerate is compromised. As Inouye points out, environmental systems and the "services" they provide are critical to the ongoing replenishment of biological and otherwise renewable resources. Though these capacities may be endangered by overuse, not all threats are rooted in scarcity dynamics. The health of both species (especially humans, as Pirages notes) and ecosystem functions (as Inouye also suggests) can be strongly affected by new interactions between organisms. These can occur at the microscopic (i.e., disease) and macroscopic scale (i.e., exotic species). Moreover, effects can be direct (e.g., predation, parasitism) or indirect, as when ecosystem disturbances enable previously benign species to become pests. Both pose significant challenges to ecological security, yet again are difficult to conceptualize in terms of scarcity.

Similarly, though the conversion of ecosystems (e.g., removing natural forests for tree plantations) may increase productivity or efficiency, it also appears to alter local capacities to provide important ecosystem services (e.g., nutrient or energy cycling). Depending on the degree of the landscape conversion, the capacity of local ecosystems to adapt to stress (e.g., global warming) may also be diminished. In her chapter, Marchak emphasizes that this raises significant questions about the ultimate sustainability of large-scale landscape conversion. Additional social impacts may derive from a narrowing of tenure or access rules on which increased investment relies (e.g., plantations that reduce access to fuelwood, as well as other nontimber forest products).

Complexity and Uncertainty

Because human impacts have become global in scale, we are not always certain whether factors originate from our actions, or from the "natural" environment. Several of our authors discuss the difficulties of identifying processes and outcomes in complex, dynamic systems. Yet biophysical and sociocultural evolution often leads to systems with exactly these characteristics. Quite often, models based on such systems produce inconsistent or indeterminate outcomes, a characteristic approaching that of a physical law—no matter how accurate our models or measurements, our ability to predict the outcomes of dynamic systems will always be limited (Byrne 1997). Thus, while criticism about the predictive capacity of the social sciences (e.g., Ruth, chapter 8, this volume) is mostly on the mark, this cannot be attributed solely to weak methodology or theory.

Even were we capable of conquering complexity, the problem of uncertainty would not necessarily be resolved. As Conca suggests, the functional value (a subset of all possible values) of environmental or social factors is often not perceived or understood except in hindsight. Thus, we may not know what is important except through loss—determining which elements are necessary or sufficient to maintain system health is not a straightforward exercise. Critical policy issues can appear in only a few decades, as several authors emphasize here. Yet as Park demonstrates, scientists have been aware of some problems for a very long time—what has been slower to emerge is a belief among policymakers or the general public that change is necessary or appropriate. Science and technology may have enabled us to expand our cognitive capacities, but we still have not escaped the limits of the "naked eye"—immediate sensations still drive our beliefs and actions. The sad truth is that public concern is more often driven by rhetoric than by reason, despite broad support for maintaining environmental quality.

Values and Environmental Policy

Our persistence as a species depends on whether we can preserve the elements necessary to our biophysical existence, but the survival of our societies and cultures is no less critical. Adaptation to ecological challenges is a value-laden endeavor, as most of our authors emphasize. Addressing a multitude of concerns requires that a delicate political balance be found, where "critical" linkages are acknowledged, but more peripheral issues remain so. This is not a simple challenge. While both Conca and Marchak emphasize the importance of developing "integrated management" strategies, Ruth notes that there is often a temptation to develop "laundry lists" in the name of inclusion and comprehensiveness. This is problematic not only where the resources available to address a problem are limited—when public policies may serve (or be seen to serve) narrower interests, it is often difficult to draw the line between "real" and "political" pressures. This is a key reason why scientific expertise has become so valued by policymaking communities (Shannon, Meidinger, and Clark 1996).

One of the most common themes in this book has been the importance of equity, both as a means of achieving ecological security and as an end in itself. One strategy to address such concerns has been to increase "stakeholder" participation, where enlightened self-interest is expected to achieve more effective, efficient, and appropriate solutions (Gregory 2000). Yet as Park argues, the breadth of stakeholder participation may be highly desirable politically, but the additional involvement greatly expands the complexity of decision making. The distribution of costs and benefits in both problems and responses is often a critical issue in environmental and resource politics. These patterns are not only geographic, but also extend forward and back through time, as Park also emphasizes. Whether it is appropriate to hold nations responsible for their historical contribution to a problem (e.g., greenhouse gas emissions), or to focus on future equity, has proven to be a key sticking point in international negotiations.

Given a limited base of political or economic resources, how do we determine which challenges to address? We cannot escape the necessity of ranking risks, and of prioritizing our efforts accordingly. These are deeply political issues, regardless of the character of the institutions (e.g., democracies, markets) we use to address them. Whether such institutions are perceived as legitimate often depends on whether their processes and outcomes reflect our particular values. While some believe that economic incentives and technological innovation will always be able to adapt to (or otherwise overcome) ecological challenges (Simon 1996), such changes often produce further unintended problems. Internalizing the costs of extraction, production, and consumption into price can be highly problematic, even for relatively simple goods—but it may be effectively impossible for larger, systemic goods. The functional value of a given ecosystem is not economic except in hindsight—again, we may only know what is important through loss. This underscores the ongoing importance of monitoring, analysis, and dialogue, even for market-based solutions.

Institutions and Change

To ensure the persistence of what we value most, institutions—the means by which societies encourage consistent behavior—are critical. Institutions are as essential and ubiquitous as language, establishing the identities, roles, and rules that condition our perceptions and actions. They are the "levers" through which durable social change is effected (Ostrom 1986).

There is often a distance between words and action in policymaking processes, usually discovered after public attention has moved on to other issues. While the environment has proven to be an enduring popular concern in many societies, the salience of any specific issue has a limited lifetime. As Park demonstrates here, issues of commitment and accountability are further complicated by domestic politics and institutions (e.g., U.S. reversal on the Kyoto Protocol). There will always be the question of whether our failure to achieve national or international goals is due to a failure of our capacity, or of our commitment to those ends. To encourage consistency and ensure accountability, many agreements often have some form of penalty for reversal, as well as monitoring and enforcement functions. However, history has shown that including such provisions reduces the number of actors willing to participate—especially those expected to bear proportionally large costs (Victor, Raustiala, and Skolnikoff 1998). The ultimate effectiveness of any policy instrument is limited, something all the more true when participants disagree about the appropriateness or validity of policy goals.

Ultimately, our ability to achieve any particular goal may be determined as much by scarcity and social capacity as by motive. As Cook and Boes suggest here, scarcity is not an absolute, but rather a function of the relationships between technology, institutions, and the underlying resource bases. Existing markets and infrastructures provide the background conditions against which new initiatives and policies must strive to establish themselves and thrive. Depending on the pace and cost of innovation, early choices may "lock in" responses that are ultimately less effective. The law of diminishing returns means that while "low-hanging fruit" are easily attained, additional gains become increasingly costly. Therefore, past choices often limit our capacity to adapt quickly, even given complete agreement as to a need for change. Transitioning to more sustainable societies will thus require us to address the distribution of effective scarcity. The range of available solutions may be determined as much by their ability to use existing infrastructures as by their life-cycle efficiency, as Ruth argues here. This encourages a certain "adaptive incrementalism," which is only strengthened by uncertainty and the need to maintain a constant supply of goods or services (Hill 1997).

We have long understood that population dynamics can pose significant ecological challenges and strongly influence the range of feasible solutions. The policy decisions of relatively few states (e.g., India, China) are likely to have increasing significance for the rest of the world, as several of our authors emphasize. While some may believe that limiting population growth is an unqualified good, Runci and Cooper note that the changing age profiles of many nations pose significant challenges as well.

Global Concerns and Local Contexts

Each of the authors in this book has demonstrated how human impacts have grown to become global in scale, yet these effects are the result of individual acts, accumulated from a multitude of social and ecological contexts. Ironic as it may seem, the only means of ensuring successful adaptation to global-level challenges is to acknowledge the diversity of local experiences and values, and to focus on understanding relationships between local and global contexts. Any efforts to mitigate even the largest impacts will require changed behavior (and values) in these diverse local places. Our understanding of ecological concerns has gradually extended to factors difficult (if not impossible) to observe directly (e.g., global warming, biodiversity); local and global actors may perceive these issues quite differently, even where they share nominal values (e.g., sustainable resource use). Because effective policies require significant local-level commitment, resolving such disagreements is a critical issue (Potoski and Prakash 2002). Success will require acknowledging the importance of the local level as the ultimate source of experience, values, and action. Adaptation requires understanding how "best" to integrate such responses within local ecological and social contexts, because such policies are themselves likely to be interpreted in terms of local values (e.g., legitimacy, equity). To paraphrase the late House Speaker Tip O'Neil, "All [implementation] is local."

Even given a clear understanding of what "must be done," the capacity to implement policy varies widely across institutional contexts. As Conca argues here, relationships between the ecological and institutional boundaries of a given problem may strongly affect our ability to respond. Because institutional boundaries may disrupt, degrade, or bias signals from ecological and other social systems, the extent of overlap conditions our ability to respond to challenges. While place-based institutions have a long history of successful adaptation (Ostrom, Walker, and Gardner 1992), their recent record is less promising, because macro-level changes (institutional and environmental) have often overwhelmed local adaptive capacities.

While it may be difficult to establish the exact moment of transition, we are clearly in the midst of a shift away from an exclusive reliance on governments to broader, less formal *governance* institutions, as many of our authors acknowledge. Many of these new approaches to policymaking and implementation (e.g., forest certification, as described in Marchak and Inouye's chapters) have been responses to perceived inadequacies of traditional institutions. As state institutions retreat and alternative institutional forms emerge, some societies may be forced to consider trade-offs between effectiveness and political legitimacy (Wapner 1995). In other words, such emerging institutional responses—though well-intentioned—may also affect the persistence of local social and environmental values. Regardless of the purity of our intentions, it is the local-global distribution of power (and costs and benefits) that may be most critical to implementing appropriate, effective, and sustainable policies.

From Environmental Scarcity to Ecological Security

We have learned a great deal about the nature of ecological limits in the past few decades. Most physical and life scientists have come to acknowledge the important role of innovation in our ability to adapt to scarcity, just as economists are much more aware of the extent to which markets and other institutions can fail to ensure that such adaptation occurs in time. The importance of resource distribution is also more appreciated, as are the norms and rules that condition our ability to access (or to bear responsibility for) natural resources. Technology has weakened the link between economic growth and increased material consumption (Goodland, Daly, and

El Serafy 1992), even as it has presented us with new and unexpected challenges. Likewise, globalization processes have facilitated the movement of people and resources to a degree almost unimaginable a generation ago. While this has undoubtedly produced improvements in human welfare, concerns for the longer-term impacts of increased consumption of renewable resources are valid, as are worries about the unanticipated consequences of the interactions of newly mobile organisms and local ecosystems. Neither disease prevention nor stewardship is easily understood in terms of scarcity. If we are to move toward a more ecologically secure world, we will have to learn how to integrate ecological factors within our economic, political, and cultural institutions.

In a world of continual change, persistence relies on adaptation; as Toynbee once argued, societies decline and dissipate once they lose the capacity to adapt to system-level changes (Toynbee and Caplan 1979). While many of the concerns detailed in this volume may be primarily ecological, it is important to remember that even these issues are understood in broader terms, including (but not limited to) wealth, opportunity, fairness, justice, and cultural identity. Looking to the future, we must consider not only the social and ecological features we want to persist, but also those we will need in order to be able to adapt and remain vital.

References

Abramovitz, Janet. 2001. *Unnatural Disasters*. Washington, DC: Worldwatch Institute.

Académie de l'Eau. 1999. La Charte Sociale de l'Eau: Une nouvelle approche de la gestion de l'eau au 21è siècle. Paris: Académie de l'Eau.

Agence France Presse. 2001. Global Food Security at Threat from Climate Change: UN Panel. *Agence France Presse*, February 13.

Al-Farouq, A. 1996. Adaptation to climate change in the coastal resources sector of Bangladesh: Some critical issues and problems. In J. B. Smith, ed., *Adapting to Climate Change*. New York: Springer-Verlag.

Allen, J. C., and D. F. Barnes. 1986. The causes of deforestation in developing countries. *Annals of the Association of American Geographers* 75 (2):163–184.

Allen-Wardell, Gordon, Peter Bernhardt, Ron Bitner, Alberto Burquez, Stephen Buchmann, James Cane, Paul Allen Cox, Virginia Dalton, Peter Feinsinger, Mrill Ingram, David Inouye, C. Eugene Jones, Kathryn Kennedy, Peter Kevan, Harold Koopowitz, Rodrigo Medellin, Sergio Medellin-Morales, Gary Paul Nabhan, Bruce Pavlik, Vincent Tepedino, Phillip Torchio, and Steve Walker. 1998. The potential consequences of pollinator declines on the conservation of biodiversity and stability of food crop yields. *Conservation Biology* 12 (1):8–17.

Alliance to Save Energy. 1997. *Energy Innovations, a Prosperous Path to a Clean Environment*. Washington, DC: Alliance to Save Energy.

Alston, Julian M., Connie Chan-Kang, Michele C. Mara, Philip G. Pardey, and T. J. Wyatt. 2000. *A Meta-Analysis of Rates of Return to Agricultural R&D: Ex Pede Herculem?* Washington, DC: International Food Policy Research Institute.

Alston, Julian M., Philip G. Pardey, and Michael J. Taylor. 2001. *Agricultural Science Policy: Changing Global Agendas*. Baltimore: Johns Hopkins University Press.

Alvarado, J., and J. Creedy. 1998. *Population Ageing, Migration, and Social Expenditure*. Cheltenham, UK: Edward Elgar.

American Wind Energy Association. 2001. *How Much Energy Does It Take to Build a Wind Energy System in Relation to the Energy it Produces?* [Internet].

American Wind Energy Association, 1998 [cited November 2001]. Available from www.awea.org/faq/bal.html.

American Wind Energy Association. 2002. *Global Wind Energy Market Report* [Internet]. American Wind Energy Association, March 2001 [cited January 2002]. Available from www.awea.org/faq/global2000.html.

Anderberg, M. 2001. Personal communication to G. Cook. Golden, CO: Renewable Resource Data Center, National Renewable Energy Laboratory.

Anderson, J. W. 2001. *The History of Climate Change as a Political Issue* [Internet]. Resources for the Future, [cited 2001]. Available from www. weathervane.rff.org/features/feature005.html.

Annan, Kofi. 1999. An increasing vulnerability to natural disasters. *International Herald Tribune*, September 10, p. 8.

Apps, Michael J., and David T. Price, eds. 1996. *Forest Ecosystems, Forest Management and the Global Carbon Cycle*. No. 40, NATO ASI Series, Berlin: Springer-Verlag.

Asian Development Bank. 1997. *Emerging Asia: Changes and Challenges*. Manila: Asian Development Bank.

Auerbach, A. J., and R. D. Lee, eds. 2001. *Demographic Change and Fiscal Policy*. Cambridge: Cambridge University Press.

Ausubel, J. H. 1991. Does climate still matter? *Nature* 350:649–652.

Ausubel, J. H. 1999. Dis the threat industry. *Technological Forecasting and Social Change* 62:119–120.

Ausubel, J. H. 2001. Some ways to lesson worries about climate change. *Electricity Journal* 14(1):24–33.

Ayres, R. U. 1978. *Resources, Environment, and Economics: Applications of the Materials/Energy Balance Principle*. New York: Wiley.

Baer, P., J. Harte, et al. 2000. Equity and Greenhouse Gas Responsibility. *Science* 289 (5488): 2287.

Balbus, J. M., and M. L. Wilson. 2000. *Human Health and Global Climate Change: A Review of Potential Impacts in the United States*. Washington, DC: Pew Center on Global Climate Change.

Barbier, E., N. Bockstal, J. Burgess, and I. Strand. 1993. *The Timber Trade and Tropical Indonesia*. London: London Environmental Economics Centre.

Barbier, E., and J. C. Burgess. 1993. *Timber Trade and Tropical Deforestation: Global Trends and Evidence from Indonesia*. York, UK: University of York, Department of Environmental Economics and Environmental Management.

Barlow, Maude. 2001. Water privatization and the threat to the world's most precious resource: Is water a commodity or a human right? In *IFG Bulletin* special water issue 1. San Francisco: International Forum on Globalization.

Barnett, T. P. 1984. The estimation of "global" sea level change: A problem of uniqueness. *Journal of Geophysical Research* 89:7980–7988.

Barney, G. O. 1999. *Threshold 2000: Critical Issues and Spiritual Values for a Global Age.* Ada, MI: CoNexus Press.

Barney, Gerald O., ed. 1980. *The Global 2000 Report to the President: Entering the Twenty-First Century.* Vol. 1. Washington, DC: Council on Environmental Quality / U.S. Department of State.

Beier, Paul, and Reed F. Noss. 1998. Do habitat corridors provide connectivity? *Conservation Biology* 12 (6):1241–1252.

Bernstein, M., and P. Bromley. 1999. *Developing Countries and Global Climate Change: Electric Power Options for Growth.* Washington, DC: Pew Center on Global Climate Change.

Berry, T., and M. Jaccard. 2001. The renewable portfolio standard: Design considerations and an implementation survey. *Energy Policy* 29:263–277.

Biomass Research and Development Board. 2001. *Fostering the Bioeconomic Revolution in Biobased Products and Bioenergy.* Golden, CO: Biomass Research and Development Board, National Renewable Energy Laboratory.

Bloom, David E., and David Canning. 2000. The health and wealth of nations. *Science* 287:1207–1208.

Böhm, R. 1998. Urban bias in temperature time series: A case study for the city of Vienna, Austria. *Climatic Change* 38:113–128.

Bongaarts, John, W. Parker Mauldin, and James F. Phillips. 1990. The demographic impact of family planning programs. *Studies in Family Planning* 21 (6): 299–310.

Bouis, Howarth E. 2000. Special issue on Improving Human Nutrition through Agriculture. *Food and Nutrition Bulletin* 21 (4).

BP AMOCO Alive. 2004. *BP Amoco Statistical Review of World Energy 2003: BP Amoco Alive* [Internet]. BP Amoco, 2003 [cited May 2004]. Available from www.bp.com/worldenergy/.

Bright, Chris. 1998. *Life Out of Bounds: Bioinvasion in a Borderless World.* New York: Norton.

Brown, Lester. 1974. *By Bread Alone.* New York: Praeger.

Bryson, Reid, and Thomas Murray. 1977. *Climates of Hunger.* Madison: University of Wisconsin Press.

Buchan, D. 2001. Big groups hover on sidelines. *Financial Times Survey,* August 8, p. iii.

Bulkley, G. 2000. Advances in medical technologies for an aging world. Paper read at Address at the Cosmos Club, December 6, Washington, DC.

Burgess, J. C. 1993. Timber production, timber trade and tropical deforestation. *Ambio* 22 (2–3):136–143.

Burton, I. 1996. The growth of adaptation capacity: Practice and policy. In J. B. Smith, ed., *Adapting to Climate Change.* New York: Springer-Verlag.

Byrne, David. 1997. Complexity theory and social research. *Social Research Update* (18):6.

Capistrano, A. D., and C. F. Kiker. 1995. Macro-scale economic influences on tropical forest depletion. *Ecological Economics* 14:21–29.

Carlson, Alvar. 1985. Ginseng: America's botanical drug connection to the Orient. *Economic Botany* 40 (2):233–249.

Catholic Relief Services. 2001. *Social Justice Issues: Third World Debt.* Baltimore, MD: Catholic Relief Services.

Center for Clean Air Policy. 2001. *Promoting Clean Power, Clean Air and Brownfield Development.* Washington, DC: Center for Clean Air Policy.

Center for Conservation Biology. 2003. The Bet. *Ecofables/Ecoscience: Countering the distortion of environmental science.* (Stanford, CA: Center for Conservation Biology.) [cited April 2004]. Available from www.standford.edu/group/CCB/Pubs/Ecofablesdocs/thebet.htm.

Chalecki, Beth. 2000. Bulk water exports and free trade. *Pacific Institute Report,* pp. 12–13.

Chalmers, B. 1976. The photovoltaic generation of electricity. *Scientific American*, October, pp. 34–43.

Chao, B. F. 1995. Anthropological impact on global geodynamics due to water impoundment in major reservoirs. *Geophysical Research Letters* 22:3533–3536.

Choucri, Nazli. 1993. Multinational Corporations and the Global Environment. In N. Choucri, ed., *Global Accord: Environmental Challenges and International Responses.* Cambridge, MA: MIT Press.

Christianson, Gale. 2000a. *Greenhouse: The 200-Year Story of Global Warming.* New York: Penguin Books.

Christianson, Gale. 2000b. *An Historian's Biography of Global Warming* [Internet]. Earth Matters, 2000 [cited March 2000]. Available from www.earthinstitute.columbia.edu/library/earthmatters/spring2000.

Christopher, Warren. 1996. American diplomacy and global environmental challenges of the 21st century. Paper read at Stanford University, Stanford, CA.

Claussen, Eileen, and Lisa McNeilly. 1998. *Equity and Global Climate Change: The Complex Elements of Global Fairness.* Washington, DC: Pew Center on Global Climate Change.

Clay, Edward J., and Olav Stokke. 2000. *Food Aid and Human Security.* London: Frank Cass.

Cohen, J. E., and C. Small. 1997. Estimates of coastal populations. *Science*, 1211–1212.

Cohen, Marc J. 1994. *Causes of Hunger: Hunger 1995.* Silver Spring, MD: Bread for the World.

Cohen, Marc J. 2000. *Food Aid and Food Security Trends: Worldwide Needs, Flows, and Channels.* The Hague: European Association of Non-Governmental Organizations for Food Aid and Emergency Aid.

Cohen, Marc J., and Per Pinstrup-Andersen. 2001. *The Case for International Agricultural Research in the 21st Century.* Durban, South Africa: Consultative Group on International Agricultural Research.

Cohen, S. J. 1996. Integrated regional assessment of global climatic change: Lessons from the Mackenzie Basin Impact Study. *Global and Planetary Change* 11 (4): 179–185.

Cohen, S. J. 1997a. *Mackenzie Basin Impact Study: Final Report.* Downsview: Environment Canada.

Cohen, S. J. 1997b. What if and so what in northwest Canada: Could climate change make a difference to the future of the Mackenzie Basin? *Arctic* 50 (4): 293–307.

Colchester, Marcus. 1990. The International Tropical Timber Organization: Kill or cure for the rainforests? *The Ecologist* (20): 166–173.

Colchester, Marcus, and Larry Lohmann. 1990. *The Tropical Forestry Action Plan: What Progress?* London: World Rainforest Movement, The Ecologist, and Friends of the Earth.

Collins, Mark, ed. 1990. *The Last Rainforests: A World Conservation Atlas.* New York: Oxford University Press.

Conca, Ken. 2000. Beyond the statist frame: Environment in a global economy. In F. P. Gale and R. M. M'Gonigle, eds., *Nature, Production, Power: Towards an Ecological Political Economy.* Cheltenham, UK: Edward Elgar.

Consultative Group on International Agricultural Research 2001a. *The Challenge of Climate Change: Poor Farmers at Risk.* Washington, DC: Consultative Group on International Agricultural Research.

Consultative Group on International Agricultural Research 2001b. *Nourishing a Peaceful Earth.* Washington, DC. Consultative Group on International Agricultural Research.

Cosgrove, W. J., and F. R. Rijsberman, 2000. *World Water Vision: Making Water Everybody's Business.* London: Earthscan Publications.

Costanza, Robert, Ralph d'Agre, Rudolf de Groot, Stephen Farber, Monica Grasso, Bruce Hannon, Karin Limburg, Shahid Naeem, Robert V. O'Neill, Jose Paruelo, Robert G. Raskin, Paul Sutton, and Marjan van den Belt. 1997. The value of the world's ecosystem services and natural capital. *Nature* 387(15): 253–259.

Crosson, P. R., and N. J. Rosenberg. 1993. An overview of the MINK study. *Climatic Change* 24 (1–2).

Culliton, T. J., and M. Warren. 1990. *Fifty Years of Population Change along the Nation's Coasts: 1960–2010.* Rockville, MD: National Oceanic and Atmospheric Administration.

Daily, Gretchen C. 1997. *Nature's Services: Societal Dependence on Natural Ecosystems.* Washington, DC: Island Press.

Daily, Gretchen C., and Katherine Ellison. 2002. *The New Economy of Nature.* Washington, DC: Island Press.

Dalby, S. 2002. *Security and Ecology in the Age of Globalization.* Washington, DC: Environmental Change and Security Project, Woodrow Wilson International Center for Scholars.

Daly, H. E. 1991. *Steady-State Economics*. Washington, DC: Island Press.

Dawkins, H. C., and M. S. Philip. 1998. *Tropical Moist Forest Silviculture and Management: A History of Success and Failure*. New York: CAB International.

Day, R. H., and E. F. Koenig. 1975. On some models of world cataclysm. *Land Economics* 51 (1):1–20.

Deacon, Robert T. 1994. Deforestation and the rule of law in a cross section of countries. *Land Economics* 70 (4):414–443.

Deaton, M. L., and J. J. Winebrake. 2000. *Dynamic Modeling of Environmental Systems*. New York: Springer-Verlag.

Deffeyes, Kenneth S. 2001. *Hubbert's Peak: The Impending World Oil Shortage*. Princeton, NJ: Princeton University Press.

De Koninck, Rudolphe. 2000. *Deforestation in Vietnam* [Internet]. International Development Resources Centre, 1999 [cited 2000]. Available from www.crdi.ca/books/focus/869/chp01.html.

Delgado, Christopher L. 1997. The Role of smallholder income generation from agriculture in Sub-Saharan Africa. In L. Haddad, ed., *Achieving Food Security in Southern Africa: New Challenges, New Opportunities*. Washington, DC: International Food Policy Research Institute.

Delgado, Christopher L., Jane Hopkins, and Valerie Kelly. 1998. *Agricultural Growth Linkages in Sub-Saharan Africa*. Washington, DC: International Food Policy Research Institute.

Dernbach, J. 2000. Moving the climate change debate from models to proposed legislation: Lessons from state experience. *Environmental Law Reporter* 30: 10933–10979.

Diaz-Bonilla, Eugenio, and Sherman Robinson, eds. 1999. *Getting Ready for the Millennium Round Trade Negotiations*. Washington, DC: International Food Policy Research Institute.

Diaz-Bonilla, Eugenio, Sherman Robinson, Marcelle Thomas, and Andrea Cattaneo. 2000. *Food Security and Trade Negotiations in the World Trade Organization: A Cluster Analysis of Country Groups*. Washington, DC: International Food Policy Research Institute.

Dobell, Rod, and Justin Longo, eds. 1996. *Politics, Management and Conflict in the Canadian Fisheries, Forum on Maritime Affairs*. Victoria, BC: Maritime Awards Society of Canada.

Donahue, John M., and Barbara Rose Johnston, eds. 1998. *Water, Culture, and Power: Local Struggles in a Global Context*. Washington, DC: Island Press.

Doornkamp, J. C. 1998. Coastal flooding, global warming and environmental management. *Journal of Environmental Management* 52:327–333.

Dore, Mohammed, Mark Johnston, and Harvey Stevens. 1997. Global market relations and the phenomenon of tropical deforestation. In, Satya Dev Gupta and Nandas K. Choudhry, eds. *Globalization and Development: Growth, Equity and Sustainability*. Amsterdam: Kluwer Academic Publishers.

Dore, Mohammed H. I., and Jorge M. Nogueria. 1994. The Amazon rain forest, sustainable development and the biodiversity convention: A political economy perspective. *Ambio* 23 (8):491–496.

Douglas, B. C. 2001a. An introduction to sea level. In B. C. Douglas, M. S. Kirney, and S. P. Leatherman, eds., *Sea Level Rise: History and Consequences.* San Diego: Academic Press.

Douglas, B. C. 2001b. Sea level change in the era of the recording tide gauge. In B. C. Douglas, M. S. Kirney, and S. P. Leatherman, eds., *Sea Level Rise: History and Consequences.* San Diego: Academic Press.

Drèze, Jean, and Amartya Sen. 1989. *Hunger and Public Action.* Oxford: Clarendon Press.

Dubash, Navroz K., Mairi Dupar, Smitu Kothari, and Tundu Lissu. 2001. *A Watershed in Global Governance? An Independent Assessment of the World Commission on Dams.* Washington, DC: World Resources Institute.

Dugan, P. J., and T. Jones. 1993. Ecological change in wetlands: A global overview. In M. Moser, R. C. Prentice, and J. van Vessem, eds., *Waterfowl and Wetland Conservation in the 1990s: A Global Perspective.* Slimbridge, UK: International Waterfowl and Wetlands Research Bureau.

Easterling, D. R., and G. A. Mehl. 2000. Climate extremes: Observations, modeling, and impacts. *Science*, 2068–2074.

Edmonds, J., and J. M. Roop. 2000. *Technology and the Economics of Climate Change Policy.* Washington, DC: Pew Center on Global Climate Change.

Ehrlich, Paul. 1968. *The Population Bomb.* New York: Ballantine Books.

Ehrlich, P. R., and J. P. Holdren. 1971. Impact of population growth. *Science* 171:1212–1217.

Ehrlich, Paul R., and Stephen Schneider. 1995. Wagering on global environment. *San Francisco Chronicle,* May 18, p. A25.

Electric Power Research Institute. 1997. *Renewable Energy Technology Characterizations.* Washington, DC: Electric Power Research Institute, U.S. Department of Energy.

Elliott, D. 2000. Renewable energy and sustainable futures. *Futures* 32:261–274.

Elliott, D. L., and M. N. Schwartz. 1993. *Wind Energy Potential in the United States.* Richland, WA: Pacific Northwest Laboratories.

Energy Information Administration. 2000. *Emissions of Greenhouse Gases in the United States: 1999.* Washington, DC: Energy Information Administration, U.S. Department of Energy.

Energy Information Administration. 2001a. *Annual Energy Outlook 2002, with Projections to 2020.* Washington, DC: Energy Information Administration, U.S. Department of Energy.

Energy Information Administration. 2001b. *Annual Energy Review 2000.* Washington, DC: Energy Information Administration, U.S. Department of Energy.

Energy Information Administration. 2001c. *International Energy Annual 1999.* Washington, DC: Energy Information Administration, U.S. Department of Energy.

Energy Information Administration. 2001d. *International Energy Outlook 2001.* Washington, DC: Energy Information Administration, U.S. Department of Energy.

Energy Information Administration. 2001e. *Annual Energy Review 2003.* Washington, DC: Energy Information Administration, U.S. Department of Energy.

Energy Information Administration. 2002. *International Energy Annual 2002.* Washington, DC: Energy Information Administration, U.S. Department of Energy.

Energy Information Administration. 2003. *Carbon Dioxide Emissions from the Generation of Electric Power in the United States 2002.* Washington, DC: Energy Information Administration, U.S. Department of Energy.

Energy Information Administration. 2004a. *Annual Energy Outlook 2004, with Projections to 2025.* Washington, DC: Energy Information Administration, U.S. Department of Energy.

Energy Information Administration. 2004b. *International Energy Outlook 2004.* Washington, DC: Energy Information Administration, U.S. Department of Energy.

Engelman, Robert. 1997. Human population prospects: Implications for environmental security. *Environmental Change and Security Project Report*, No. 3, pp. 47–54. Washington, DC: Woodrow Wilson International Center for Scholars.

Epstein, P. 2000. Is global warming harmful to health? *Scientific American, August*, pp. 50–57.

European Wind Energy Association. 2004. Wind Industry: Worth € 80 Billion/Year by 2020 [Internet]. Available from http://www.ewea.org. Posted May 13, 2004; accessed May 27, 2004.

Evans, David L. 2001. *Commerce, Science, and Transportation.* In testimony to U. S. Senate Committee. Washington, DC: Office of Oceanic and Atmospheric Research, NOAA.

Faeth, P. 1994. *Evaluating the Carbon Sequestration Benefits of Forestry Projects in Developing Countries.* Washington, DC: World Resources Institute.

Fan, Shenggen, Peter Hazell, and Sukhadeo Thorat. 1999. *Linkages between Government Spending, Growth, and Poverty in Rural India.* Washington, DC: International Food Policy Research Institute.

Fisher-Vaden, Karen. 1997. *International Policy Instrument Prominence in the Climate Change Debate: A Case Study of the United States.* Cambridge, MA: Kennedy School of Government, Harvard University.

Flores, R., and S. Gillespie, eds. 2001. *Health and Nutrition: Emerging and Reemerging Issues in Developing Countries.* Washington, DC: International Food Policy Research Institute.

Foley, G. 1999. The looming environmental refugee crisis. *The Ecologist* 29(2): 96–97.

Frankhauser, S. 1996. The potential costs of climate change adaptation. In J. B. Smith, ed., *Adapting to Climate Change.* New York: Springer-Verlag.

Frederick, K. D., and P. H. Gleick. 1999. *Water and Global Climate Change.* Washington, DC: Pew Center on Global Climate Change.

French, Hilary. 2000. *Vanishing Borders: Protecting the Planet in the Age of Globalization.* New York: Norton.

Fusaro, Peter C. 2002. The future importance of oil: Geopolitical lynchpin or common commodity? In L. P. Bloomfield Jr., *Global Markets and National Interests: The New Geopolitics of Energy, Capital, and Information.* Washington, DC: Center for Strategic and International Studies.

Gabre-Madhin, Eleni Z., and Steven Haggblade. 2001. *Successes in African Agriculture: Results of an Expert Survey* 2001 [cited July 16, 2001]. Available from www.ifpri.org/divs/mtid/dp/papers/mssdp53.pdf.

Gallopin, Gilberto C., and Frank Rijsberman. 2000. Three global water scenarios. In William J. Cosgrove and Frank R. Rijsberman for the World Water Council, *World Water Vision: Making Water Everybody's Business.* Paris: World Water Council. CD-ROM edition.

Gambolati, G., and P. Teatini. 1999. Coastline regression of the Romagna region, Italy, due to natural and anthropogenic land subsidence and sea level rise. *Water Resources Research* 35 (1):163–184.

Gardner, Gary, and Brian Halweil. 2000. *Overfed and Underfed: The Global Epidemic of Malnutrition.* Washington, DC: Worldwatch Institute.

Garrett, James L., and Marie T. Ruel, eds. 2000. *Achieving Urban Food and Nutrition Security in the Developing World.* Washington, DC: International Food Policy Research Institute.

Garrett, Laurie. 1994. *The Coming Plague: Newly Emerging Diseases in a World Out of Balance.* New York: Farrar, Straus and Giroux.

Geels, F. W., and W. A. Smit. 2000. Failed technology futures: Pitfalls and lessons form a historical survey. *Futures* 32:867–885.

Gibbons, Ann. 1993. Where are new diseases born? *Science* 261:680–681.

Gillespie, Stuart, and Lawrence Haddad. 2000. *Attacking the Double Burden of Malnutrition in Asia.* Washington, DC: International Food Policy Research Institute.

Gleick, Peter H. 1998a. The human right to water. *Water Policy* 1:487–503.

Gleick, Peter H. 1998b. *The World's Water 1998–1999: The Biennial Report on Freshwater Resources.* Washington, DC: Island Press.

Gleick, Peter H. 2000. *The World's Water 2000–2001.* Washington, DC: Island Press.

Global Committee for the Water Contract. 1998. *The Water Manifesto: The Right to Life.* Lisbon: Global Committee for the Water Contract.

Global Water Partnership. n.d. *IWRM at a Glance.* Stockholm: Global Water Partnership.

Godwin, Obasi. 1999. Protection of the atmosphere: Achievements and challenges. In A. K. Hegazi, ed., *Environment 2000 and Beyond.* Cairo: Horus.

Gokhale, S. D., P. V. Ramamurthi, N. Pandit, and B. S. Pendse, eds. 1999. *Ageing in India*. Mumbai, India: Somaiya Publications Private Limited.

Gómez-Pompa, A., and F. W. Burley. 1991. The Management of Natural Tropical Forests. In A. Gómez-Pompa, T. C. Whitmore, and M. Hadley, eds., *Rain Forest Regeneration and Management*. Paris: UNESCO and the Parthenon Publishing Group.

Goodland, R., E. Ashley, J. Post, and M. Dyson. 1990. *Tropical Moist Forest Management: The Urgent Transition to Sustainability*. Washington, DC: World Bank.

Goodland, Robert J. A., Herman E. Daly, and Salah El Serafy. 1992. *Population, Technology, and Lifestyle: The Transition to Sustainability*. Washington, DC: Island Press.

Grainger, Alan. 1993. *Controlling Tropical Deforestation*. London: Earthscan.

Greenberg, Russell, Peter Bichier, Andrea Cruz Angon, and Robert Reitsma. 1997. Bird populations in shade and sun coffee plantations in central Guatemala. *Conservation Biology* 11 (2):448–459.

Gregory, Robin. 2000. Using stakeholder values to make smarter environmental decisions. *Environment* 42 (5):34–44.

Gritsevskyi, A., and N. Nakicenovic. 2000. Modeling uncertainty of induced technological change. *Energy Policy* 28:907–921.

Grübler, A., and N. Nakicenovic. 1999. Modeling technological change: Implications for the global environment. *Annual Review of Energy and Environment* 24:545–569.

Guppy, Nicolas. 1984. Tropical Deforestation: A Global View. *Foreign Affairs* 62 (4–5):928–965.

Gwilliam, K. M. 1993. *On Reducing Transport's Contribution to Global Warming*. Paris: Organization for Economic Cooperation and Development.

Hamner, J., and A. Wolf. 1997. Patterns in international water resource treaties: The transboundary freshwater dispute database. *Colorado Journal of International Environmental Law and Policy* (1997 Yearbook).

Han, X., and L. Chatterjee. 1997. Impacts of growth and structural change on CO_2 emissions of developing countries. *World Development* 25:395–407.

Hanemann, W. Michael. 1986. Economics and the preservation of biodiversity. In E. O. Wilson, ed., *Biodiversity*. Washington, DC: National Academy Press.

Hannon, B., and M. Ruth. 2000. *Dynamic Modeling*. New York: Springer-Verlag.

Hansen, J., and M. Sato. 2000. Global warming in the twenty-first century: An alternative scenario. *Proceedings of the National Academy of Sciences* 97 (18):9875–9880.

Hardin, Garrett. 1968. The tragedy of the commons. *Science* 162:1243–1248.

Hardin, Garrett. 1974. Living in a life boat. *Bioscience* 24 (10): 561–568.

Hardin, Garrett, and J. Baden, eds. 1977. *Managing the Commons*. New York: W. H. Freeman.

Hardner, Jared, and Richard Rice. 2002. Rethinking green consumerism. *Scientific American*, May, pp. 88–95.

Harris, Michael. 1998. *Lament for an Ocean: The Collapse of the Atlantic Cod Fishery—a True Crime Story*. Ontario: McClelland & Stewart.

Hartshorn, G. S. 1983. *Sustained Yield Management of Natural Forests: A Synopsis of the Palcazu Development Project in the Peruvian Amazon*. San José, Costa Rica: Tropical Science Center.

Hazell, Peter B. R. 1999. *Agricultural Growth, Poverty Alleviation, and Environmental Sustainability: Having It All*. Washington, DC: International Food Policy Research Institute.

Hecht, Susanna, and Alexander Cockburn. 1989. *The Fate of the Forest: Developers, Destroyers, and Defenders of the Amazon*. New York: Verso.

HelpAge International. 1999. *The Ageing and Development Report*. London: Earthscan.

Herd, G. 2001. *Russia's Population Crisis: Demography as Destiny?* [Internet]. Resources for the Future, November 8, 2001 [cited November 9, 2001]. Available from www.rff.org.

Heywood, V. H. 1993. *Flowering Plants of the World*. New York: Oxford University Press.

Hicks, D. 2000. Questioning the millennium: Shared stories of past, present and future. *Futures* 32:471–485.

Higgins, Matthew, and Jeffrey G. Williamson. 1997. Age structure dynamics in Asia and dependence on foreign capital. *Population and Development Review* 23 (2):261–293.

Hill, Michael. 1997. Implementation theory: Yesterday's issue? *Policy and Politics* 25 (1):375–385.

Hingane, L. S. 1996. Is a signature of socio-economic impact written on the climate? *Climatic Change* 32:91–102.

Hobhouse, Henry. 1990. *Forces of Change: An Unorthodox View of History*. New York: Arcade Publishing.

Hoffert, M. I. 1998. Energy implications of future stabilization of atmospheric CO_2 content. *Nature* 395:881–884.

Holdren, John P., Paul R. Ehrlich, and Anne J. Ehrlich. 1980. Bad news: Is it true? *Science* 210:1296–1301.

Homer-Dixon, Thomas F. 1991. On the threshold: Environmental changes as causes of acute conflict. *International Security* 16 (2):76–116.

Homer-Dixon, Thomas F. 1994. Environmental scarcities and violent conflict: Evidence from cases. *International Security* 19 (1):5–40.

Houghton, Richard A. 1996. Land-use change and terrestrial carbon: The temporal record. In Michael J. Apps and David T. Price, eds., *Forest Ecosystems, Forest Management and the Global Carbon Cycle*. NATO ASI Series, vol. 1, no. 40. Berlin: Springer-Verlag.

Huang, G. H., and S. J. Cohen. 1998. Land resources adaptation planning under changing climate—a study for the Mackenzie Basin. *Resources Conservation and Recycling* 24 (2):95–119.

Hughes, W. S., and R. C. Balling. 1996. Urban influences on South African urban temperature trends. *International Journal of Climatology* 16 (8):935–940.

Hunter, Malcolm L., Jr. 1996. *Fundamentals of Conservation Biology.* Cambridge, MA: Blackwell Science.

Iltis, Hugh H. 1986. Serendipity in the exploration of biodiversity: What good are weedy tomatoes? In E. O. Wilson, ed., *Biodiversity.* Washington, DC: National Academy Press.

Institute of Medicine. 1995. *Best Intentions: Unintended Pregnancy and the Well-Being of Children and Families.* Washington, DC: National Academy Press.

Intergovernmental Panel on Climate Change. 2001a. *Climate Change 2001: The Scientific Basis.* Geneva: Intergovernmental Panel on Climate Change.

Intergovernmental Panel on Climate Change. 2001b. *Intergovernmental Panel on Climate Change, Working Group I, Third Assessment Report, Summary for Policymakers.* Shanghai: Intergovernmental Panel on Climate Change.

International Energy Agency. 2000. *World Energy Outlook 2000* [Internet]. [cited September 17 2004]. Available from www.iea.org/dbtw-wpd/testbase/nppdf/free/2000/weo2000.pdf.

International Federation of Red Cross. 2001. *World Disasters Report* [Internet]. International Federation of Red Cross and Red Crescent Societies, [cited 2001]. Available from www.ifrc.org/publicat/wdr2001.

International Food Policy Research Institute. 1993. *The Political Economy of Food and Nutrition Policies.* Baltimore: Johns Hopkins University Press.

International Food Policy Research Institute. 2000. *Women: The Key to Food Security.* Washington, DC: International Food Policy Research Institute.

International Food Policy Research Institute. 2001. *International Conference on Sustainable Food Security for All by 2020.* [cited. Available from www.ifpri.org/2020conference/program/program.asp.

International Fund for Agricultural Development. 2001. *Rural Poverty Report 2001.* Rome: International Fund for Agricultural Development.

International Labour Organization. 2001. *Life at Work in the Information Economy: World Employment Report 2001.* Geneva: International Labour Organization.

Ipsen, D., and R. Rösch. 2001. Cooperation in global climate policy: Potentialities and limitations. *Energy Policy* 29:315–326.

Ismael, Yousouf, Richard Bennett, and Stephen Morse. 2001. *Farm Level Impact of Bt Cotton in South Africa.*

IUCN. 2000. *Red List of Threatened Species.* Gland, Switzerland: World Conservation Union.

Jackson, Robert B., Stephen R. Carpenter, Clifford N. Dahm, Diane M. McKnight, Robert J. Naiman, Sandra L. Postel, and Steven W. Running. 2001. Water in a changing world. *Issues in Ecology* (9): 2–18.

Jacobson, Susan K. 1990. Graduate education in conservation biology. *Conservation Biology* 4 (4):431–440.

James, Clive. 2001. *Preview—Global Review of Commercialized Transgenic Crops: 2001*. Ithaca, NY: International Service for the Acquisition of Agri-biotech Applications.

Jervis, Robert. 1997. *System Effects*. Princeton, NJ: Princeton University Press.

Johnson, Nels, and Bruce Cabarle. 1993. *Surviving the Cut*. Washington, DC: World Resources Institute.

Jordan, C. F. 1991. Nutrient cycling processes and tropical forest management. In A. Gómez-Pompa, T. C. Whitmore, and M. Hadley, eds., *Rain Forest Regeneration and Management*. Paris: UNESCO and the Parthenon Publishing Group.

Jorgenson, D. W., and R. J. Goettle. 2000. *The Role of Substitution in Understanding the Cost of Climate Change Policy*. Washington, DC: Pew Center on Global Climate Change.

Kahn, J. R., and J. A. Mcdonald. 1995. Third-World debt and tropical deforestation. *Ecological Economics* 12 (2):107–123.

Kaul, Inge, Isabelle Grunberg, and Marc A. Stern, eds. 1999. *Global Public Goods: International Cooperation in the 21st Century*. New York: Oxford University Press.

Kay, J. J., and E. D. Schneider. 1994. Embracing complexity. *Alternatives* 20 (3):32–39.

Kearney, M. S., A. S. Rogers, J. R. G. Townshend, J. C. Stevenson, J. T. Stevens, E. Rizzo, and K. Sundberg. 2002. Large scale decline of coastal marshes in Chesapeake Bay and Delaware Bay, USA, determined from Landsat imagery. *Eos* 83 (16):173–178.

Kearns, C. A., and D. W. Inouye. 1997. Pollinators, flowering plants, and conservation biology. *BioScience* 47 (5):297–307.

Kearns, Carol A., David W. Inouye, and Nickolas M. Waser. 1998. Endangered mutualisms: The conservation of plant-pollinator interactions. *Annual Review of Ecology and Systematics* 29:83–112.

Keck, Margaret, and Kathryn Sikkink. 1998. *Activists beyond Borders: Advocacy Networks and International Politics*. Ithaca, NY: Cornell University Press.

Keller, C. F. 2002. *Global Warming: An Update* [Internet]. Los Alamos National Laboratories, June 1998 [cited January 11, 2002]. Available from www.igpp.lanl.gov/climate.html.

Kerr, John, and Shashi Kolavalli. 1999. *Impact of Agricultural Research on Poverty Alleviation: Conceptual Framework with Illustrations from the Literature*. Washington, DC: International Food Policy Research Institute.

Kherallah, Mylène, Christopher Delgado, Eleni Gabre-Madhin, Nicholas Minot, and Michael Johnson. n.d. *The Road Half Traveled: Agricultural Market Reform in Sub-Saharan Africa*. Washington, DC: International Food Policy Research Institute.

Kimble, Melinda. 1988. Buenos Aires climate conference. Paper read at monthly meeting of the Women in International Trade Forum, October 12, Buenos Aires.

King, Neil, Jr., Geraldo Samor, and Scott Miller. 2004. WTO rules against US cotton aid. *Wall Street Journal*, April 27, p. 2.

Kirk, Dudley. 1996. Demographic transition theory. *Population Studies* 50:361–387.

Klein, R. J. T., and R. J. Nicholls. 1999. Assessment of coastal vulnerability to climate change. *Ambio* 28 (2):182–183.

Kopp, R. J. 2001. *An Analysis of the Bonn Agreement*. Washington, DC: Resources for the Future.

Lebel, Louis Philip. 1999a. *Illegal Log Exports to Laos from Cambodia* [posted message online]. Sea-Span-L, March 29, 1999 [cited 2000].

Lebel, Louis Philip. 1999b. *Logging in Cambodia: Politics and Plunder* [posted message online]. Sea-Span-L, March 24, 1999 [cited 2000].

Lebel, Louis Philip. 1999c. *New Indonesian Forestry Act* [posted message online]. Sea-Span-L, September 27, 1999 [cited 2000].

Lalasz, R. 2002. *Infectious Diseases and Global Change: Threats to Human Health and Security—a Meeting Report*. Washington, DC: Environmental Change and Security Project, Woodrow Wilson International Center for Scholars.

Langenkamp, R. Dobie. 2000. Outlook US "Big Oil" companies, getting smaller in real world. *Houston Chronicle*, December 31, p.

Lemons, J., and D. A. Brown, eds. 1995. *Sustainable Development: Science, Ethics and Public Policy*. Dordrecht, The Netherlands: Kluwer Academic Publishers.

Licking, Ellen. 1999. They're here, and they're taking over. *Business Week*, May 24.

Lomborg, Bjørn. 2001. *The Skeptical Environmentalist: Measuring the Real State of the World*. Cambridge: Cambridge University Press.

Longstreth, J. 1999. Public health consequences of global climate change in the United States: Some regions may suffer disproportionately. *Environmental Health Perspectives* 107 (1):1–11.

Lovejoy, T. 1993. Global change and epidemiology: Nasty synergies. In S. S. Morse, ed., *Emerging Viruses*. Oxford: Oxford University Press.

Ludwig, D., R. Hilborn, and C. Walters. 1993. Uncertainty, resource exploitation, and conservation: Lessons from history. *Science* 260 (2):17–52.

Lutz, W. 1994. Global population trends. In L. Arizpe, M. P. Stone, and D. C. Major, eds., *Population and Environment: Rethinking the Debate*. Boulder, CO: Westview Press.

Lutz, Wolfgang, Warren Sanderson, and Sergei Scherbov. 2001. The end of world population growth. *Nature* 412:543–545.

Mack, Richard N., Daniel Simberloff, W. Mark Lonsdale, Harry Evans, Michael Clout, and Fakhri A. Bazzaz. 2000. Biotic invasions: Causes, epidemiology, global consequences, and control. *Ecological Applications* 10 (3):689–710.

Maini, J. S., and O. Ullsten. 1993. Conservation and sustainable development of forests globally: Issues and opportunities. In K. Ramakrisna and G. M. Woodwell, eds., *World Forests for the Future: Their Use and Conservation*. New Haven, CT: Yale University Press.

Marchak, M. P. 1995. *Logging the Globe*. Montreal: McGill–Queen's University Press.

Marland, G., and A. M. Weinberg. 1988. Longevity of infrastructure. In J. H. Ausubel and R. Herman, eds., *Cities and Their Vital Systems: Infrastructure Past, Present, and Future*. Washington, DC: National Academy Press.

Martens, W. J. M. 1996. Global atmospheric change and human health: An integrated modelling approach. *Climate Research* 6 (2):107–112.

Martens, W. J. M. 1998. Climate change, thermal stress and mortality changes. *Social Science and Medicine* 46 (3):331–344.

Matthew, Richard A. 2002. In *Defense of Environment and Security Research*. Washington, DC: Environmental Change and Security Project, Woodrow Wilson International Center for Scholars.

Matthews, Jessica. 1997. Power shift. *Foreign Affairs* 76 (1):50.

Maycock, P. 2001. *PV News* 20 (2).

Maycock, P. 2004. *PV News* 23 (3).

Maycock, P. 2001. *PV News* 20 (12).

McCaffrey, Stephen C. 2001. *The Law of International Watercourses: Non-Navigational Uses*. Oxford: Oxford University Press.

McCann, Kevin Shear. 2000. The diversity-stability debate. *Nature* 405:228–233.

McCarl, B. A., and U. A. Schneider. 2001. Greenhouse gas mitigation in US agriculture and forestry. *Science* 294:2481–2482.

McCarthy, James J., Osvaldo F. Canziani, Neil A. Leary, David J. Dokken, and Kasey S., eds. 2001. *Climate Change 2001: Impacts, Adaptation, and Vulnerability: Contribution of Working Group II to the Third Assessment Report of the Intergovernment Panel on Climate Change. Edited by Intergovernment Panel on Climate Change, Third Assessment Report*. New York: Cambridge University Press.

McCulloch, Anna Knox, Ruth Meinzen-Dick, and Peter Hazell. 1998. *Property Rights, Collective Action, and Technologies for Natural Resource Management: A Conceptual Framework*. Washington, DC: International Food Policy Research Institute.

McCully, Patrick. 2001. *Silenced Rivers: The Ecology and Politics of Large Dams*. London: Zed Books.

McDevitt, Thomas. 2000. *Knowledge-Based Population Projections: New Statistical Evidence and a Word on Making Projections under Real World Conditions*. Los Angeles: Population Association of America.

McDevitt, Thomas M., Karen A. Stanecki, and Peter O. Way. 1999. *World Population Profile: 1998*. Washington, DC: U.S. Census Bureau.

McNeely, Jeffrey A., and Sara J. Scherr. 2001. *Common Ground, Common Future: How Ecoagriculture Can Help Feed the World and Save Wild Biodiversity*. Washington, DC: IUCN/Future Harvest.

McNeill, William. 1976. *Plagues and Peoples*. Garden City, NY: Anchor Press.

Meadows, Dennis L., Donella H. Meadows, William W. Behrens, and Jørgen Randers. 1992. *The Limits to Growth: A Report for the Club of Rome's Project on the Predicament of Mankind*. New York: Universe Books.

Meadows, Donella, Jørgen Randers, and Dennis Meadows. 2004. *Limits to Growth: The 30-Year Update*. South Burlington, VT: Chelsea Green Publishing.

Mehl, G. A., and T. Karl. 2000. An introduction to trends in extreme weather and climate events: Observations, socioeconomic impacts, terrestrial ecological impacts, and model projections. *Bulletin of the American Meteorological Society* 81 (3):413–416.

Meinzen-Dick, Ruth S., Lynn R. Brown, Hillary Sims Feldstein, and Agnes R. Quisumbing. 1997. Gender and property rights: Overview. *World Development* 25 (8):1299–1302.

Messer, Ellen, Marc J. Cohen, and Jashinta D'Costa. 1998. *Food from Peace: Breaking the Links between Conflict and Hunger*. Washington, DC: International Food Policy Research Institute.

Messer, Ellen, Marc J. Cohen, and Thomas Marchione. 2001. *Conflict: A Cause and Effect of Hunger*. Washington, DC: Environmental Change and Security Project, Woodrow Wilson International Center for Scholars.

Mitchell, Alison. 1997. Climate pact: Health care revisited. *New York Times*, December 13, p. 6.

Modified oil cited in tuna ban. 2000. *Bangkok Post*, March 25.

Mohan, Uday. 2000. *Bridging the Digital Divide*. Washington, DC: International Food Policy Research Institute.

Morse, S. S., ed. 1993. *Emerging Viruses*. Oxford: Oxford University Press.

Mowery, D. C., and Nathan Rosenberg. 1998. *Paths of Innovation*. Cambridge: Cambridge University Press.

Myers, N. 1984. *The Primary Source: Tropical Forests and Our Future*. New York: Norton.

Myers, Norman. 1997. The rich diversity of biodiversity issues. In M. L. Reaka-Kudla, D. E. Wilson, and E. O. Wilson, eds., *Biodiversity II: Understanding and Protecting Our Biological Resources*. Washington, DC: Joseph Henry Press.

Myers, Norman, Russell A. Mittermeier, Cristina G. Mittermeier, Gustavo A. B. Da Fonseca, and Jennifer Kent. 2000. Biodiversity hotspots for conservation priorities. *Nature* 403:853–858.

Nabhan, Gary Paul, and S. L. Buchmann. 1997. Services provided by pollinators. In G. C. Daily, ed., *Nature's Services: Societal Dependence on Natural Ecosystems*. Washington, DC: Island Press.

Naeem, S., J. M. H. Knops, D. Tilman, K. M. Howe, T. Kennedy, and S. Gale. 2000. Plant diversity increases resistance to invasion in the absence of covarying extrinsic factors. *Oikos* 91 (1):97–108.

Naik, Gautum. 2003. Forget SARS: WHO expert fears the flu. *Wall Street Journal,* May 29.

National Academy of Sciences. 2001a. *Abrupt Climate Change: Inevitable Surprises.* Washington, DC: National Academy of Sciences.

National Academy of Sciences. 2001b. *Climate Change Science: Analysis of Some Key Questions.* Washington, DC: National Academy of Sciences.

National Intelligence Council. 2002. *The Next Wave of HIV/AIDS: Nigeria, Ethiopia, Russia, India, and China.* Washington, DC: National Intelligence Council.

National Renewable Energy Laboratory. 1999. *Pv Faqs: Energy Payback—Clean Energy from Pv.* Washington, DC: National Renewable Energy Laboratory.

National Renewable Energy Laboratory. 2001. *Advancing Technology to Address Climate Change, Renewable Energy Technologies.* Washington, DC: National Renewable Energy Laboratory.

Nautilus Institute. 2004. *Energy, Environment and Security in Northeast Asia: Defining a U.S.-Japan Partnership for Regional Comprehensive Security* [Internet]. Nautilus Institute and Center for Global Communications (GLOCOM), December 1999 [cited 2004]. Available from www.nautilus.org/papers/ energy/ESENAfinalreport.html.

New World Oil Reserves Lag Growing Consumption. 2001. Reuters.

Ni, Weidou, Zheng Li, and Yuan Xue. 2000. *National Energy Futures Analysis and Energy Security Perspectives in China: Strategic Thinking on the Energy Issue in 10th Five-Year Plan of China.* Berkeley, CA: Nautilus Institute.

Nicholls, R. 1995. Coastal megacities and climate change. *GeoJournal* 37 (3):369–379.

Nicholls, R. J., and F. M. J. Hoozemans. 1996. The Mediterranean: Vulnerability to coastal implications of climate change. *Ocean and Coastal Management* 31 (2–3):105–132.

The Non-Governmental Order. 1999. *The Economist,* December 11, pp 20–21.

Nord, Mark, Nader Kabbani, Laura Tiehen, Margaret Andrews, Gary Bickel, and Steven Carlson. 2002. *Household Food Security in the United States.* Washington, DC: U.S. Department of Agriculture.

Norton, Bryan. 1986. Commodity, amenity, and morality: The limits of quantification in valuing biodiversity. In E. O. Wilson, ed., *Biodiversity,* Washington, DC: National Academy Press.

Noss, Reed F., E. T. LaRoe III, and J. M. Scott. 1995. *Endangered Ecosystems of the United States: A Preliminary Assessment of Loss and Degradation.* Washington, DC: United States Department of the Interior.

Nye, J., and W. Owens. 1996. America's information edge. *Foreign Affairs,* March-April, pp. 20–36.

Obasi, Godwin. 1999. Protection of the atmosphere: Achievements and challenges. In A. K. Hegazi, *Environment 2000 and Beyond*. Cairo: Horus.

O'Brien, K. L., and R. M. Leichenko. 2000. Double exposure: Assessing the impacts of climate change within the context of economic globalization. *Global Environmental Change* 10:221–232.

Office of Science and Technology Policy. 1997. *Climate Change: State of Knowledge*. Washington, DC: Office of Science and Technology Policy, Executive Office of the President.

Oksanen, Tapani, Matts Heering, Bruce Cabarle, and Caroline Sargent. 1993. *A Study on Coordination: Sustainable Forestry Development—Report to the Tropical Forestry Action Program Forestry Advisers' Group*. Kuala Lumpur, Malaysia, United Nations Food and Agriculture Organization (FAO).

Olson, David M., and Eric Dinerstein. 1998. The global 200: A representation approach to conserving the earth's most biologically valuable ecoregions. *Conservation Biology* 12 (3):502–515.

Organization for Economic Cooperation and Development. 2000a. *Development Cooperation*. Paris: Organization for Economic Cooperation and Development.

Organization for Economic Cooperation and Development. 2000b. *Energy Balances of Non-OECD Countries*. Paris: Organization for Economic Cooperation and Development.

Organization for Economic Cooperation and Development. 2001. Development Cooperation. Paris: Organization for Economic Cooperation and Development.

Ostrom, Elinor. 1986. An agenda in the study of institutions. *Public Choice* 48:3–25.

Ostrom, Elinor, James Walker, and Roy Gardner. 1992. Covenants with and without a sword: Self-enforcement is possible. *American Political Science Review* 86 (2):404–417.

Oud, Engelbertus, and Terence C. Muir. 1997. Engineering and economic aspects of planning, design, construction and operation of large dam projects. Paper read at Conference on Large Dams: Learning from the Past, Looking at the Future, April 11–12, Gland, Switzerland.

Paarlberg, Robert L. 2000. *Governing the GM Crop Revolution: Policy Choices for Developing Countries*. Washington, DC: International Food Policy Research Institute.

Paddock, William, and Paul Paddock. 1967. *Famine 1975! America's Decision: Who Will Survive*. Boston: Little, Brown.

Palo, M., G. Merey, and J. Salmi. 1987. Deforestation in the tropics: Pilot scenarios based on quantitative analysis. In P. Salmi and J. Salmi, eds., *Deforestation or Development in the Third World?* Helsinki: Division of Social and Economic Forestry, Finnish Forest Research Institute.

Pan, P. 2001. Scientists issue dire warning on climate change. *Washington Post*, January 23, p. A1.

Panayotou, Theodore, and Peter S. Ashton. 1992. *Not by Timber Alone: Economics and Ecology for Sustaining Tropical Forests.* Washington, DC: Island Press.

Pardey, Philip G., Julian M. Alston, Jason E. Christian, and Shenggen Fan. 1996. *Hidden Harvest: US Benefits from International Research Aid.* Washington, DC: International Food Policy Research Institute.

Pardey, Philip G., and Nienke M. Beintema. 2001. *Slow Magic: Agricultural R&D a Century After Mendel.* Washington, DC: International Food Policy Research Institute.

Parikh, Jyoti. 2000. Inequity: A root cause of climate change. In *International Human Dimensions Programme (IHDP) Update,* 2. International Human Dimensions Programme.

Pauly, Daniel, Villy Christensen, Sylvie Guénette, Tony J. Pitcher, U. Rashid Sumaila, Carl J. Walters, R. Watson, and Dirk Zeller. 2002. Towards sustainability in world fisheries. *Nature* 418 (6898):689–695.

Pearce, D. 1991. Evaluating the socioeconomic impacts of climate change: An introduction. In D. Pearce, ed., *Climate Change: Evaluating the Socioeconomic Impacts.* Paris: Organization for Economic Cooperation and Development.

Peel, Q. 2001. Relaxing the rules of entry. *Financial Times,* May 28, p. 2.

Pender, John, and Peter B. R. Hazell. 2000. *Promoting Sustainable Development in Less Favored Areas.* Washington, DC: International Food Policy Research Institute.

Peterson, P. 1999a. Gray dawn: The global aging crisis. *Foreign Affairs,* January-February, pp. 42–55.

Peterson, Peter G. 1999b. *Gray Dawn: How the Coming Age Wave Will Transform America—and the World.* New York: Times Books.

Pettifor, Ann. 2000. *Pursuing Debt Relief.* Washington, DC: International Food Policy Research Institute.

Phantumvanit, D., and Theodore Panayotou. 1990. Natural resources for a sustainable future: Spreading the benefits. Paper read at TDRI End-Year Conference on Industrializing Thailand and Its Impact on the Environment, December 8–9, Chon Buri, Thailand.

Philips, D. R., ed. 2000. *Ageing in the Asia-Pacific Region.* New York: Routledge.

Pianin, Eric. 2001. US report forecasts crises brought on by global warming. *Washington Post,* February 20, p. 6.

Pieterse, J. N. 2000. Globalization and human integration: We are all migrants. *Futures* 32:385–398.

Pimental, David, L. Lach, R. Zuniga, and D. Morrison. 1999. Environmental and economic costs associated with non-indigenous species in the United States. *Bioscience* 50: 53–65.

Pinstrup-Andersen, Per, ed. (1993). *The Political Economy of Food and Nutrition Policies.* Baltimore, MD: Johns Hopkins University Press.

Pinstrup-Andersen, Per, and Marc J. Cohen. 1998. *Aid to Developing Country Agriculture: Investing in Poverty Reduction and New Export Opportunities.* Washington, DC: International Food Policy Research Institute.

Pinstrup-Andersen, Per, and Marc J. Cohen. 2001. Modern agricultural biotechnology and developing country food security. In C. N. Gerald, ed., *Genetically Modified Organisms in Agriculture: Economics and Politics*. London: Academic Press.

Pinstrup-Andersen, Per, Rajul Pandya-Lorch, and Mark W. Rosegrant. 1997. *The World Food Situation: Recent Developments, Emerging Issues, and Long-Term Prospects*. Washington, DC: International Food Policy Research Institute.

Pinstrup-Andersen, Per, Rajul Pandya-Lorch, and Mark W. Rosegrant. 1999. *World Food Prospects: Critical Issues for the Early Twenty-First Century*. Washington, DC: International Food Policy Research Institute.

Pirages, D. 2000. Diversity and social progress in the next millennium: An evolutionary perspective. *Futures* 32:513–523.

Pirages, Dennis, and Theresa DeGeest. 2004. *Ecological Security: An Evolutionary Perspective on Globalization*. Lanham, MD: Rowman & Littlefield.

Poore, Duncan. 1993. The sustainable management of tropical forests: The issues. In S. Rietbergen, ed., *The Earthscan Reader in Tropical Forestry*. London: Earthscan.

Population Reference Bureau 2003. *2003 World Population Data Sheet*. Washington, DC: Population Reference Bureau.

Population Reference Bureau. 2004. *2004 World Population Data Sheet*. Washington, DC: Population Reference Bureau.

Poquet, Guy. 1978. The limits to global modelling. *International Social Science Journal* 30 (2):284–300.

Portney, P. R., and J. P. Weyant, eds. 1999. *Discounting and Intergenerational Equity*. Washington, DC: Resources for the Future.

Postel, Sandra, and Stephen Carpenter. 1997. Freshwater ecosystem services. In G. C. Daily, *Nature's Services: Societal Dependence on Natural Ecosystems*. Washington, DC: Island Press.

Potoski, Matthew, and Aseem Prakash. 2002. Protecting the environment: Voluntary regulations in environmental governance. *Policy Currents* 11 (4):8.

Pöyry, Jaakko. 1996. Overhead figures provided at conference on Paper read at Conference on Sustaining Ecosystems and People in Temperate and Boreal Forests, September, Victoria, BC.

Pray, Carl, Danmeng Ma, Jikun Huang, and Fanbin Qiao. 2001. Impact of Bt Cotton in China. *World Development* 29 (5):813–825.

Price, L., and L. Michaelis. 1998. Sectoral trends and driving forces of global energy use and greenhouse gas emissions. *Mitigation and Adaptation Options for Global Change* 3:263–319.

Quisumbing, Agnes R., Lynn R. Brown, Hilary Sims Feldstein, Lawrence Haddad, and Christine Peña. 1995. *Women: The Key to Food Security*. Washington, DC: International Food Policy Research Institute.

Raffelshausen, B. 2001. Aging fiscal policy, and social insurance. In A. J. Auerbach and R. D. Lee, eds., *Demographic Change and Fiscal Policy*. Cambridge: Cambridge University Press.

Randel, Judith, and Tony German. 2001. *Reality Check 2001.* Somerset, UK: Reality of Aid.

Raustiala, Kal. 1997. States, NGOs, and international environmental institutions. *International Studies Quarterly* 41:719.

Ravetz, J. 1999. The maturing of science at the millennium. *Bulletin of Science, Technology and Society* 19 (4):268–270.

Recer, P. 2001 Study: Cycling Drugs May Curb Aids [Internet]. *Associated Press Online.* December 4 [cited December 5 2001]. Available from www.aegis.com/ news/ap/2001/AP011206.html.

Repetto, R., and S. S. Baliga. 1996. *Pesticides and the Immune System.* Washington, DC: World Resources Institute.

Republic of South Africa. 1998. *National Water Act August 20, 1998* [cited No. 36.] Available from www.dwaf.gov.za/Documents/Legislature/nw act/NWA.htm.

Revenga, Carmen, Siobhan Murray, Janet Abramovitz, and Allen Hammond. 1998. *Watersheds of the World: Ecological Value and Vulnerability.* Washington, DC: World Resources Institute.

Roberts, Callum M. 2002. Deep impact: The rising toll of fishing in the deep sea. *Trends in Ecology & Evolution* 17 (5):242–245.

Roberts, Callum M., James A. Bohnsack, Fiona Gell, Julie P. Hawkins, and Renata Goodridge. 2001. Effects of marine reserves on adjacent fisheries. *Science* 294 (5548):1920–1923.

Robinson, W. A. 2001. *Modeling Dynamic Climate Systems.* New York: Springer-Verlag.

Rodenberg, Eric. 1992. *Eyeless in Gaia: The State of Global Environmental Monitoring.* Washington, DC: World Resources Institute.

Roe, Emery. 1998. *Taking Complexity Seriously: Policy Analysis, Triangulation, and Sustainable Development.* Dordrecht, The Netherlands: Kluwer Academic Publishers.

Rosegrant, Mark W. 1997. *Water Resources in the Twenty-First Century: Challenges and Implications for Action.* Washington, DC: International Food Policy Research Institute.

Rosegrant, Mark W., and Peter B. R. Hazell. 2000. *Transforming the Rural Asian Economy: The Unfinished Revolution.* New York: Oxford University Press for the Asian Development Bank.

Rosegrant, Mark W., Michael S. Paisner, Siet Meijer, and Julie Witcover. 2001. *Global Food Projections to 2020: Emerging Trends and Alternative Futures.* Washington, DC: International Food Policy Research Institute.

Rosegrant, Mark W., and Claudia Ringler. 2000. Impact on food security and rural development of transferring water out of agriculture. *Water Policy* 1 (6):567–586.

Rosenbaum, Walter. 1998. *Environmental Politics and Policy.* Washington, DC: Congressional Quarterly Press.

Rosenberg, N. J. 1993. An overview of the MINK study. *Climate Change* 24 (1–2): 159–173.

Rosenberg, N. J., ed. 1993. *Towards an integrated impact assessment of climate change: The MINK study*. Dordrecht, The Netherlands: Kluwer Academic Publishers.

Rosenberg, N. J., and P. R. Crosson. 1993. The MINK methodology— Background and base-line. *Climatic Change* 24 (1–2):

Rubinoff, Ira. 1982. "Tropical Forests: Can We Afford Not to Give Them a Future?" *The Ecologist* 12(6): 153–158.

Ruddle, K. 1987. *Administration and Conflict Management in Japanese Coastal Fisheries*. Rome: Food and Agriculture Organization. (FAO) Fisheries Technical Paper.

Runyan, Curtis. 1999. Action on the front lines. *World Watch*, November-December, pp. 12–21.

Russia and the WTO: Shaping up for the club. 2001. *The Economist*, November 24, 68.

Ruth, M. 1993. *Integrating Economics, Ecology and Thermodynamics*. Dortdrecht, The Netherlands: Kluwer Academic Publishers.

Ruth, M., and B. Davidsdottir. 2000. Impacts of market-based climate change policies on the US pulp and paper industry. *Energy Policy* 28:259–270.

Ruth, M., and B. Hannon. 1997. *Modeling Dynamic Economic Systems*. New York: Springer-Verlag.

Ruth, M., and P. Kirshen. 2001. Integrated impacts of climate change upon infrastructure systems and services in the Boston metropolitan area. *World Resources Review* 13(1):106.

San Martin, R. L. 1989. *Environmental Emissions from Energy Technology Systems: The Total Fuel Cycle*. Washington, DC: U.S. Department of Energy.

Sarewitz, Daniel, and Roger Pielke. 2000. Breaking the global-warming deadlock. *Atlantic Monthly*, July, p. 92.

Saunders, D. A., R. J. Hobbs, and C. R. Margules. 1991. Biological consequences of ecosystem fragmentation: A review. *Conservation Biology* 5:18–32.

Schelling, T. C. 1992. Some economics of global warming. *American Economic Review* 82(1):1–14.

Scherr, Sara J. 1999. *Soil Degradation: A Threat to Developing-Country Food Security by 2020?* Washington, DC: International Food Policy Research Institute.

Schilling, K. E., and E. Z. Stakhiv. 1998. Global change and water resources management. *Water Resources Update* 112:1–5.

Schioler, Ebbe. 1998. *Good News from Africa*. Washington, DC: International Food Policy Research Institute.

Schipper, L., and S. Meyers, eds. 1992. *Energy Efficiency and Human Activity: Past Trends, Future Prospects*. Cambridge: Cambridge University Press.

Schmandt, J., and J. Clarkson, eds. 1992. *The Regions and Global Warming: Impacts and Response Strategies*. New York: Oxford University Press.

Schneider, S. 2002. Global warming: Neglecting the complexities. *Scientific American*, January, pp. 62–65.

Schultz, Jim. 2000. Bolivia's water war victory. *Earth Island Journal*, Autumn, pp. 28–29.

Sen, Amartya. 1999. *Development as Freedom*. New York: Knopf.

Serageldin, I. (1999). Biotechnology and Food Security in the 21st Century. Science 285: 387–389.

Shannon, Margaret A. Errol E. Meidinger, and Roger N. Clark. 1996. Science advocacy is inevitable: Deal with it. Paper presented at the Annual Meeting of the Society of American Foresters, Albuquerque, NM, November 11.

Shapiro, Kevin A. 2001. Too darn hot? *Commentary*, June, pp. 25–29.

Shell International. 1995. *The Evolution of the World's Energy Systems*. London: Shell International.

Shell International. 2001. *Energy Needs, Choices and Possibilities: Scenarios to 2050*. Shell International.

Shiklomanov, I. 1998. *World Water Resources and World Water Use*. St. Petersburg, Russia: State Hydrological Institute.

Simmons, Matthew R. 2000. *Revisiting the Limits to Growth: Could the Club of Rome Have Been Correct, After All?* Houston, TX: Simmons & Company International.

Simon, J. L. 1980. Resources, population, environment: An oversupply of false bad news. *Nature* 208:1431–1437.

Simon, J. L. 1996. *The Ultimate Resource*. 2nd ed. Princeton, NJ: Princeton University Press.

Simon, Julian L., and Herman Kahn. 1984. *The Resourceful Earth: A Response to Global 2000*. London: Blackwell.

Sizer, Nigel. 1996. *Profit without Plunder: How to Reap Revenue from Tropical Forests without Destroying Them—the Guyana Case Study*. Washington, DC: World Resources Institute.

Sizer, Nigel. 2000. *Opportunities to Save and Sustainably Use the World's Forests through International Cooperation* [Internet]. International Institute for Sustainable Development [cited 2000]. Available from www.iisd.ca/linkages/ forestry/sizer.html.

Sizer, N., and R. Rice. 1995. *Backs to the Wall in Suriname: Forest Policy in a Country in Crisis*. Washington, DC: World Resources Institute.

Smil, V. 1997. *Cycles of life: Civilization and the Biosphere*. New York: Scientific American Library.

Smith, Lisa C., and Lawrence Haddad. 2000. *Explaining Child Malnutrition in Developing Countries: A Cross-Country Analysis*. Washington, DC: International Food Policy Research Institute.

Solar Energy [Internet]. 2001. The Online Encyclopedia of Science & Technology, McGraw-Hill, February 26, 2001 [cited December 14, 2001]. Available from www.accessscience.com/server-java/Arknoid/science/AS.

Soulé, M. E. 1980. Thresholds for survival: Criteria for maintenance of fitness and evolutionary potential. In M. E. Soulé and B. M. Wilcox, eds., *Conservation Biology: An Evolutionary-Ecological Perspective*. Sunderland, MA: Sinauer Associates.

Soulé, M. E., and B. A. Wilcox, eds. 1980. *Conservation Biology: An Evolutionary-Ecological Perspective*. Sunderland, MA: Sinauer.

Southwick, E. E., and L. Southwick Jr. 1992. Estimating the economic value of honey bees (Hymenoptera: Apidae) as agricultural pollinators in the United States. *Journal of Economic Entomology* 85 (3):621–633.

Sprout, H., and M. Sprout. 1965. *The Ecological Perspective on Human Affairs with Special Reference to International Politics*. Princeton, NJ: Princeton University Press.

Stopford, John. 1999. Multinational corporations. *Foreign Policy* 113 (Winter):16.

Swaney, James A. 1991. Julian Simon versus the Ehrlichs: An institutionalist perspective. *Journal of Economic Issues* 25 (2):499–509.

Tayanc, M., and H. Toros. 1997. Urbanization effects on regional climate change in the case of four large cities of Turkey. *Climatic Change* 35:501–524.

Taylor, J. A., and J. Lloyd. 1992. Sources and sinks of atmospheric CO_2. *Australian Journal of Botany* 40:407–418.

This year was the 2nd hottest, confirming a trend, UN says. 2001 Associated Press, Wednesday, December 19, A5: 3.

Thomson, Jennifer A. 2001. Biotechnological approaches to sustainable food production. Paper read at Conference on Sustainable Food Security for All by 2020, September 4–6, Bonn, Germany.

Thussu, Daya Kishan. 2001. Lost in space. *Foreign Policy*, May-June, pp. 70–71.

Tien, H. Y. 1992. China's demographic dilemmas. *Population Bulletin* 47 (1):38–39.

Tierney, John. 1990. Betting on the planet. *New York Times*, December 2, p. 52.

Tilman, D. 1999. The ecological consequences of changes in biodiversity: A search for general principles. *Ecology* 80 (5):1455–1474.

Timmerman, P., and R. White. 1997. Magahydropolic: Coastal cities in the context of global environmental change. *Global Environmental Change* 7 (3):205–234.

Toman, M., and R. Bierbaum. 1996. An overview of adaptation to climate change. In J. B. Smith, ed., *Adapting to Climate Change*. New York: Springer-Verlag.

Toynbee, Arnold Joseph, and Jane Caplan. 1979. *A Study of History*. New York: Weathervane Books.

Trombulak, Stephen C., and Christopher A. Frissell. 2000. Review of ecological effects of roads on terrestrial and aquatic communities. *Conservation Biology* 14 (1):18–30.

Tweeten, Luther G., and Donald G. McClelland. 1997. *Promoting Third-World Development and Food Security*. Westport, CT: Praeger.

UN Administrative Committee on Coordination, Sub-Committee on Nutrition. 1997. *3rd Report on the World Nutrition Situation*. Geneva: UN Administrative Committee on Coordination, Sub-Committee on Nutrition.

UN Administrative Committee on Coordination, Sub-Committee on Nutrition/International Food Policy Research Institute. 2000. *4th Report on the World Nutrition Situation*. Washington, DC: UN Administrative Committee on Coordination, Sub-Committee on Nutrition / International Food Policy Research Institute.

UNAIDS. 2000. *Report on the Global HIV/AIDS Epidemic*. Geneva: UN Joint Programme on HIV/AIDS.

UNAIDS. 2001. AIDS Epidemic Update. Geneva: United Nations AIDS.

UNAIDS. 2002. AIDS Epidemic Update. Geneva: United Nations AIDS.

UN Commission on Sustainable Development. 1997. *Comprehensive Assessment of the Freshwater Resources of the World*. Report of the Secretary-General, fifth session, April 7–25. New York: UN Commission on Sustainable Development.

UN Conference on Environment and Development. 1992. Non-legally binding authoritative statement of principles for a global consensus on the management, conservation and sustainable development of all types of forests. New York: United Nations Conference on Environment and Development.

UN Department of Economic and Social Affairs. 1998. *World Population Projections to 2150*. New York: UN Department of Economic and Social Affairs.

UN Department of Economic and Social Affairs. 1999. *World Population Prospects: The 1998 Revision*. New York: UN Department of Economic and Social Affairs.

UN Department of Economic and Social Affairs. 2000. *Below Replacement Fertility*. New York: UN Department of Economic and Social Affairs.

UN Department of Economic and Social Affairs. 2001. *World Population Prospects: The 2000 Revision*. New York: UN Department of Economic and Social Affairs.

UN Development Program. 1994. *Human Development Report*. New York: Oxford University Press.

UN Development Program. 2000. *Human Development Report*. New York: UN Development Program.

UN Development Program. 2001. *Human Development Report*. New York: UN Development Programme.

UN Environment Programme. 1995. *Global Biodiversity Assessment*. Cambridge: Cambridge University Press.

UN Food and Agriculture Organization of the 1991. *Production Yearbook FAO*. Rome: UN Food and Agriculture Organization.

UN Food and Agriculture Organization of the 1993. *Forest Resources Assessment, 1990: Tropical Countries*. Rome: UN Food and Agriculture Organization.

UN Food and Agriculture Organization of the 1996a. *Investment in Agriculture: Evolution and Prospects*. Rome: UN Food and Agriculture Organization.

UN Food and Agriculture Organization of the 1996b. *The Sixth World Food Survey*. Rome: UN Food and Agriculture Organization.

UN Food and Agriculture Organization of the 1999. Assessment of the world food security situation. Paper read at 25th Session of the Committee on World Food Security, May 31–June 2, Rome.

UN Food and Agriculture Organization of the 2000a. *Agriculture toward 2015/2030, Technical Interim Report*. Rome: UN Food and Agriculture Organization.

UN Food and Agriculture Organization of the 2000b. *The State of Food and Agriculture*. Rome: UN Food and Agriculture Organization.

UN Food and Agriculture Organization of the 2000c. *The State of Food Insecurity in the World*. Rome: UN Food and Agriculture Organization.

UN Food and Agriculture Organization of the 2001a. *Final Report of the World Food Summit, Part I*. UN Food and Agriculture Organization, 1996 [cited June 24, 2001]. Available from www.fao.org/wfs/index_en.htm.

UN Food and Agriculture Organization of the 2001b. *Mobilizing Resources to Fight Hunger: Report to the 27th Session of the Committee on World Food Security*. UN Food and Agriculture Organization, 2001 [cited June 29, 2001]. Available from www.fao.org/docrep/meeting/003/Y0006E/Y0006E00.htm.

UN Food and Agriculture Organization of the 2001c. *The State of Food Insecurity in the World, 2001*. Rome: UN Food and Agriculture Organization.

UN Framework Convention on Climate Change of the 1992. *United Nations Framework Convention on Climate Change*. New York: United Nations.

UN Framework Convention on Climate Change. 1997. *Kyoto Protocol to the United Nations Framework Convention on Climate Change*. New York: United Nations.

UNICEF. 2000. *The State of the World's Children*. New York: Oxford University Press.

UNICEF. 2001. *Goals for Children and Development in the 1990s* [Internet] [cited June 24, 2001]. www:unicef.org/wsc/goals.htm.

Union of Concerned Scientists. 2001. *Clean Energy Blueprint, a Smarter National Energy Policy for Today and the Future*. Cambridge, MA: Union of Concerned Scientists, American Council for an Energy Efficient Economy, and Tellus Institute.

United Nations. 1975. Report of the World Food Conference. Paper read at World Food Conference, November 5–16, Rome.

United Nations. 1998. *World Population Projections to 2150*. New York: UN Department for Economic and Social Affairs.

United Nations. 2000. *The Aging of the World's Population* [Internet]. UN Division for Social Policy and Development, 2000 [cited 2000]. Available from www.un.org/esa/socdev/ageing/agewpop.htm.

United Nations. 2003. *World Population Prospects: The 2002 Revision*. New York: UN Department of Economic and Social Affairs.

UN Office for the Coordination of Humanitarian Affairs. 2002. *Consolidated Appeals Process Mid-Year Review Status Report.* New York and Geneva: UN Office for the Coordination of Humanitarian Affairs.

UN Population Division. 1999. *World Population Prospects: The 1998 Revision.* New York: United Nations.

UN Population Division. 2000a. *Below Replacement Fertility.* New York: UN Department of Economic and Social Affairs, Population Division.

UN Population Division. 2000b. *World Urbanization Prospects: The 1999 Revision.* New York: UN Department of Economic and Social Affairs.

UN Population Division. 2001. *World Population Prospects: The 2000 Revision.* New York: United Nations.

Unruh, G C. 2000. Understanding carbon lock-in. *Energy Policy* 28:817–830.

UN World Food Programme. 2001a. *Projects—Colombia* [Internet]. UN World Food Program, 2002 [cited May 24, 2001]. Available from www.wfp.org/country_brief/Americas/Colombia/projects_c.html.

UN World Food Programme. 2001b. *Statistics* [Internet]. *UN World Food Program, 2001* [cited June 27, 2001]. Available from www.wfp.org.

UN World Food Programme. 2001c. *WFP in Statistics 2001* [Internet]. UN World Food Program, 2002 [cited June 5, 2001]. Available from www.wfp.org.

U.S. Census Bureau. 1979. *Illustrative Projections of World Populations to the 21st Century.* Washington, DC: U.S. Department of Commerce.

U.S. Census Bureau. 2001a. *International Data Base* [Internet]. U.S. Department of Commerce, 2001 [cited June 4, 2001]. Available from www.census.gov/ipc/www.

U.S. Census Bureau. 2001b. *Population Change and Distribution, 1990–2000: Census 2000 Brief.* Washington, DC: U.S. Department of Commerce.

U.S. Census Bureau. 2004. *Global Population Profile: 2002.* Washington, DC: U.S. Department of Commerce.

U.S. Department of Energy and U.S. Environmental Protection Agency. 2000. *Carbon Dioxide Emissions from the Generation of Electric Power in the United States.* Washington, DC: U.S. Department of Energy and U.S. Environmental Protection Agency.

U.S. Environmental Protection Agency. 2001. *Global Warming: Climate, Our Changing Atmosphere* [Internet]. Environmental Protection Agency, April 6, 2001 [cited November 12, 2001]. Available from www.epa.gov/globalwarming/climate/index.html.

U.S. Global Change Research Program. 1997. *Global Change* [Internet]. [cited September 1997]. Available from *www.globalchange.org/moderall/97sep32d.htm.*

U.S. Geological Service. 2004. *Resource Assessment Summaries of the Countries of the World* [Internet]. USGS Central Region Energy Resources Team, 2004 [cited May 2004]. Available from http://energy.cr.usgs.gov/energy/stats_ctry/Stat2.html.

U.S. Photovoltaic Industry. 2001. *Solar Electric Power: The U.S. Photovoltaic Industry Roadmap*. U.S. Photovoltaic Industry.

Valdmanis, Richard. 2000. Climate talks may be moot amid green power advances. Reuters.

Valemoor, S., and P. Heydon. 2000. Exploring the next thousand years. *Futures* 32:509–512.

van Wijk, C., E. de Lange, and D. Saunders. 1998. Gender aspects in the management of water resources. *Natural Resources Forum* 20 (2):91–103.

Victor, D. G., K. Raustiala, and E. B. Skolnikoff, eds. 1998. *The implementation and effectiveness of international commitments: Theory and practice*. Cambridge, MA: MIT Press.

Vig, Norman, and Michael Kraft, eds. 1997. *Environmental Policies in the 1990s*. Washington DC: Congressional Quarterly Press.

von Hippel, David. 2000. *A Framework for Energy Security Analysis and Application to a Case Study of Japan*. Berkeley: Nautilus Institute.

Wallensteen, Peter, and Ashok Swain. 1997. *International Fresh Water Resources: Conflict or Cooperation?* Stockholm: Stockholm Environment Institute.

Wapner, Paul. 1995. Politics beyond the state: Environmental activism and world civic politics. *World Politics* 47 (3):312.

Water Fights. 2000. *The World in 2000*. London: The Economist Group.

Watkins, Kevin. 2001. *The Oxfam Education Report*. London: Blackwell.

Westoby, J. 1989. *Introduction to World Forestry: People and their Trees*. Oxford, UK: Basil Blackwell.

What worries Americans. 1999. *Washington Post*, November 7, p. 14.

Whitmore, T. C. 1990. *An Introduction to Tropical Rainforests*. Oxford: Clarendon Press.

Wigley, T. M. L. 1999. *The Science of Climate Change*. Washington, DC: Pew Center on Global Climate Change.

Wilson, Edward O. 1992. *The Diversity of Life*. New York: Norton.

Wilson, Sara E. 2001. *Global Warming Changes the Forecast for Agriculture*. Washington, DC: International Food Policy Research Institute.

Wolf, Aaron T. 1999. Water and human security. Aviso 3:2.

Wolf, Aaron T., Jeffrey A, Natharius, Jeffrey J. Danielson, Brian S. Ward, and Jan K. Pender. 1999. International river basins of the world. *International Journal of Water Resources Development* 15(4).

Wood, Stanley, Kate Sebastian, and Sara J. Scherr. 2001. *Pilot Analysis of Global Ecosystems: Agroecosystems*. Washington, DC: International Food Policy Research Institute/World Resources Institute.

World Bank. 1994. *Averting the Old Age Crisis*. New York: Oxford University Press.

World Bank. 1997. *Rural Development: From Vision to Action*. Washington, DC: World Bank.

World Bank. 2000a. *Cities, Seas, and Storms: Managing Change in Pacific Island Economies.* Washington, DC: World Bank.

World Bank. 2000b. *World Development Report.* New York: Oxford University Press.

World Bank. 2001a. *Poverty Trends and Voices of the Poor* [Internet]. [cited June 15, 2001]. Available from www.worldbank.org/poverty/data/trends/scenario.htm.

World Bank. 2001b. *World Development Indicators.* Washington, DC: World Bank.

World Commission on Dams. 2000. *Dams and Development: A New Framework for Decision-Making. The Report of the World Commission on Dams: An Overview.* Cape Town, South Africa: World Commission on Dams.

World Commission on Environment and Development. 1987. *Our Common Future.* Oxford: Oxford University Press.

World Energy Council and International Institute for Applied Systems Analysis. 1995. *Global Energy Perspectives to 2050 and Beyond.* London: World Energy Council and International Institute for Applied Systems Analysis.

World Energy Council and International Institute for Applied Systems Analysis. 1998. *Global Energy Perspectives, 1998.* London: World Energy Council and International Institute for Applied Systems Analysis.

World Health Organization. 1999. *Removing Obstacles to Healthy Development: Report on Infectious Diseases.* World Health Organization.

World Health Organization. 2001. *Nutrition.* World Health Organization, 2001 [cited June 24, 2001]. Available from www.who.int/nut.

World Health Organization. 2003. *Removing Obstacles to Healthy Development: Report on Infectious Diseases.* World Health Organization, 1999 [cited 2003]. Available from www.who.int/infectious-disease-report/index-rpt99.html.

World Resources Institute. 1992. *World Resources 1992–93.* New York: Oxford University Press.

World Resources Institute. 1994. *World Resources 1994–95.* New York: Oxford University Press.

World Resources Institute. 1996. *World Resources 1996–97.* New York: Oxford University Press.

World Resources Institute. 1998. *World Resources 1998–99.* New York: Oxford University Press.

World Resources Institute. 2000. *World Resources 2000–2001.* Washington, DC: World Resources Institute.

World Resources Institute. 2004. World Resources 2002–2004: Decisions for the Earth: Balance, Voice, and Power [Internet]. Available from http://governance.wri.org/pubs_pdf.cfm?PubID=3764. Last modified, April 2. 2004; accessed May 20, 2004.

World Water Commission. 2000. *A Water Secure World: Vision for Water, Life, and the Environment.* Paris: World Water Commission.

World Water Council. 2000. Statement of the Gender Ambassadors to the Ministerial Conference. Paper read at Second World Water Forum and Ministerial Conference: Final Report, July.

Worldwide report. 2000. *Oil & Gas Journal.* Available from: http://ogj.pennet.com/datasets/survey.cfm.

Yelle, L. E. 1979. The learning curve: Historical survey and comprehensive survey. *Decision Sciences* 10:302–334.

Yohe, G., and J. Neuman. 1996. The economic cost of greenhouse-induced sea-level rise for developed property in the United States. *Climatic Change* 32:387–410.

Yudelman, Montague, Annu Ratta, and David Nygaard. 1998. *Pest Management and Food Production: Looking to the Future.* Washington, DC: International Food Policy Research Institute.

Zhou, Fengqi. 2000. *Discussion of Macro Assumptions in the Future Evolution of the Chinese Energy System and the Impact of Energy Security Considerations on Planning.* Berkeley, CA: Nautilus Institute.

Contributors

Kali-Ahset Amen is a research assistant at Population Action International, holding a BA in African regional studies from Columbia University and an MPhil in environmental management from the University of Cape Town. She has served as a research fellow at the Centre for African Research and Transformation in Durban, South Africa, and at the Southern African Political Economy Series Trust in Harare, Zimbabwe. Ms. Amen has also conducted environmental education in South Africa, Madagascar, and Lesotho. Her recent research concerns reproductive health policy issues associated with young people and with HIV transmission.

Eldon Boes is director of energy analysis for the National Renewable Energy Laboratory. Boes began work in renewable energy at Sandia National Laboratories in 1974. Since 1991, he has worked on developing and managing a strong energy analysis program at NREL, in support of the planning, management, and representation of renewable energy and energy efficiency programs at NREL and the Department of Energy. Boes has a PhD in mathematics from Purdue University and has taught for eight years.

Richard Cincotta is an ecologist and a senior research associate at Population Action International. Cincotta has five years of overseas field research experience in applied ecological and agricultural projects in Asia and North Africa, and has written extensively in scientific journals on topics in ecology, demography, mathematical modeling, and public health. His opinion columns on population and environmental topics have appeared in the *Washington Post,* the *Oregonian* and the *Hindu* (India). He has also served as a policy fellow in the U.S. Agency for International Development's Population, Health, and Nutrition Center.

Amy Coen is president and CEO of Population Action International, a nongovernmental organization committed to advancing universal access to family planning and related health services, and to educational and economic opportunities, especially for girls and women. Ms. Coen has more than 30 years of experience in reproductive health and rights advocacy. She currently serves as a trustee on several boards of reproductive health organizations and in a coalition of CEOs of America's leading environmental organizations.

Marc J. Cohen is a research fellow and special assistant to the director general at the International Food Policy Research Institute (IFPRI) in Washington, D.C. He has written extensively about global food security, conflict, humanitarian aid, human rights, and biotechnology. Cohen received his PhD in political science from the University of Wisconsin-Madison.

Ken Conca is director of the Harrison Program on the Future Global Agenda and an associate professor of government and politics at the University of Maryland. His teaching and research interests include global environmental politics, social movements in world politics, international political economy, the politics of science and technology, alternative security, and the transformation of sovereignty. He also teaches in the campuswide interdisciplinary undergraduate program in environmental science and policy. Dr. Conca has been a visiting professor at Mount Holyoke College (USA) and Nankai University (People's Republic of China), and a visiting scholar at the Massachusetts Institute of Technology (USA) and Federal University of Rio de Janeiro (Brazil).

Heather Conley has been deputy assistant secretary, U.S. Department of State for European and Eurasian Affairs since September 2001. Prior to her appointment at the State Department, Ms. Conley worked with the international consulting firm Armitage Associates, serving as senior associate law clerk after 1997. From February 1992 to June 1994, Ms. Conley served as a special assistant to the coordinator of U.S. assistance to the New Independent States (NIS) of the former Soviet Union. Ms. Conley received a BA from West Virginia Wesleyan College, and an MA in international relations from the Paul H. Nitze School of Advanced International Studies, Johns Hopkins University. She has received two State Department Meritorious Honor Awards.

Gary Cook is senior science writer at the National Renewable Energy Laboratory (NREL), where he has worked since 1979. In his time at the Laboratory, he has written scores of papers on a wide range of technical, scientific, analytical, and policy subjects concerning renewable energy and the environment. Currently, he serves as team leader for NREL corporate communications and as the executive editor of the laboratory's journal, the *Research Review*. He has a BS in physics and is working toward a doctorate in the philosophy of science.

Chester Cooper is the deputy director, special programs for the Environment and Health Sciences Division of the Pacific Northwestern National Laboratory. For more than four decades, Cooper has been deeply involved in public policy issues and international negotiations. He served on the White House National Security Council, was a key staff member of the Presidential Commission on Environmental Quality, and currently serves on the planning group for the Aspen Institute Energy Policy Forum. His career has included involvement in academia, the military, national intelligence, national security, foreign affairs, environment, and energy. He is the author or editor of many books and papers on foreign affairs and science policy.

Ken Cousins is a doctoral candidate in the Department of Government and Politics at the University of Maryland. His dissertation centers on nonstate, market-based policies to promote sustainability, with a case study focusing on the certification of forest management systems in the Chilean forest products industry. He is a member of the International Studies Association, the International Ecological Economics Association, and the Forest Stewards Guild.

Robert Engelman is vice president for research at Population Action International. He is author of more than a dozen reports on global demography and its connection to specific renewable natural resources, and to community development. Mr. Engelman has also written numerous scientific papers and book chapters on these connections. A former newspaper reporter and a founding (now honorary) member of the Society of Environmental Journalists, Mr. Engelman's writing has appeared in the *Washington Post*, the *Wall Street Journal*, and the *Boston Globe*. He also chairs the board of the Center for a New American Dream, a nonprofit organization dedicated to enhancing the quality of North American life while reducing consumption of natural resources.

David Inouye is director of the University of Maryland's graduate program in Sustainable Development and Conservation Biology and a faculty member in the Department of Biology. He studies wildflowers and wildlife at the Rocky Mountain Biological Laboratory in Colorado, and his studies there since 1973 are providing insight into the changes occurring as a result of climate change.

Patricia Marchak is professor emeritus of anthropology and sociology at The University of British Columbia. She is also a faculty representative on the UBC Board of Governors and a member of the BC Forest Appeals Commission. Dr. Marchak has conducted extensive research in environmental issues and resource industries. Her many books include *Logging the Globe* (1995) and *Green Gold: The Forest Industry in British Columbia* (1983). She received her PhD from UBC in 1970 and joined the faculty on a full-time basis in 1973. She has been professor emeritus since 2001.

Jacob Park is assistant professor of business and public policy at Green Mountain College in Vermont, specializing in the teaching and research of community-based sustainable development, global environment and business strategy, NGOs/global governance, and corporate social responsibility. Park is also a senior fellow of the Environmental Leadership Program and serves on the International Planning Board of the Greening of Industry Network, the IUCN/World Conservation Union's Commission on Ecosystem Management, the Steering Committee of the North American Green Purchasing Initiative, and the Board of Directors of the Center for Environmental Citizenship, a Washington DC-based nonprofit group. His most recent book is *The Ecology of the New Economy: Sustainable Transformation of Global Information Technology, Communication, and Electronics Industries* (Greenleaf Publishing, 2002).

Warren Phillips is professor emeritus of government and politics at the University of Maryland. His research interests include international development, international political economy, the information revolution, and environmental politics. For over thirty years, Phillips has also served as a consultant to various governmental, nongovernmental, and private sector organizations, including the Departments of State and Defense, the Arms Control and Disarmament Agency, the Ford Foundation, and IBM. He is currently the CEO of Maryland Moscow, which helps governments in Central Europe and the former Soviet Union make the transition to market-based economies. In addition, Phillips founded and now consults for International Initiatives, a firm that works with American businesses and their international ventures.

Dennis Pirages is Harrison professor of international environmental politics at the University of Maryland. He is author or editor of fifteen books including, most recently, *Global Ecopolitics, Global Technopolitics, Building Sustainable Societies,* and *Ecological Security: An Evolutionary Perspective on Globalization*. He is a lifetime fellow of the American Association for the Advancement of Science and currently co-chair of the Board of the World Future Society.

Paul Runci is an independent consultant in Kensington, Maryland. He has worked as an energy and environmental policy researcher for the Pacific Northwest National Laboratory, with the Joint Global Change Research Institute, and the Aspen Institute. He holds a PhD in political science from the University of Maryland.

Matthias Ruth is the director of the Environmental Policy Program at the University of Maryland's School of Public Affairs and an associate professor of environmental economics and policy. His research and teaching focus on dynamic modeling of human-environment interactions, with a special focus on energy, industrial and environmental economics, and policy. Ruth has taught in the United States and in many other countries on dynamic modeling and ecological economics.

Index